Gardening with Heirloom Seeds

Gardening with

Lynn Coulter

Heirloom Seeds

TRIED-AND-TRUE FLOWERS,
FRUITS, AND VEGETABLES FOR
A NEW GENERATION

Fitzhenry & Whiteside

*Gardening with Heirloom Seeds: Tried-and-True Flowers,
Fruits, and Vegetables for a New Generation* by Lynn Coulter.
Copyright © 2006 by the University of North Carolina Press.

This edition has been published for sale in Canada by
arrangement with the University of North Carolina Press,
Chapel Hill, North Carolina 27514, USA
www.uncpress.unc.edu

First published in paperback 2007 in Canada by Fitzhenry &
Whiteside

Fitzhenry and Whiteside Limited
195 Allstate Parkway
Markham, Ontario L3R 4T8
www.fitzhenry.ca   godwit@fitzhenry.ca

Fitzhenry & Whiteside acknowledges with thanks the Canada
Council for the Arts, and the Ontario Arts Council for their support
of our publishing program. We acknowledge the financial support
of the Government of Canada through the Book Publishing
Industry Development Program (BPIDP) for our publishing
activities.

ONTARIO ARTS COUNCIL
CONSEIL DES ARTS DE L'ONTARIO

Canada Council   Conseil des Arts
for the Arts   du Canada

Library and Archives Canada Cataloguing in Publication
Coulter, Lynn
Gardening with heirloom seeds : tried-and-true flowers, fruits &
vegetables for a new generation / Lynn Coulter.
Includes bibliographical references and index.
ISBN-13: 978-1-55455-016-6
ISBN-10: 1-55455-016-5
1. Seeds. 2. Gardening. I. Title.
SB117.C74 2007   635   C2006-904455-4

1 3 5 7 9 10 8 6 4 2

Printed in China

To Bill
Like Muir, a
mountain-dweller

With thanks to
Michael for the
love and chocolate
chip cookies

In memory of
James and Juanita
Baxter

Contents

Acknowledgments

Gardeners are generous people. The seeds they sow produce a bounty of flowers and vegetables that others can enjoy. In that tradition of sharing, many people have contributed to this project. I am sincerely grateful for the wonderful images, seed packets, seeds, and gardening expertise provided by the following heirloom gardeners, photographers, and seed sellers. Thank you all for your gracious help and support.

Marilyn Barlow, of Select Seeds
Professor David W. Bradshaw, Department of Horticulture, Clemson University
David Cavagnaro, of David Cavagnaro Photography
John Coykendall, heirloom gardener
Wesley Greene, garden historian, Colonial Williamsburg Foundation
Renee Shepherd, of Renee's Garden Seeds
Aaron Whaley, Diane Whealy, and Kent Whealy, of Seed Savers Exchange

Text from William Curtis's *Botanical Magazine* is courtesy of the National Agricultural Library, Agricultural Research Service, U.S. Department of Agriculture. Heartfelt thanks to Roseanne Key for her friendship and encouragement.

Gardening with Heirloom Seeds

A Celebration of Seeds

There are heirloom seeds asleep in my refrigerator, tucked into brown paper envelopes wound with rubber bands. They have been there since last fall, when I collected them from my garden and dropped them into the crisper alongside some shriveled radishes. I'd almost forgotten them until I heard the rumble of a neighbor's rototiller and suddenly realized it's time to plant.

There's a science to seed keeping, but I'm a laid-back kind of gardener who doesn't stress over it. For me, it's enough that a farmer at a roadside stand gives me a sandwich bag filled with ebony seeds and promises they will grow the sweetest melons I ever put in my mouth. I don't mind driving around to find a deserted house I've passed just once before, when some starry yellow blossoms were beginning to open in a patch of weeds. In the fall, when the blossoms fade, I will return and shred them for their ripened seeds. Keeping seeds this way—dumping them into baggies and stuffing them into pockets—may seem slightly disrespectful, especially when you consider what I'm keeping. Heirloom seeds are much more than the promise of next summer's crookneck squash or mammoth sunflowers. They are living antiques, handed down from one generation to another. They are an inheritance of flavor or beauty from long ago and, often, far away.

Heirloom seeds have proved to be excellent travelers through time and space. I can expect the old time turnips I will plant this year to have the same rosy skin and sweet flesh as the ones my grandmother grew behind her Depression-era rental house. Once my scarlet runner beans are up, their brilliant red flowers will lure just as many thirsty hummingbirds. What is wonderful about heirloom seeds is that most of them will thrive almost anywhere in North America.

Some heirlooms, of course, have been around for a very long time. You can't get out of elementary school without learning that corn was an important native crop. Early peoples were already cultivating its ancestor, mahiz, when Columbus stepped onto their shores. Exotic amaranths, with their dangling ropes of red, purple, and chartreuse flowers, were known in ancient Greece. Julius Caesar's troops carried cabbages with them when they marched into Britain in 55 B.C. Two Englishmen were among the most influential early plant collectors and distributors. John Gerard, gardener to one of Queen Elizabeth's advisors, described many new discoveries in his 1597 *Herbal*, or *Generall Historie of Plantes*. John Parkinson, apothecary for James I, cataloged other botanical finds in his 1629 *Paradisi in Sole, Paradisus Terrestris*.

Eventually, heirloom seeds traveled in the other direction. Immigrants pouring into the New World often carried with them seeds from their cottage gardens, fields, and vegetable patches so they could continue to enjoy the flowers they had always grown or satisfy their cravings for familiar foods in a strange and different land. Many seeds were smuggled in, hidden under suitcase linings and hatbands or sewn into dress seams to avoid confiscation by sharp-eyed officials. There are even stories of tiny lettuce and tomato seeds being glued to the backs of postage stamps on letters mailed from behind the Iron Curtain to North America.

Over time, all this seed saving has changed. What started as a quest for previously unknown species or new varieties has become a way to remember our ancestors or native lands. More and more, we are saving seeds as a link to the past.

Luckily, Iowa gardener Diane Whealy saved her own green heritage before it disappeared. Whealy's great-grandparents were Bavarian immigrants who sailed to America in 1867, bringing with them seeds from the morning glories they had grown around their European home. Their son (and Whealy's grandfather) Baptist John Ott kept the flowers going. Whealy remembers visiting his Iowa farm, sitting beside him on a porch draped in a curtain of velvety purple blossoms with heart-shaped leaves. On one visit, Grandpa Ott gave Whealy and her husband, Kent, a small bottle of morning glory seeds and the seeds of his favorite tomato, German Pink. Grandpa Ott died soon after their trip, and Diane realized the seeds would have been lost if she had not taken them. There would have been no one left to tend the morning glories and tomatoes, no one left to save more seeds.

The Whealys decided to share the flower seeds, now christened Grandpa Ott's morning glory, with other gardeners who loved old plants. Interest in antique varieties started to spread, and by 1975 the Whealys' efforts had blossomed into the Seed Savers Exchange of Decorah, Iowa. To date, the nonprofit organization has preserved an astounding 24,000 varieties of vegetables, fruits, and grains. Its network of more than 10,000 members allows gardeners from all over the world, including Canada, to trade their antique seeds. An offshoot group, the Flower and Herb Exchange, links some 3,000 gardeners equally devoted to heirloom varieties. Today, there are mail order seed companies across the United States and Canada that carry these wonderful old varieties; a sampling appears in the back of this book. You can order online from many of them, which makes heirloom gardening easier than ever.

If you are wondering exactly what an heirloom seed is or how old a plant has to be before it is considered an antique, the answer is a little tricky. Is that battered cedar chest your aunt left you really an antique, or just old? Most gardeners agree that a plant becomes an heirloom when it's been around longer than fifty years, while others set the bar at a century. But others don't hold to a strict definition. Why not include the chili seeds your father brought into Canada from Barbados or Jamaica some forty-odd years ago, as long as you love the fiery bite of the peppers and you think of him when you plant the seeds? It's not just the age of that old chest that makes it valuable; it's also where it came from and who gave it to you.

But there are a couple of things that help us identify heirloom seeds, even if we do relax the age barrier. Most heirlooms are open-pollinated varieties, which means that they can reproduce themselves from seed. Their seeds grow true to type, resulting in plants that look like the parents.

Hybrid plants result from the cross of two different varieties, and these plants are widely sold in today's garden centers and nurseries. Hybrids may bear sterile seeds or seeds that produce plants that revert to one of the parental forms. In other words, you can plant the seeds from a hybrid petunia, but you will not get baby petunias that look like the one you started with. If the seeds are sterile, you won't get any petunias at all. There are a few exceptions, newer hybrids that have been stabilized through generations of breeding to grow true from seeds, but not many.

Most gardeners also consider a plant an heirloom if it has a back story. Some plants, like the vegetables introduced to the New World by the French and the Irish, have a long and interesting history. Their past is intricately wound up with the cuisine, politics, folklore, or science of Europe or the Far East or wherever they came from. Other seeds are native to North America, and their stories start right where we live. Of course, stories don't have to be ancient to be fascinating. The squash seeds originally grown by an Iroquois woman living along the Great Lakes may or may not be very old. But if they could speak, they would tell us a lot about her culture. And in some ways, heirlooms do speak to us, by giving us a glimpse into the way they were cooked or used or enjoyed.

Finally, by way of definition, heirlooms are often flowers and vegetables that have adapted over time to whatever climate and soil they have grown in. Thanks to their genetics, heirlooms are unusually resistant to pests, diseases, and extremes of weather. (Try ignoring a modern hybrid rose in your garden and see how long it lasts. Black spot or Japanese beetles can take it down in a matter of days.) Besides being undemanding and easy to grow, many heirloom seeds produce wildflowery, sweet-scented blossoms or delicious fruits and vegetables.

So how did our heirlooms start slipping away, with so much going for them? Why have some already vanished? Sadly, some disappeared as our personal tastes changed. Fashion has had a lot to do with it, especially in the flower world. Certain plants have gone out of style, much like miniskirts or big band music. Victorians were once passionate about amaranths, but gardeners who live in today's townhouses want neat, easy-to-maintain flowers, not twelve-foot giants with gaudy, blood-red blossoms.

Commerce has driven changes in the vegetable world. Improved transportation and modern refrigeration allowed us to truck more watermelons to market than ever before — until grocers started complaining that cannonball-shaped melons took up too much space on their shelves and tended to roll around. Demand grew for oblong melons that stacked better. Consumers became more sophisticated, too, turning up their noses at warty-looking tomatoes or funny-colored carrots. The marketplace responded to these pressures. When we opened our arms to new hybrids, seduced by flowers with big blossoms or vegetables with perfect shapes, we snuggled up to the work of enterprising growers. There is nothing wrong with that, except that when we stop buying older varieties, sellers stop selling them. Eventually growers stop growing them, and antique plants disappear.

Of course, some improvements really are improvements. Hybridizers have given us disease-resistant tomatoes, carving pumpkins with less stringy pulp, cucumbers that won't make us burp after lunch, stockier sunflowers, frillier petunias, and more colors than you can name in just about every plant.

But all this genetic tinkering has had a dark side; there have been trade-offs. Plants have lost some desirable characteristics while gaining others. Those round tomatoes don't have much old-fashioned flavor anymore, even though the red balls make a nice pyramid in grocery stores. Modern sweet peas have lost their rich, intense perfumes.

Fortunately, you don't have to climb onto a political bandwagon or paste a bumper sticker on your car to help save heirloom seeds. Many have already survived in the wild without us—that's where they came from in the first place—and others will save themselves once enough people find out how fun and rewarding they are to grow. Still more heirlooms are being preserved through the efforts of dedicated researchers like those at Seeds of Diversity, one of Canada's premier seed exchanges. Its member network is composed of farmers, historians, gardeners, teachers, scientists, seed sellers, and many others who recognize the value of propagating and sharing antique Canadian varieties.

In that spirit, the Canadian edition of this book is designed as a sampler for heirloom seeds. Under the seasonal chapters, you will find descriptions of fifty different flowers and vegetables, along with growing tips and suggested varieties. The sources section will help you find seeds available for sale or trade and gardens you can visit to see them growing.

You can use this book as a journal, too, a place to make notes about your plants. Maybe you'll record the weight of your biggest pumpkin or tomato. You might press antique pansies between its pages or jot down the names of the elderly gentleman who gave you a handful of heirloom beet seeds. As your garden progresses, take time to track some of the practical stuff: your planting dates, weather conditions, harvest dates, and amounts of rainfall. List the plants that grew successfully for you and the ones that failed. Good records are invaluable when you're preparing for next year. As a journal keeper, you will be following in some big footsteps. Catharine Parr Traill, for instance, recorded her descriptions of many of the flowers she saw growing in *Canadian Wild Flowers* 1868: "The wild Columbine is perennial and very easily cultivated. Its blossoms are eagerly sought out by the bees and humming birds. On sunny days you may be sure to see the latter hovering over the bright drooping bells, extracting the rich nectar with which they are so bountifully supplied. Those who care for bees, and love humming birds, should plant the graceful red-flowered Columbine in their garden borders."

As time goes on, you'll be creating an heirloom of your own, a personalized garden book to pass on to your children, to give to a friend or new neighbor, or to keep for your own use. You may wait to include news about what's going on in the world as you garden, about how you sowed heirloom poppies to commemorate the service of our veterans when they came home from duty, or about the summer you planted beans to make a living, leafy playhouse for your five-year-old. Maybe you'll keep a favorite recipe here after you make pickles from heirloom cukes or a casserole from delicious antique squash.

After all, heirloom seeds aren't just about gardening. Throughout the centuries, they have been intricately linked with medicine, love, romance, exploration, discovery, and poisons. They have been a part of history, science, cooking, literature, fairy tales, genetics, and wildlife. They are wrapped up in farming, travel, local fairs, archaeology, philosophy, and so much more.

When you plant your heirloom seeds, remember where they've been. Keep them going.

The Garden in Spring

The earth has a rhythm, as every gardener knows. We see it every year when the leaves stored in tulip bulbs push tiny green mouse ears toward the sun. We hear it when the frogs emerge from hibernation and raise a raspy chorus on the first warm, rainy night. When it arrives, spring rushes in with an invisible, irrepressible spirit that affects everything.

Whether you're planting flowers or vegetables, this is your busy season, the time to haul out the tiller or sharpen the good shovel. But before you turn that first clump of dirt, make sure you have a plan in place so you won't waste your time and money.

Before you plant any veggies, consider the size of your family and their tastes in foods. You won't need many tomato plants if you're only serving fresh, sliced tomatoes in salads or sandwiches. But you will need a lot more if you want to freeze or can enough spaghetti sauce to last throughout the winter.

On the other hand, beware of plants that bear prolifically, and plant accordingly. More than one gardener has been overwhelmed with zucchinis and desperately tried to sneak the grated veggies into every muffin or loaf of bread the family consumes. When gardeners' spouses and children finally rebel, the zucchini-rich find themselves staging late-night runs to drop their surplus on the doorsteps of unsuspecting neighbors.

After you decide what to grow, measure your garden spot and make a sketch or drawing of its dimensions so you'll know how to arrange your rows and hills. If you're observant, you'll already know which side of your garden gets the morning sun. That will help you avoid putting tall plants, like sunflowers, in front of shorter ones, where they'll cast shadows as the day progresses. Then again, if you live in the South, you can use the changing sunlight to shelter your cool-season crops. Lettuce, for instance, appreciates some shade during the hottest, brightest time of the day, so southern gardeners can tuck those plants close to taller ones.

Hang on to your sketch so you won't make the mistake of planting the same

"To own a bit of ground, to scratch it with a hoe, to plant seeds, and watch the renewal of life—this is the commonest delight of the race, the most satisfactory thing a man can do."

Charles Dudley Warner,
My Summer in a Garden
(1870)

things in the same garden spot year after year. Many diseases, weeds, and insects overwinter in the soil, so rotating your plants can minimize or prevent problems. Minerals in the soil also become depleted over time; this is another good reason to alternate crops. You can actually restore some nutrients to the ground when you grow different crops and then till them under after they die and decompose.

Fall or early winter is the best time to get a soil analysis, but if you haven't gotten one yet, it may not be too late. Check with your county extension agent. Tell the agent what you're growing, so he or she can recommend the right additives and fertilizers, in the right amounts, for your particular needs. If your agent is too busy for this in the spring—and many are—you can purchase a home test kit and do your own. Because improving the soil is a work in progress for most of us, save your test results. Then you can compare them to next year's and see how your soil is changing.

Ideally, you will have bought or traded for your heirloom seeds sometime last fall or winter. If not, don't waste any time now gathering the ones you want. Seed sellers and collectors run out fast in the spring, and some heirlooms are rare and hard to find anyway.

As you thumb through the following chapters, you will find that some of the seeds featured here, such as sunflowers or beans, are easy even for beginners to grow. Others, like pansies, may challenge you, so read over their growing requirements before you dive in.

To avoid disappointment, you may also want to take a look around and see what your neighbors are growing. For many years, northern gardeners seldom grew cosmos, simply because the plants required so many days to go from seed to flower. Who wanted to bother, when the first winter freeze killed the plants before they ever opened a single bloom? In other words, if you don't see a particular plant in the yards around you, there's probably a good reason. Check to see if it's recommended for your region before you try it.

Once the weather conditions are right, it's time to prepare your ground. In general, the smaller the seed, the more you will need to dig or till the seed bed. Tiny seeds need finely tilled soil, while larger ones, like corn, can muscle through earth that's not quite as well prepared.

If you are buying commercially packaged seeds, compare the size of your garden to the information on the backs of the packages. You may be surprised to find how many feet of row you can sow from a single packet, so don't over-buy. Also, remember that you do not have to plant an entire package of seeds all at once. A 4.5-gram packet of radishes, for example, may contain 400 quick-sprouting seeds, enough to plant 15 feet of row. Can your family eat that many fresh radishes at once? If not, sow only the seeds you need and save the rest. Many will stay viable for a few years if you store them in an airtight bag or jar and keep them in a cool, dark place.

Of course, some seeds need to be started indoors, especially if you live where the growing season is short. Again, check the cultural requirements for each variety and don't rush things. Prematurely sown seeds can become stunted, lanky, or weak if you have to keep them inside too long. When your seeds finally sprout and put out their second set of leaves, the so-called true leaves, it's time to harden them off. This means you acclimate the seedlings to the world outside by gradually exposing them to cooler temperatures and bright sunlight. Then transplant them into their permanent location in the garden. If necessary, be ready to protect the tender seedlings in case of a late freeze.

Now that spring is here, it's time to get a little dirt under your fingernails. It's time to get those heirloom seeds into the ground.

BEET—*Beta vulgaris*

Beets are such earthy, humble vegetables. They hide their delicious roots under the soil and don't demand much care in the garden. Just give them some cool weather and regular water, and they will bring plenty of flavor and nutrients to your table.

Prehistoric peoples in the Mediterranean region were the first to use beet leaves, probably for medicinal purposes. The plants did not immediately catch on with the early Romans who tried them; Pliny scorned their roots as "those scarlet nether parts." But by the second and third centuries, Roman chefs were adding beet roots to their recipes and praising them as better than cabbage—which may say something about their taste, if you're not a cabbage fan.

Only a few types of garden beets were grown throughout the seventeenth and eighteenth centuries, when the plants were commonly referred to as

"The beet root is a better emblem of modesty than the rose. The color is as fine; it conceals itself from the view more completely; moreover, it is good to eat, and will make excellent sugar."
English author
Samuel Butler
(1835–1902)

Colorful mixed beets. (Courtesy of David Cavagnaro)

"blood turnips" because of their dark, turniplike roots. English gardeners were limited to just two varieties, the Red and the Long Red.

Choices were limited in the United States as well, where seed sellers offered only three or four kinds of beets as late as 1828. Today we can sample from a broad array of these cold-hardy root crops. Look for them in a range of colors, including gold, garnet, dark purplish-red, orange, maroon, vermilion, red, white, and striped.

DETROIT DARK RED

D. M. Ferry & Company introduced this all-purpose variety in 1892, and it has since become one of the most popular beets for backyard gardeners and commercial growers. The 2- to 4-inch globes have a sweet, tender flesh with a uniform color and texture that's nice for canning. A descendant of the nineteenth-century Early Blood Turnip, this one matures about 60 days after sowing.

BULL'S BLOOD

This old Victorian-era beet was originally grown for its attractive leaves. Some gardeners still turn up their noses at the roots and never bring them to the table, preferring to grow Bull's Blood strictly as an ornamental. The near-black leaves can be eye-catching, especially when mingled with silvery foliage or flowers in cut arrangements or in beds and borders.

Give the plants 35 days from sowing if you plan to eat the foliage. Otherwise, the roots need 58 days to mature. Pull them while they are small, for the best flavor.

CHIOGGA

Italy claims this fast-growing variety, which first popped up in seed lists in the mid-1800s. When sliced, the roots show alternating rings of white and rosy pink. Even the green stems have pale pink stripes. Nicknamed the "candy cane beet," Chiogga needs 55 days from sowing.

CROSBY'S EGYPTIAN

Developed from a German beet, this variety came into the United States around 1880. The flattened, heart-shaped roots are ready in about 50 days.

A versatile heirloom root crop. (Courtesy of David Cavagnaro)

Inside, the deep red flesh is sweet and tender. Despite its name, this beet has no clear, direct link to Egypt.

GOLDEN BEET

This gourmet favorite has an attractive golden yellow flesh and light green leaves with gold veins. It is ready in 55 days from sowing; harvest the buttery sweet roots at 2 inches in diameter for the best taste. These beets will not bleed when sliced or cooked. Unfortunately, this variety has a reputation for poor germination, so soak the seeds in lukewarm water before planting them, and sow extra to avoid disappointment.

ALBINA VERDUNA, **also known as Snow White**

White beet sugar was once made from this old Dutch variety. The white roots have a sweet flavor and no dark juice to bleed into salads or stain your fingers. Allow 55 days from planting.

LUTZ GREEN LEAF (WINTER KEEPER)

Make extra room in your garden for these big beets, which can grow to 6 inches in diameter. The smooth-skinned, reddish-purple roots are slow to mature, needing 60 to 80 days. They are good keepers, though, perhaps because this variety was developed in the era before refrigeration. Lutz is one of the sweetest heirloom varieties, said to become sweeter in storage. The pink-veined leaves, which resemble chard, stay tender into the fall.

Growing Tips

Beets are short-season crops, but they crave full sun and good drainage. Give them a head start by clearing your ground of rocks and sticks and working their soil to 8 to 10 inches deep. Add some organic material to help loosen their bed.

Since beets need cool temperatures, start them in early spring or before the first frost in fall. Gardeners in mild climates can grow them year-round.

Each beet seed is actually a cluster of embryos that can produce from three to five plants. That's why you'll find lots of seedlings coming up close together, no matter how carefully you space the seeds.

Before you plant, soak the seeds overnight. Then scatter them over the soil directly into your garden. It is not a good idea to start them indoors, as beets dislike transplanting.

Beet seeds germinate between temperatures of 50° and 85°F. Don't forget to plant extras of the golden and pale heirloom varieties, as they have low germination rates.

Sow your seeds ½ inch deep and 1 to 2 inches apart in single or wide rows. Allow 18 to 24 inches between the rows. You can toss out some fast-sprouting radishes, too, to help mark the location of the beets until they sprout.

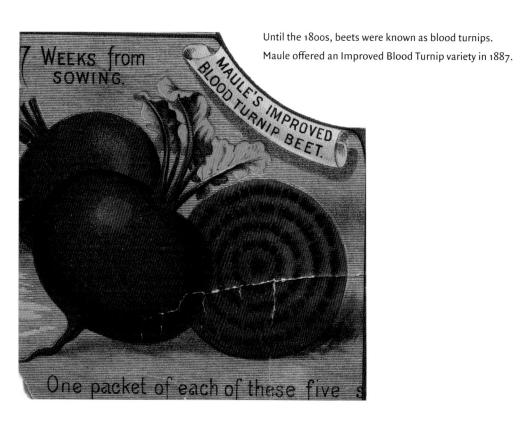

Until the 1800s, beets were known as blood turnips.
Maule offered an Improved Blood Turnip variety in 1887.

When the seedlings appear, thin them to every 3 inches for small varieties and every 6 inches for larger ones. If you're accidentally pulling up neighboring seedlings, try snipping the sprouts with scissors. Water regularly as the beets grow so the roots won't turn woody.

You can start harvesting when the roots are about the size of golf balls. Modern varieties may become bigger if you leave them in the ground.

If you're saving seeds, remember that beets are biennials. Gardeners who live in mild areas can mulch their roots and let them overwinter. The following spring, seed stalks will form after the mulch is removed.

But if you live where the winter temperature drops to freezing, you'll need a different strategy to save beet seeds. Instead of leaving the roots outdoors, dig them up and stash them in damp sand in a cellar where the temperature stays slightly above freezing. The following spring, replant them outside. After seed stalks appear, let the seeds ripen before you collect them. Saving beet seeds is difficult, so most gardeners will opt to buy or trade for new seeds each year.

For true-to-type seeds and to avoid cross-pollination, don't grow garden beets alongside sugar beets or chards.

Beets can tolerate light frost, which often makes them taste better and store longer. If you have lots of room, you can follow the advice from a 1908 seed catalog and store the roots for winter use "in barrels with five or six inches of sand on top in a cool cellar just above the freezing point."

For a continuous supply of fresh beets, sow more seeds every two to three weeks in the spring, or up to a month before the first expected fall frost. Growing early and late varieties will also help stretch your supply.

Ruby Queen beet seeds.

Eat Your Beets

Beets are nutritious, from their buttery, green tops to their tasty roots. Just a half-cup of cooked beets provides vitamin A, folate, phosphorus, potassium, and more.

Think beyond salads when you bring beets to the kitchen. American colonists once roasted the tough-skinned roots in coals, and today we can bake, steam, sauté, mash, shred, and pickle them. Young beet leaves are also good whether stir-fried, steamed, or tossed with vinegar for salads.

CABBAGE—*Brassica oleracea* var. *capitata*

You might not suspect it, but cabbage comes from a big family. This famously smelly vegetable, which is related to kale, broccoli, collards, kohlrabi, cauliflower, and Brussels sprouts, probably originated in the Mediterranean region over 4,000 years ago. Early Romans were fond of the heads; it has even been said that the philosopher Diogenes consumed nothing but cabbage leaves and water. And we know from the writings of Pliny that the plants were once used medicinally. In the 1760s, a doctor aboard Captain Cook's sea voyage stretched their uses even further, wrapping the wounds of storm-battered sailors in huge cabbage leaves.

Julius Caesar's troops carried cabbages with them to Britain when they invaded in 55 B.C. The leaves must have been good provisions for warriors, because Genghis Khan took them along, too, when his Mongols ransacked Europe.

In 1541, cabbages made their way into Canada with the French explorer

"The cabbage surpasses all other vegetables. If, at a banquet, you wish to dine a lot and enjoy your dinner, then eat as much cabbage as you wish, seasoned with vinegar, before dinner, and likewise after dinner eat some half-dozen leaves. It will make you feel as if you had not eaten, and you can drink as much as you like."

Marcus Porcius Cato, Roman general and politician (234–149 B.C.)

Jacques Cartier, who noted in his journal, "We sowed seeds of cabbage, lettuce, turnips, and others of our country, which came up in eight days."

Settlers in the New World also cultivated cabbages and discovered that the vegetables grew best in cooler regions. The plants became a food staple for both people and livestock, and Jamestown minister Alexander Whitaker sounded pleased when he wrote in 1612, "Our English seeds thrive very well heare, as Peas, Onions, Turnips, Cabbages, Coleflowers, . . ."

By the eighteenth century, twenty-two different kinds of cabbage were offered for sale in a Williamsburg newspaper. Most are no longer available, probably because these biennials do not set seeds until their second year and perish in the first hard freeze in most of the country. Cabbage plants also require cross-pollination and simply don't produce as many usable seeds as other, self-pollinating vegetables—all of which makes collecting their seeds a dicey proposition.

British author Jane Grigson complained that cabbage could smell terrible while cooking and generally "ruin a meal with its wet flab." Worse still, she added, in *Jane Grigson's Vegetable Book* (1979), the stinky but nutritious vegetables are good for us.

EARLY YORK

"One of the premier cabbages of the late eighteenth century through the mid-nineteenth century. This variety, as far as I can tell, has disappeared but seems to be similar to the 'Early Jersey Wakefield,' a mid-nineteenth century variety still available. Both have a tendency to burst if left in the ground too long, particularly in rainy weather."

Wesley Greene, Garden Historian, Colonial Williamsburg Foundation

In 1865, Fearing Burr recorded a story about a soldier who introduced this cabbage to England in the mid-1700s. The soldier, Burr said, eventually sold seeds in Yorkshire, hence the variety's name. Philadelphia nurseryman Bernard McMahon forwarded some of the seeds to Thomas Jefferson, who liked it so well he planted it more often than any of the other eighteen cabbage varieties he grew at Monticello. Early York forms mild-tasting, cone-shaped heads early in the season. The seeds have become rare and hard to find.

JANUARY KING

From Victorian England, this very cold-hardy cabbage holds up well even during the heat of summer. The firm, blue-green heads, which are wrapped in purple-tinged outer leaves, may be flattened or globe-shaped. Gardeners in the Pacific Northwest say they successfully overwinter this variety and harvest 2- to 4-pound heads the following spring. Try it for its sweet flavor and crisp, crunchy texture. It needs 100 to 120 days to mature.

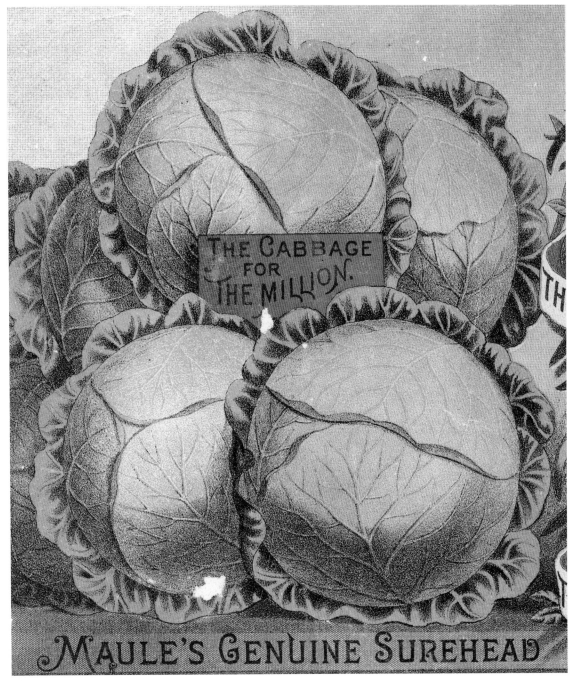

The 1887 catalog boasted that just seven heads of Maule's cabbage weighed 218 pounds.

LATE FLAT DUTCH

German immigrants carried the seeds of these big, flat-headed cabbages into America around 1840. The short-stemmed heads can weigh up to 15 pounds and measure up to a foot across. Lots of blue-green leaves surround the creamy white centers. Don't expect the plants to perform well in midsummer, but they'll perk back up when cooler temperatures return. Use this variety for making kraut, or store the long-lasting heads through the winter. Space the seeds 18 inches apart and harvest them about 100 days after sowing.

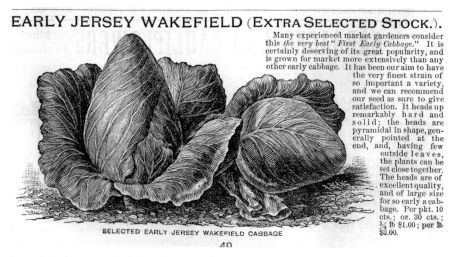

Burpee's Early Jersey Wakefield cabbage, an 1891 variety, formed conical heads.

EARLY JERSEY WAKEFIELD

Gardeners with limited space like these early cabbages, which reach maturity in 60 to 75 days. The cone-shaped, pale green heads have a tender, crisp taste and form few outer leaves. Introduced to New Jersey from England around 1840, this variety became widely popular. By 1888, Burpee's listed it as the most commonly grown early cabbage in the United States. It is still a great choice for backyard gardens, although you'll want to pick the heads before they develop a strong flavor in hot weather. Heirloom gardener and author William Woys Weaver recommends that southerners skip this variety, unless they are planting in the fall, and grow Charleston Wakefield, which was developed in 1892 for hot climates.

MAMMOTH RED ROCK

Each hefty, purple-red head of this variety can weigh 6 or more pounds. Although they take from 90 to 100 days to mature, the cabbages keep for an exceptionally long time, and they're excellent boiled, processed, or pickled. The slightly flattened heads are tightly formed and resist splitting, with color that goes all the way to the core. From Europe, this one dates back to 1889.

Growing Tips

Like its leafy *Brassica oleracea* cousins, kale and collards, cabbage performs best in cool weather. Give the plants a garden spot with full sun to light shade and well-drained soil.

Cabbage should be started early so the heads can develop before hot weather sets in. Sow your seeds indoors in flats 4 to 6 weeks before the last spring frost and cover them with ¼ to ½ inch of soil. After the last heavy frost, harden off the seedlings and transplant them. Space the young plants 12 to 18 inches apart in rows set 2 feet apart. If you prefer, direct-sow cabbage seeds into the garden.

Cabbages are thirsty plants, so give them an inch of water each week. The heads may split if they become dry and then receive a lot of moisture, so try to water evenly and regularly. Mulching also helps. Cabbages are heavy feeders, so dress them generously with compost.

The cabbage heads have matured when they're firm and solid. Cut the stems at soil level, discard the outer leaves, and gather the whole plants; or leave about an inch of stem in the ground and check periodically to see if new, smaller heads are forming. Cabbages can tolerate light frost, so you can allow them to grow until a killing freeze.

To extend your harvest, plant early and late varieties, or sow more seeds a few weeks apart. Northern gardeners who want a fall crop can sow early to midseason cabbages until midsummer. Southerners can plant a little later.

Since cabbages are biennials, only gardeners with mild winters can leave them to overwinter and produce seeds. To save seeds, gardeners in cold-winter areas have to dig up the plants, overwinter them where the temperature remains just above freezing, and then return them to the garden the following year. It is usually much easier to treat cabbages as annuals and buy fresh seeds each season.

Burpee's introduced a sweet-flavored Surehead cabbage in 1877.

Don't Lose Your Head

Old-timey gardeners have a trick to keep cabbages from splitting: they give the heads a quick quarter-twist while they're developing, or they tug them gently up out of the ground. This seems to slow the uptake of moisture by severing some of the roots.

COLUMBINE—*Aquilegia*, also known as Granny's Bonnets, European Crowfoot, Meeting Houses, Garden-Honeysuckle, and Doves-Round-A-Dish

Columbines always seem to make gardeners think of birds. The plants' botanical name, *aquila*, is believed to come from the Latin word for "eagle," because many of these delicate flowers have curved spurs that resemble a bird's talons. But it is also possible that the scientific name comes from *aquilegus*, which means "water container" or "drawing water." While not as obvious, there is a connection to birds there, too. Columbine spurs are actually hollow tubes packed with nectar, so they're wildly attractive to hummingbirds. Even the common name, columbine, is derived from *columba*, or "dove," perhaps because early gardeners thought the blossoms looked like doves perched in a circle. Medieval artists saw them as doves, too, and often painted columbines as symbols of the Holy Spirit.

Columbines are native to North America and Europe. The short-spurred *A. vulgaris* is a wild European plant that pops out of the soil early each spring. It is easy to grow, usually preferring dappled shade to full sun, and is widely available in pink, deep purple, mauve, blue, and white.

A. canadensis is a North American native. Around 1640, its scarlet and yellow blossoms caught the eye of plant collector John Tradescant the Younger, who shipped samples home to England. British gardeners were fascinated by the plants' novel colors and quickly made room for them in their gardens. Striped columbines also became fashionable in Europe around the same time; but passions for those unusual beauties inexplicably cooled, and today columbines with streaked blossoms seem to have disappeared.

In America, *A. canadensis* stayed popular through the mid-nineteenth century, until hybrids with bigger blossoms nudged them out of beds and bor-

"These flowers are of colour sometimes blewe, at other times of a red or purple, often white, or of mixt colours which to distinguish severally would be to small purpose, being things so familiarly known to all."

   John Gerard, Herball
   (1597)

"There's fennel for you, and columbines; there's rue for you; and here's some for me."

   William Shakespeare,
   Hamlet

ders. Today, most of us grow *A. vulgaris* columbines in single or double forms. Try these charmers in a wildlife garden, as they're a magnet for butterflies.

TOWER PINK

In 1597, English botanist John Gerard described this frilly columbine as "very double, that is to say, many of those little flowers are thrust into the belly of another." Its deep mauve-pink petals are frosted with greenish-white "icing" on the edges.

TOWER BLUE

True blue blossoms are hard to find for the garden, but this double variety, planted in masses, provides a sweep of watercolor, or powder, blue to purple blue. The flowers have short spurs and delicate petals that overlap in a honey-comb effect. By late spring, the plants can reach 2 to 3 feet tall. Their stems are usually sturdy enough to cut for bouquets.

NORA BARLOW

Nora, with its doubled sepals, is often called a rose columbine. While rose types can be traced to the 1600s, Nora, in name at least, is modern. Some sources speculate that an English grower renamed this variety in the early 1980s to honor Charles Darwin's granddaughter. Nora is unusual because it lacks spurs and cups. Its densely clustered flowers, which look like miniature dahlias, may be fuchsia and white or deep pink and white, tinged with pale green. The plants mature at 1 to 2 feet tall.

BLACK BARLOW

These modern, doubled flowers are actually deep violet. Some gardeners report that their plants also produce maroon or deep purple stems. For a unique cutting garden, grow this one with other dark flowers, such as Black Beauty hollyhocks, Black Boy cornflowers, Bowles Black violas, and modern Molly Sanderson pansies. Or try a striking black-and-white color scheme, mingling snowy white blossoms with its shadowy shades.

GRANDMOTHER'S GARDEN

Grandmother probably did grow these large, nodding blossoms, which come in rose, violet, white, burgundy, and deep red. Watch for clumps of ferny foliage to shoot up in late spring. This variety, which is believed to have originated in Germany, grows 2 feet tall.

RUBY PORT

Once found in monastery gardens of the 1600s, Ruby Port nearly disappeared for centuries, and the seeds have become hard to find. The bell-shaped blossoms range from wine to ruby red, while the young foliage starts out burgundy and matures to bluish-green. Expect this roselike columbine to reach about 2½ feet tall.

IRISH ELEGANCE

These ivory white flowers streaked with green, or dipped in green at their tips, look like miniature pom-poms. This easy-to-grow beauty matures at 24 to 30 inches high. Some gardeners say that the temperature affects the amount of green that appears on the blossoms.

MRS. SCOTT ELLIOTT

Introduced around 1918, Mrs. Scott Elliott bears star-shaped flowers with long spurs. Look for them in red, yellow, blue, and purple color combinations. With its larger-than-usual blooms, this variety is a good choice for the middle or back of the border, where it often tops out at 3 to 4 feet tall.

GREEN APPLE

Spurless columbines date back to the late 1500s. While this newer cultivar is rare and hard to find, it is worth the search. Each creamy white flower is lightly brushed with apple or lime green on the back. The heavily petaled blossoms are slightly flattened, so they look like small stars as they open. Some gardeners report that this variety blooms later in the spring than other columbines and continues to open into the summer.

Grandmother's
Garden columbines.
(Courtesy of Select Seeds)

Growing Tips

If plants were people, we would call columbines shameless hussies, because they cross-pollinate with abandon and scatter their small, black seeds everywhere. Unfortunately this causes their colors to become mixed and mingled until the blossoms eventually turn out muddy looking. For columbines that stay true to type, you'll need to plant only one variety at a time or keep different varieties isolated from one another.

As short-lived perennials, columbines are easily grown from seed. For best results, chill the seeds briefly and then scatter them over a moistened growing mix placed in pots or trays. Press the seeds lightly into the mix but do not cover them, as columbine seeds need light to germinate. Refrigerate the trays or pots at 40°F for 4 to 5 weeks.

Now you'll need patience, as the seeds can take 20 to 25 days to sprout. Pot up the seedlings when they appear, but wait until summer to move the hardened-off plants outside. They will be ready to move from their pots into beds and borders by fall or by early the following spring.

If this sounds like too much trouble, you can simply sow columbine seeds directly into the garden from fall until early spring. As long as the nights are cold, nature will do the work for you. Just put them where you really want them, as the plants form long taproots and detest being moved.

These fragile-looking flowers need well-drained soil that stays on the damp side. To help retain moisture, give them some organic mulch and provide a little extra water during dry spells. While columbines can take partial to full sun in some areas, they'll appreciate partial shade in the hot South. The plants should bloom for up to 6 weeks starting from spring until early summer.

If you want your columbines to self-sow, allow the flowers to dry on the plants. The pods will burst open when the seeds are ripe.

With their graceful forms and wildflowery blossoms, columbines are great for naturalizing in woodlands. Their green or blue-green foliage is especially attractive in a bed of ferns. *A. canadensis*, with its bold, firecracker colors, can be tricky to use in a mixed bed, but it works well with white or yellow flowers. You can also cool its fiery colors by planting it near a bed of dark green ferns.

GARDEN PEA—*Pisum sativum*

Think some of your canned vegetables have been on the shelf for a long time? The oldest wild peas on record, found in a cave on the border between Thailand and Burma, have been carbon-dated to 9750 B.C. Historians think that's where the plants originated, or perhaps in northern India, where the climate would have suited these cool-weather vegetables.

Peas were known to the Greeks and Romans around 500 B.C., when street vendors in Athens hawked hot pea soup. By the seventh century, Chinese gardeners were cultivating snow peas and eating them, pods and all.

Peas also caught on in France during the reign of King Louis XIV, whose wife, Madame de Maintenon, complained that an obsession for green peas had swept through the court: "The subject of Peas, continues to absorb all others." She added, "The anxiety to eat them, the pleasure of having eaten them, and the desire to eat them again. . . . It is both a fashion and a madness."

In early America, Thomas Jefferson was so fond of peas, he raised at least thirty different varieties. During one session at the White House, he even took time to pen a note to his gardener at Monticello, directing him to sow "Ravenscroft peas, which you will find in a canister in my closet."

Essayist William Wallace Irwin confessed an appetite for garden peas in his 1952 book, *The Garrulous Gourmet*. But he admitted he once had trouble sacrificing the tender vegetables for the sake of his stomach. Nothing was as innocent, he mourned to his readers—probably as he held a handful of raw peas over a pot of steaming water—"as the small green face of the freshly shelled spring pea." But hunger pangs apparently won out over conscience, and there was nothing to do, Irwin concluded, but heat the water and throw the victim in. "Let him boil—and that's that," he wrote.

Although peas fall into various classifications, most of us are simply interested in whether they're good for shelling, snapping, drying, or freezing.

Shelling Peas

These are the most popular garden peas. When allowed to dry on the vine, they're excellent in homemade soups.

Burpee's debuted a vigorous, sweet-tasting pea known as Profusion in 1891.

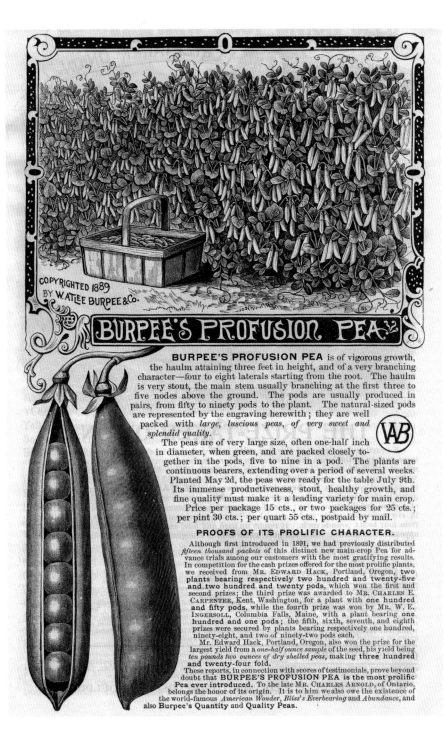

COPYRIGHTED 1889
BY W. ATLEE BURPEE & Co.

BURPEE'S PROFUSION PEA

BURPEE'S PROFUSION PEA is of vigorous growth, the haulm attaining three feet in height, and of a very branching character—four to eight laterals starting from the root. The haulm is very stout, the main stem usually branching at the first three to five nodes above the ground. The pods are usually produced in pairs, from fifty to ninety pods to the plant. The natural-sized pods are represented by the engraving herewith; they are well packed with *large, luscious peas, of very sweet and splendid quality.*

The peas are of very large size, often one-half inch in diameter, when green, and are packed closely together in the pods, five to nine in a pod. The plants are continuous bearers, extending over a period of several weeks. Planted May 2d, the peas were ready for the table July 9th. Its immense productiveness, stout, healthy growth, and fine quality must make it a leading variety for main crop.

Price per package 15 cts., or two packages for 25 cts.; per pint 30 cts.; per quart 55 cts., postpaid by mail.

PROOFS OF ITS PROLIFIC CHARACTER.

Although first introduced in 1891, we had previously distributed *fifteen thousand packets* of this distinct new main-crop Pea for advance trials among our customers with the most gratifying results. In competition for the cash prizes offered for the most prolific plants, we received from Mr. EDWARD HACK, Portland, Oregon, two plants bearing respectively **two hundred and twenty-five and two hundred and twenty pods**, which won the first and second prizes; the third prize was awarded to Mr. CHARLES E. CARPENTER, Kent, Washington, for a plant with **one hundred and fifty pods**, while the fourth prize was won by Mr. W. E. INGERSOLL, Columbia Falls, Maine, with a plant bearing **one hundred and one pods**; the fifth, sixth, seventh, and eighth prizes were secured by plants bearing respectively one hundred, ninety-eight, and two of ninety-two pods each.

Mr. Edward Hack, Portland, Oregon, also won the prize for the largest yield from a *one-half ounce sample* of the seed, his yield being *ten pounds two ounces of dry shelled peas*, making **three hundred and twenty-four fold.**

These reports, in connection with scores of testimonials, prove beyond doubt that **BURPEE'S PROFUSION PEA is the most prolific Pea ever introduced.** To the late Mr. CHARLES ARNOLD, of Ontario, belongs the honor of its origin. It is to him we also owe the existence of the world-famous *American Wonder, Bliss's Everbearing* and *Abundance,* and also Burpee's **Quantity** and **Quality Peas.**

ALDERMAN OR ALDERMAN POLE

Many gardeners insist that this is the best tall variety, with vines that run to 6 feet long. Introduced in 1881, Alderman bears dark green pods containing 8 to 10 big peas each. An early Burpee's catalog boasted, "It is a grand sort, giving us as late a supply as we can have before the season of mildew, which blights our peas when the hot, dry weather of August sets in." Give it 70 days from planting.

LINCOLN, also known as Homesteader

Northern gardeners are usually successful with this dwarf variety, which matures in 65 to 70 days. The vines run 18 to 30 inches long and produce slender pods that shell easily. In commercial production until the mid-1960s, this popular heirloom is still widely available. The cream-colored peas are sweet and tender, fine for eating fresh or freezing.

WANDO

Summer heat takes a toll on most garden peas, but Wando, a 1943 introduction from the South Carolina Vegetable Breeding Lab, stays productive even if sown late in the season. It's also resistant to cold. The pods hold medium-sized peas on 30-inch vines. It needs 70 days from sowing. Called the "hot weather pea," this variety is recommended for southern and coastal gardens.

BRITISH WONDER

This rare pea has become hard to find from commercial sources. Introduced to England in 1890, it's a heavy yielder, bearing sweet, dark green pods on 2- to 3-foot vines. As late as 1904, the peas were displayed at the Louisiana Purchase Exhibition as some of the most commonly grown vegetables in New York State.

Edible-Podded Peas

Also known as sugar or snow peas, these plants produce flattened pods. Their French name is *mange-tout*, meaning "eat everything."

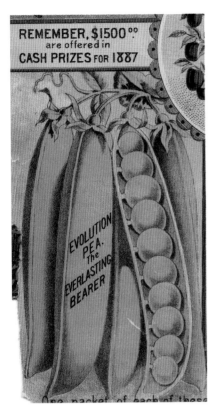

In 1887 the W. Henry Maule Company offered $1,500 in cash prizes for gardeners who grew their Evolution Peas and other vegetables.

DWARF GRAY SUGAR

You'll enjoy the pretty lavender blooms on this snow pea, which is one of the earliest of the edible-podded types. The bushy vines grow to 2 feet long and produce light green pods that mature in about 75 days. The pods are rather flat but meaty and, for the best flavor, should be picked before the seeds completely develop. Try this variety, which predates 1773, in Oriental recipes.

GOLDEN SWEET

India is the homeland of this rare "wax snow pea." Its purple and violet flowers form lemon-colored pods about 65 days after planting. Give the 5-foot vines some support and they'll produce heavily throughout the season. The pods aren't really sweet; some gardeners describe their taste as spicy or perfumelike. But they add welcome color to fresh spring salads. This one can withstand hot, dry summers.

RISSER EARLY SUGAR

Grown by four generations of the Risser family in Lancaster County, Pennsylvania, this pea predates 1850. The tall vines are heavy yielders and bear sweet, edible pods in 55 to 60 days. Risser Sickle Peas, with their sickle-shaped pods, also hail from Pennsylvania, where they were cultivated by colonial English and German settlers. The peas are good for eating in the pod or shelling out.

AMISH SNAP

Keep these vigorous plants picked and they'll bear tender, crisp pods for up to 6 weeks. You'll need to trellis the 6-foot vines. The Maine Seed Saving Network is credited for helping restore this variety, which was introduced by Amish immigrants from Europe.

MAMMOTH MELTING SUGAR

This variety's thick, tender pods are ready to pick about 65 days from sowing. This is one of the largest and sweetest snow pea types. For the best flavor, harvest the pods before the creamy white peas plump up inside. The vigorous, 5-foot vines are wilt resistant and produce for a long time. Mammoth likes cool weather, so sow it in summer for a fall crop.

Growing Tips

Green peas signal the start of the spring garden. Because they love cool weather, they should be planted as early in spring as the ground can be worked.

Sow your pea seeds 1 inch deep, 2 to 3 inches apart in double rows. Keep the rows 2 feet apart for dwarf varieties and 3 feet apart for taller types, or 4 to 6 feet apart if you're using trellises. You can also stick bushy branches into the ground around the plants for support, or let them catch hold of a fence.

Be wary of giving your plants too much nitrogen, which yields lush vines but few pods. Peas don't generally need extra watering unless the soil becomes quite dry while the pods are forming.

To extend your harvest, plant both early and late varieties, or sow more seeds every few weeks. For a fall crop, plant at least two months before the first frost.

"BURPEE'S BEST"
EXTRA EARLY PEA.

Prior to introducing this strain in 1889 we distributed among Pea growers in the spring of 1888 about three thousand packages of these peas, *for careful comparative trials*, with the result that all, so far as heard from, unite in pronouncing **"Burpee's Best"** *the very earliest, most uniform*, and **best** *of all Extra Early Peas*. The sample reports published herewith render any additional words of praise entirely unnecessary.

Per package 15 cts.; pint 25 cts.; per quart 45 cts., by mail, postpaid. By freight or express, per quart 30 cts.; 2 quarts 50 cts.; 4 quarts 75 cts.; peck $1.25; per bushel $4.50.

BURPEE'S BEST.—The Earliest of All.

J. MILTON BERGER, Jamaica, N. Y., Jan. 20, 1892, writes:—It is not necessary for me to comment on your seeds after sending you another order, still I will say that I find your BEST EXTRA EARLY PEAS to be the earliest of all that I planted.

HENRY FACOVITE, Troy, Ohio, writes:—I planted BURPEE'S BEST EXTRA EARLY PEAS the last week in April, and just six weeks from that time they were ready for the table; they are the best I ever raised.

Ten Days Earlier Than any Other.

LEWIS A. LARCOMB, Upper Sandusky, Ohio, writes:—My BURPEE'S BEST EXTRA EARLY PEAS were in the market ten days earlier than any other variety.

Gardeners praised Burpee's Best Extra Early Pea in field trials conducted in 1888.

Shelling peas should be harvested when the pods feel filled out. Snap types are usually ready soon after the flowering stage. For best results, pick the snaps before the peas mature inside. Snow peas are also ready soon after flowering, while the pods are still flat. The sugar in peas converts to starch soon after picking, so cook or process them as soon as possible after harvest.

If you're saving seeds, isolate different varieties to ensure purity. Let the pods turn brown on the vine. When the seeds inside rattle, they are ready to collect.

Peas in Troy

In the late 1800s, archaeologist Heinrich Schliemann discovered several large storage jars while digging through the ruins of Troy. While damaged, the jars held the remains of 4,000-year-old dried peas. According to legend, Schliemann couldn't resist dining on them.

LARKSPUR—*Consolida* (formerly *Delphinium ajacis*), also known as Rocket Larkspur, Lark's Heel, Lark's Claw, Lark's Toe, and Doubtful Knight's Spur

If you've ever thought that larkspurs look a little like plain-Jane delphiniums, you're right. These classic cottage garden plants are related to delphiniums as members of the *Ranunculaceae*, or buttercup, family. But larkspurs are hardy annuals, while true delphiniums are biennials or perennials. And while both send up graceful spires of shrimp pink, pale blue, purple, or snow white blossoms, larkspurs, which are shorter, simply are not as glamorous. Their flower spikes are also arranged more loosely, so they're better suited to less formal gardens.

Native to southern Europe and the Mediterranean area, larkspurs were introduced to Britain around the mid-1500s and to America by 1572. Jefferson reportedly saw them growing near his birthplace in Shadwell, Virginia, in the summer of 1767. By April 1810, he was cultivating larkspurs at Monticello. These cool-season flowers are still grown today in Monticello's roundabout flower border.

Larkspurs found a welcome in American gardens from the seventeenth through the mid-nineteenth centuries. They're not as widely grown as they once were; their popularity seemed to fade with the casual, cottage garden style of landscaping. But there are plenty of hybrid strains on the market, and a few wonderful old heirlooms are still around.

Larkspurs take their common names from the shape of their blossoms, which are splayed like birds' feet.

EARL GREY

Gardeners disagree over the color of this unusual larkspur, which has been described as slate gray, silvery mauve, gunmetal, misty blue-gray, or simply silver. Earl Grey sends up strong, straight flower spikes on 2- to 3-foot-high plants. The stems are densely packed with doubled blossoms that lure butterflies—and bees, so plant them away from doorways or porches.

opposite: Earl Grey. (Courtesy of Renee's Garden)

BUNNY BLOOM

This larkspur's name is as charming as its flowers. Look closely, and you will spot a bunny's face in each rose, blue, or purple blossom. This single-bloomed variety, which matures at 2 to 3 feet tall, was named a Texas SuperStar Selection, an honor given to plants that grow successfully even in harsh conditions. In some parts of the country, Bunny Bloom hops right into spring by flowering around Easter. Once the petals age and loosen, the bunny's face disappears.

FRENCH ALOUETTE IMPERIAL LARKSPUR

Pied-d'alouette, the French nickname for larkspurs, translates as "foot of the lark." This hard-to-find French strain comes in salmon, rose, lilac, purple, and pure white. The plants produce an abundance of doubled blooms and fine-cut foliage; they mature at 3 to 4 feet tall. Cut the stems to use in fresh arrangements, or hang them upside down to dry in bunches for everlasting use.

BLUE BELL

Another rare heirloom, this larkspur fills a bed or border with lilac or periwinkle blue flower spikes. The plants top out at 2 to 3 feet tall and flower in 70 to 80 days after sowing. An All-American Selections winner from 1934, Blue Bell flowers resist shattering even after they're cut for vases. Butterflies find them irresistible.

GIANT IMPERIAL

Often sold as a mix of lilac, rose, white, red, salmon, pink, lavender, and dark blue, these wonderful old larkspurs can be counted on to bloom generously throughout the cool growing season. The spires are covered with double florets and feathery foliage. This is another good choice for a cutting garden. Plan to space these big larkspurs at least 10 inches apart.

WHITE KING

Sometimes listed as Imperial White King, this rare beauty bears double white blossoms set against bright green, fernlike foliage. The plants grow 2 to 3 feet tall. Like Blue Bell, this variety resists shattering.

BLUE CLOUD

C. regalis, a species of larkspur, produces soft sprays of marine blue or purple flowers that look like baby's breath. The thin stems form lots of small branches and delicate foliage, making Blue Cloud useful as a filler for bare garden spots. The butterfly-friendly blossoms dry nicely and hold their color. Give the plants full sun, and be careful when pulling up weeds around them, as their roots are shallow.

Growing Tips

Sometimes it's tempting to buy bedding plants for your garden instead of trying to coax them up from seeds that take weeks to germinate. But don't count on doing that if you want larkspurs. Nurseries seldom offer these delightful annuals as seedlings. That's okay, because larkspur seeds sprout easily. They are relatively undemanding, too, content with ordinary to rich garden soil.

One warning: larkspurs do not like transplanting, so sow your seeds directly into beds and borders. Gardeners in southern regions can sow in fall as long as there is sufficient time for the seeds to sprout and begin growing before the onset of frost. Gardeners in colder climates should wait until early spring to sow larkspurs—after the last chance of frost has passed but as soon as the ground can be worked.

Larkspurs can be slow to sprout, needing 14 to 21 days, so be patient with them. They also do not germinate well when the temperature rises to 75°F or higher. If you expect to get a late start preparing your spring garden, it may be helpful to chill your seeds at 35° to 40°F for 1 to 2 weeks before planting them.

Give larkspurs a spot in the yard that receives full sun to partial shade. Since some of the older forms can look rather spindly when planted alone, use them in drifts or clusters.

Larkspur seeds are small, so cover them lightly, or about ⅛ inch deep. After the seedlings emerge and produce their first set of true leaves, thin them to every 6 inches. Keeping the plants fairly close together will encourage them to hold one another up, so you won't have to do a lot of staking. Their feathery foliage can also lace together, helping fill in empty spots as neighboring perennials go in and out of bloom.

These plants will appreciate regular waterings, especially during periods of drought. They are at their best where the summers are cool and moist. To extend their display of star-shaped blooms, sow more seeds at 2-week intervals. Once their flowers fade, larkspurs will perish.

Fortunately, larkspurs self-sow readily. Don't be surprised if you find seedlings popping up some distance from where your flowers were originally planted.

If you're saving seeds, store your larkspur seeds in the refrigerator. For maximum germination, you will need to plant them within 4 to 6 months after collecting them. The seeds should be viable for about a year, but after that, the germination rate quickly drops to less than 50 percent. To compensate for this problem, you can simply sow extra seeds when you're planting.

Do make sure to keep larkspurs away from children and pets, as the seeds and all parts of these plants are poisonous.

Since larkspur blossoms open from the base of the stem first and continue toward the tip, pick the flowers for indoor arrangements as soon as the lowest blossoms are completely open. They are relatively short lived in vases, but the blooms will last longer if you recut the stems under water and keep them in a solution of water and floral preservative.

ANNUAL LARKSPUR

In beds and borders, try mixing larkspurs with pansies, cornflowers, and Shirley poppies. Their feathery foliage also looks nice when mingled with white bishop's lace or baby's breath.

LETTUCE—*Lactuca sativa*

You might suspect that Iceberg lettuce is a relative newcomer to the garden. After all, it sounds like a hybridizer's dream. The compact heads don't take up much space even in small gardens, and they are easy to grow, tolerating filtered sun or shade as long as the temperature stays cool. Icebergs pack and ship well for market, too, unlike some other heirloom veggies.

But Iceberg lettuce, sometimes called crisphead, has actually been around

A bed of heirloom lettuce leaves. (Courtesy of Renee's Garden)

for over a century. We have been layering its crunchy leaves in our sandwiches or drizzling them with oil and vinegar in salad bowls since Burpee's introduced the variety in 1894.

Lettuce, of course, has been around much longer than that. The greens we eat today are probably related to *L. serriola*, a prickly weed that has grown wild in the eastern Mediterranean region since ancient times.

Archaeologists point to Egyptian paintings for evidence that early gardeners once grew a type of lettuce with erect leaves. Once called Cos, for the Greek island of Cos, this lettuce is now known as romaine. The Greek historian Herodotus wrote that lettuce was served to the royals of Persia in 550 B.C., and the physician Hippocrates described it as a sleep aid in 430 B.C. Other ancient users believed lettuce could alleviate pain, aid digestion, or serve as an aphrodisiac. Not bad for a vegetable that nutritionists say is mostly water!

Botanists think that lettuce arrived in the Bahamas with Columbus around 1494 and that heading types were introduced to Europe by the 1500s. Lettuces of various colors, and those with oaklike or curly leaves, showed up a century later.

Sources disagree about how lettuce was used in colonial America. Some researchers think only slaves or poor whites gathered the greens for their tables, while others believe the plants were more widely consumed. In the 1790s, an Englishman named Richard Parkinson visited the Chesapeake region and wrote of early Americans, "Indeed, in the spring they boil everything that is green, for use at the table."

Lettuce takes its name from the Latin word *lactuca*, which refers to the white liquid that oozes out of its broken or crushed stems.

The habit of serving a salad course before an entrée is an old one. The custom probably started near the beginning of the Christian era, when Roman diners dished up the greens as an appetizer.

AMISH DEER TONGUE

Named for its long, green, pointed leaves, this 1840 looseleaf is prolific and dependable, although it has a slightly sharp taste. Red Deer Tongue, which forms loose heads, has a bronzy red tint and a tender flavor. Both need about 50 to 55 days from sowing.

TOM THUMB

As diminutive as its name, this English butterhead dates to around 1853. The leaves have a "soft" bite and a mild, buttery flavor. Each head grows only 3 to 5 inches across—the size of a baseball—to make a perfect salad for one. Try this miniature, which matures in 50 days, in window boxes or pots or as a decorative border around other plants. Lettuces like Tom Thumb were traditionally pickled with cloves to preserve them through the winter.

RED LEPRECHAUN

Jazz up an ordinary salad with this colorful romaine variety. The puckered, bumpy-looking leaves are dark purple or burgundy and fade to pinkish cream at the base. Give this variety, which has a slight bite, about 60 days to mature. The plants grow 8 to 12 inches tall.

BLACK-SEEDED SIMPSON

This lettuce has been a home-garden favorite since its introduction by New York's Peter Henderson & Company in the 1870s. Able to withstand some drought and heat, the curly, light green leaves are ready to pick 45 days after

A mix of Speckled Troutback, Blush Butter Cos, Red Ruffled Oak, Devil's Tongue, and Sucrine lettuces. (Courtesy of Renee's Garden)

✤ Renee's Garden ✤

Baby Leaf Lettuce
Heirloom Cutting Mix

"Set a table in the garden"
–Renee Shepherd

sowing. For the sweetest, most tender flavor, be sure to harvest them before the weather heats up.

Growing Tips

Lettuce is easy to grow, but it is not always easy to categorize. The problem originated with early seedsmen who sometimes switched the names of popular varieties. They intended to lure unsuspecting customers into thinking they were buying new varieties of these popular greens—an unscrupulous marketing ploy that worked. Gardeners snapped up many "new" offerings.

Unfortunately, this practice also blurred the plants' lineage. In 1923, Lester Morse of C. C. Morse and Company tried to determine the number of distinct lettuce varieties. His field tests showed that only about 140 of 1,100 listed varieties were unique—and that allowed for even tiny differences.

But while you may find one lettuce sold under many different names, the plants fall into four basic categories: looseleaf; butterhead; romaine, or Cos; and crisphead, or Iceberg. Looseleaf types are generally the easiest to cultivate, even in poor soil, and tend to resist bolting longer than the others when the weather turns hot and dry.

Maule's 1887 Improved Hanson promised big, dense heads of lettuce.

Lettuce loves cool weather, so it's a great spring or fall crop. In the South, sow your lettuce seeds directly into the garden 2 to 4 weeks before the last spring frost. Elsewhere, start them indoors under bright lights or in a greenhouse 3 to 4 weeks before the last frost. If you wait longer to plant, remember that lettuce seeds won't germinate above 85°F.

Most lettuce seeds should be covered with ¼ inch of loose, well-drained soil. Others, especially those with white seeds, need light to germinate and should not be covered at all but pressed firmly into the ground. Check the requirements for each variety that you grow.

When your seedlings appear and put out two or three leaves, thin them to every 12 inches for Iceberg types or 8 to 10 inches for other types. Keep your lettuce rows about 18 inches apart. The baby plants that are thinned out can be tossed into your salad bowl.

Lettuce is ready to harvest at almost any stage, or when heading types form firm heads. Pick a few leaves at a time, or cut the entire head at the soil line.

Key Lime, Amish Deer Tongue, Red Leprechaun, and Heirloom Cutting Mix (courtesy of Renee's Garden) lettuce seeds.

For a steady supply of fresh greens, sow more seeds at 10- to 14-day intervals. You can also plant different varieties as the seasons change, switching to heat-tolerant types that are slow to bolt as summer approaches.

Lettuce is a self-pollinating crop that does not depend on wind or insects to reproduce. Varieties that flower at the same time should be kept at least 20 feet apart, however, if you're saving seeds. Some lettuce seeds, if stored properly, may remain viable for up to 3 years, although many gardeners prefer to buy or trade for fresh seeds each year.

Once lettuce plants bolt, or set flower heads, the leaves become tough and bitter, so harvest the seeds when the temperature hits about 70°F. The seeds are ripe when the plants turn yellow and the flower heads start to look like small dandelion heads. Just as the heads start to open, cut them off and drop them upside down in a paper bag. Let them dry in a well-ventilated room, out of direct sunshine, for a month. When they're completely dry, roll the flower heads between your fingers or rub them between your palms, letting the seeds fall into the bag. It's easier to separate the seeds from the chaff if you shake them in a fine sieve. If the seeds prove difficult to clean, you can simply plant them, chaff and all.

As with all seeds, label your varieties and store them in a cool, dark place. A 1-gram package of lettuce seeds holds about 830 seeds and will plant a row approximately 30 feet long.

PINK—*Dianthus*, also known as Gillyflower, Coronation, Carnation, Indian Pink, Sweet William, Spice Pink, Clove Pink, Sops-in-Wine, Julyflower, and Sweet John

Don't pay too much attention to the common name for dianthus, especially if you're not fond of pink flowers. With more than 300 known species, you can find these cottage garden favorites in plenty of other colors, including fuchsia, shrimp, salmon, crimson, white, red, rose, lavender, cherry, and magenta. There are even blossoms with speckles and stripes. Of course, many dianthus really are pink. But it's not their color that gives these plants their nickname; it's their blossoms. The petals have fringed or jagged edges, as if they've been snipped with pinking shears.

Pinks, as they are widely known, have been cultivated for at least 2,000 years. The genus includes *D. barbatus*, the beloved Sweet William grown in old cottage gardens; *D. caryophyllus*, also known as the clove pink and as our modern carnation; *D. knappii*, a wild species with sulphur yellow flowers; and *D. superbus*, the so-called lilac pink that bears a jasmine perfume. Then there are the small maiden pinks, *D. deltoides*, that make nice groundcovers for rock gardens or slopes.

D. gratianopolitanus, the Cheddar pink, is another wonderful perennial dianthus with blue-green foliage. Like the famous cheese, it hails from the Cheddar Gorge region of Somerset, England. China pinks, or *D. chinensis*, are often sold as plants, but they will bloom from seeds in the first year. Look for Heddewigii, a sweetly scented rose, red, or pink charmer that dates back to an 1888 Burpee's catalog.

Sweet William

Prolific, self-seeding *D. barbatus* are probably native to the Pyrenees or southern Europe. Everyone in England seems to have grown these biennials at one time, from Henry VIII at Hampton Court to ordinary cottage dwellers who were cultivating double varieties by 1634. In the 1900s, gardening author Louise Beebe Wilder recommended mixing drifts of salmon-colored Sweet Williams with white foxgloves and bunches of white-and-green-striped grasses for a show-stopping display.

Sweet Williams have tightly packed flower clusters and long, stiff stems that are good for cutting. The fringed blossoms, with their light, delicate fragrance, remind many gardeners of phlox. Some sources suggest the plants were named to honor William the Conqueror.

These pinks are not fond of hot weather, so give the plants partial shade if you live in the South. Depending on your region, you may see skippers and Painted Lady butterflies visiting the frilly flowers.

NEWPORT PINK

Flower lovers see different shades of pink in these fringed beauties, including salmon, coral, and watermelon. First listed in an 1828 seed catalog, this one can tolerate light shade in the South.

"Sometimes a cultivator is fortunate enough to raise one with rose-leaved edges; but it is rare and thought much of. . . . The great beauty of this flower depends on the distinctness and brilliancy of the color round the edge of the petals called the lacing."
Horticulture *magazine (1835)*

"Of course all the Pinks marry and intermarry, and bring forth many a soft-coloured, sweet-breathed surprise for me, and I should miss them more than any of the garden's children. They are plants for sunny nooks and corners, friendly things to be tended by loving hands and enjoyed by those who care for what is sweet and simple. As old Parkinson knew, they are 'of a most fragrant scent, comforting the spirits and senses afar on.'"
Louise Beebe Wilder, My Garden *(1920)*

DIANTHUS,—CHINESE AND JAPANESE PINKS.

The China and Japan Pinks are deservedly very popular, as few flowers can equal them in beauty and profusion of bloom. They comprise many distinct and most beautifully-marked varieties, of rich and varied colors. They bloom continually all summer and fall, until overtaken by severe frost; they are alike ornamental in the garden and for bouquets.

DWARF FIREBALL. The dwarf compact habit of growth of this distinct novelty is accurately shown in the illustration, which also shows a flower natural size. The plants are covered with brilliant *blood-red* double flowers in profusion. Per pkt. 15 cts.

DWARF SNOWBALL. A fitting companion to the preceding, differing only in the flowers, which are *double white*. Per pkt. 10 cts.

THE BRIDE. A charming new variety of beautifully marked Japan Pink. The very large and handsome single flowers are pure white with deep purplish-red center, surrounded by a still darker ring. Pkt. 10 cts. *The three new Pinks as above for 25 cts.*

Chinensis (Double Chinese Pinks), large clusters of small double flowers; mixed. Pkt. 5 cts.; oz. 50 cts.

Chinensis albus fl. pl., double white. Per pkt. 5 cts.

Diadematus fl. pl. (Double Diadem Pink). Hieroglyphically marked, in the middle down to the base of each petal; very double, large flowers, magnificent in color and variety. Per pkt. 5 cts.

Heddewiggii, Finest Single, Mixed, magnificent flowers, 2 to 3 inches across. Per pkt. 5 cts.; oz. 75 cts.

Heddewiggii fl. pleno, finest double, mixed in great variety; extra choice. Per pkt. 5 cts.; oz. 75 cts.

Heddewiggii albus pleno, double white. Per pkt. 5 cts.

—— atrosanguineus fl. pl., double, dark red. 5 cts.

—— Mourning Cloak. Very double, large flowers of dark mahogany, *almost black*, each petal edged with a *clear-cut* margin of *pure white*. Per pkt. 10 cts.

Crimson Belle, very large, single, dark red flowers. 5 cts.

Eastern Queen, magnificent single flowers, 2 to 4 inches across, splendidly striped and stained. Pkt. 5 cts.

Imperialis fl. pl. (Double Imperial Pinks), finest mixed, many bright colors. Per pkt. 5 cts.; oz. 75 cts.

Laciniatus, large, single fringed flowers; mixed. 5 cts.

Laciniatus, fl. pl., magnificent, large, perfectly double and deeply-fringed flowers; finest mixed. Per pkt. 5 cts.

—— Double Red Blotched. The flowers are of the purest snowy white, blotched with red. 10 cts.

Our own mixture of all the above splendid varieties. Per pkt. 5 cts.; ¼ oz. 35 cts.; per oz. 60 cts. *The entire collection, of 18 pkts., mailed for 75 cts.*

COPYRIGHTED 1890.

DWARF FIREBALL DIANTHUS.

NIGRICANS

These large, deep ruby flowers have white anthers and a spicy, carnationlike scent. Swallowtail butterflies love the dark blossoms—some gardeners say they're actually oxblood red—that appear on 12- to 18-inch stems. Nigricans dates back to 1870.

SOOTY

Small but fragrant, each of these diminutive, maroon-black blossoms measures less than an inch across. Use the chocolate-red stems, which grow 12 to 15 inches tall, in cut arrangements. When the plants mature, their green foliage turns a rich mahogany color.

Grass or Clove Pink

This species of pink is known for its grasslike foliage, which grows in tufts. It's hardier than other dianthus, sometimes blooming into fall. Eleventh-century monks introduced the plants to Britain, where they continue to grow wild around many old castles.

IPSWICH PINK

Blue-gray foliage surrounds these blossoms, which may be white, mauve, magenta, rose, or pink with dark centers. The dwarf plants spread nicely, making them an excellent groundcover, and reach 9 to 12 inches tall. They take their name from Ipswich, Suffolk, England, where the Thompson & Morgan seed company was founded in 1855. Joseph Sangster, who joined the company as a partner and breeder in the early 1900s, helped popularize this variety. The fragrant flowers appear from late spring through summer.

ESSEX WITCH

Introduced in 1908 and sold by the Ohio firm of Storrs, Harrison, and Company, this is another very fragrant dianthus. Its semidouble, pink blossoms are lightly fringed along the edges. They are carried on slender stems that grow 8 to 12 inches long, with blue-green foliage.

BAT'S DOUBLE RED

Believed to have been introduced by grower Thomas Bat in the late 1700s or early 1800s, these wine red, carnationlike flowers have a distinctive clove scent. The plants reach 15 inches tall and produce blue-gray foliage. Choose this one for blossoms that last into the autumn. Bat's Double Red has been grown at the University of Oxford Botanic Garden since 1717.

Growing Tips

Dianthus make life easy for gardeners, because these lovely flowers like full sun, except in the deep South, and fertile, well-drained soil. To start them indoors, sow the seeds in peat pots or flats 6 to 8 weeks before your last spring frost. Cover the seeds lightly and water them gently to settle them into a good quality germinating mix. Annual and biennial dianthus seeds generally sprout in 7 to 10 days, while perennials can take up to 3 weeks. To speed up the process, cover the seeds with clear plastic and place them in a room where the temperature stays around 70°F.

Once the seedlings appear, remove the plastic and keep them moist but not soggy. Harden them off after their first true leaves appear. Don't worry if you transplant the biennial or perennial types a little early and they're hit by a late frost. They can withstand some cold. But do wait until after the last frost to transplant annual dianthus and *D. barbatus*, which is treated like an annual.

Dwarf dianthus can be spaced 6 to 8 inches apart in beds and borders. Plant taller varieties or those that form thick mats up to 1 foot apart.

If you would rather sow dianthus seeds directly outside, wait until midsummer. Gardeners with mild winters can plant in the fall for flowers the following spring. Dianthus prefer neutral to alkaline soil, so you may want to add some ground limestone if your garden is acidic.

Unlike most plants, dianthus do not like mulching, which can cause crown rot. With their dense foliage, they don't need it anyway, as they can often crowd out competing weeds. If you do mulch, try small gravel, since straw or bark can impede good air circulation.

Deadhead your plants to encourage more flowers, or simply shear them back after the blooms fade.

Most dianthus self-sow freely. They also cross-pollinate, so seed savers should plant only one variety at a time.

A Flower by Many Other Names

Colonial gardeners knew carnations as "gillyflowers," which may have come from the French word for their family name, *gelofres*. Early Romans used pinks instead of cloves to spice their beverages, leading to another nickname, "sops-in-wine." Their botanical name, dianthus, comes from the Greek *dios*, for divine, and *anthos*, for flower.

POPPY—*Papaver*

For all their beauty, poppies have a rather nasty reputation. An old Eurasian legend says that they first appeared when Buddha, desperate to stay awake, cut off his eyelids and flung them to the ground. Scarlet flowers sprang up from his spilled blood, and anyone who touched them was cursed to suffer a troubled sleep. In the ancient Greek myth of changing seasons, Demeter ate poppies to forget her grief after her daughter, Persephone, was kidnapped.

It doesn't seem fair that these flamboyant flowers pop up in such notorious tales, but some poppies do have dangerous narcotic properties. Even their Latin name, *papa*, means "thick milk" and refers to the juice from certain poppies that can be made into opium, heroin, and morphine.

About fifty species of poppies are native to Europe, while many more grow in temperate regions of North America. Some are annuals with single blossoms, while others are double-flowered perennials. Some bear silky and shiny petals, while others have a wrinkled, crinkly look, like crepe paper.

Poppies also vary widely in size, from dainty corn poppies with 2-inch blooms to showy orientals, whose blossoms spread a foot across. Peony types are lush and full, with frilly flower heads that look like ruffled petticoats. Their seed pods remind us that poppies once symbolized fertility, since a single peony poppy case can hold an astounding 32,000 seeds—that's according to Linnaeus, who supposedly counted them all.

Opium poppies, also known as lettuce poppies, have been both used and misused as drugs, although most poppies have simply been enjoyed as ornamentals.

Wherever they are found, poppies are as admired for their brilliant blooms as for their attractive seed pods, which generously spill their tiny contents over the garden at the end of each growing season.

Opium Poppies—P. somniferum

These sun-worshipping annuals are also known as lettuce poppies because their light green to gray-green foliage resembles young lettuce leaves. They are especially showy when planted in masses for late spring or summer bloom.

These opium plants were probably the first poppies to be grown in American gardens. But they're actually quite old, with roots reaching back to lower Mesopotamia around 3400 B.C. The Sumerians discovered that the plants could bring on sleep or produce euphoric feelings. Nicknamed Hul Gil, or the "joy plant," lettuce poppies quickly spread into Assyria, Babylon, and Egypt, and by 1300 B.C. a flourishing opium trade took them into Carthage, Greece, and Europe.

"These creations of heat and light, of silken gauze and crinkled crepe, have no peers for colour and texture in the floral kingdom. They are like dainty bits of finery, and as such must we use them in the garden, for their beauty is ephemeral and they leave sad blanks behind them."
Louise Beebe Wilder,
My Garden *(1920)*

For centuries, people believed that opium poppies, which could induce a deep sleep, were magical. But by 460 B.C., Hippocrates seized on the idea of using the plants medicinally, for alleviating pain or producing a kind of hypnotic state.

Opium use was tolerated in many countries until the Inquisition swept through Europe in the 1300s. Then religious leaders started accusing those who ate, drank, or smoked opium of sinning with the devil's own drug. Frightened of reprisals, addicts took their habit underground.

Meanwhile, gardeners in the Far East continued to raise poppies to treat dysentery and other illnesses. Opium treatments resurfaced in European medicine during the Reformation, and by 1803, opium was once again accepted as a drug to relieve suffering. Canadian physician Sir William Osler was finally inspired to pronounce morphine "God's own medicine."

DANISH FLAG

These 4- to 5-inch flowers are lovely when they flutter in a passing breeze. This is a very old plant; some form of Danish Flag has been cultivated for about 3,000 years. The fringed blossoms may be single or semidouble. Each

fire engine red blossom carries 4 white marks in the center that form a cross.
These easy-to-grow annuals yield large seed pods that are beautiful in dried
arrangements.

HUNGARIAN BLUE BREAD SEED

Rare and hard to find, this heirloom poppy has striking purple-blue flowers. When the seed pods are dry enough to rattle, you can open them and harvest a bounty of gray-blue seeds. Chefs store the nutty-tasting seeds in airtight jars until they are ready to bake them in breads, cakes, and muffins.

Corn Poppies—P. rhoeas

Corn poppies, or field poppies, are native to European meadows. Thomas Jefferson referred to them as his "Lesser Poppies" when he cultivated them at Monticello. In England, syrup makers once paid children to gather their petals for cough medicine. This handsome flower was immortalized in the World War I poem "In Flanders Fields," by Canadian John McCrae, and many people still wear corn poppies in their buttonholes to honor disabled veterans.

SHIRLEY POPPIES

In 1880, an English vicar discovered a fiery red flower with a snowy lip growing in a corner of his garden. The vicar, Rev. W. Wilks, also happened to be the secretary of the Royal Horticultural Society in England, and his fascination with this unusual flower led him to experiment with its seeds.

Wilks gradually changed the centers of his poppies from black to yellow to white and altered the petals from bright red to rose and salmon pink to white. The strain he developed, Shirley, is named for the village where he grew up. The plants are still available in many luscious colors.

In the early 1900s, Luther Burbank bred a blue form of Shirley poppies after discovering what he described as a smoky blue pigment in one specimen. Burbank's Sunset Shades are now quite rare.

FLEMISH ANTIQUE—*P. PAEONIFLORUM*

This gorgeous peony-type poppy, with its tightly packed, doubled blossoms, nearly edged out carnations as the most popular flower of the eighteenth century. Its creamy white petals are ruffled and streaked with deep pink or cherry,

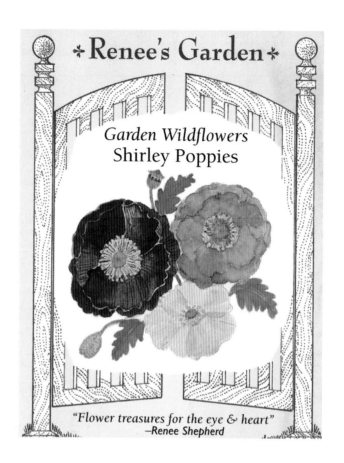

❧ Renee's Garden ❧

Garden Wildflowers
Shirley Poppies

"Flower treasures for the eye & heart"
—Renee Shepherd

sometimes so heavily that you would describe the entire flower as red or pink. Look for these in the old masterpieces painted by Dutch and Flemish artists.

ORIENTAL POPPIES—*P. ORIENTALE*

Oriental poppies, which are native to Persia and the Mediterranean area, were greatly admired in the court of Louis XIV. In 1741, a Quaker seedsman saw the plants growing in England and shipped some of their seeds to his partner, Philadelphia botanist John Bartram. They have been popular in America ever since.

Oriental poppies are stunners, with vermilion to pastel pink blossoms and mounds of fernlike foliage. Their only fault is that they bloom early, leaving gaps in most perennial beds and borders. Designer Gertrude Jekyll suggested planting airy Baby's Breath between them as a filler.

Flemish Antique peony poppy. (Courtesy of David Cavagnaro)

Growing Tips

Tiny poppy seeds are not too hard to sow if you mix them with a little sand or sprinkle them into the palm of your hand and simply blow them over the garden. They do need light to germinate, however, so press them gently into the earth and don't bury them.

Poppies hate transplanting, so start them directly in the garden in late fall,

New Cardinal poppies
and other flowers sold by
Burpee's in 1894.

or in early spring in cold regions, and give them a site with full sun. When seedlings appear, thin them to 9 to 12 inches apart. To ensure continuous blooms, sow another batch of seeds while the first plants are blooming. Two plantings per year may yield both early and late blooms if you're careful to sow while the temperature is still cool.

Like other poppies, Oriental types need full sun and cool temperatures to germinate and moderately rich, well-drained soil. They'll behave as perennials if you live where the nights are cool. Elsewhere, use them as annuals.

When your poppies drop their petals, watch for the seed pods to fatten up. They will eventually burst and self-sow nicely, or you can wait to collect the seeds when they ripen.

Shirley Poppies seeds.
(Courtesy of Renee's Garden)

RADISH—*Raphanus sativus*

You've got to have a little sympathy for radishes, vegetables that once enjoyed a regular place at the American dinner table. An 1888 Burpee's catalog listed 17 different varieties of these members of the cabbage family and even recommended serving them "for breakfast, dinner, and supper, three times a day, they are an appetizing and wholesome relish." Other catalogs of the era offered a wide selection of English radishes guaranteed to mature throughout the spring, summer, fall, or winter.

Today, of course, radishes are largely absent from our tables (although they are still among the most widely grown vegetables in Japan). We seldom use them except as a garnish for green salads or as a novelty on appetizer trays, where they're carved into frilly roses or shaped into long-tailed mice.

Botanists suspect radishes originated in China, where they were mentioned by the philosopher Confucius around 479 B.C. But they are likely much older. At the Great Pyramid in Giza, Herodotus reportedly saw an inscription listing the 1,600 talents spent by Pharaoh for feeding radishes, onions, and garlic to his enslaved masons. Early Egyptians were also known to use radish seed oil in their cooking, much as we use olive oil today.

The ancient Greeks were fond of radishes as well, often dishing them up on golden platters to present to the gods. But in Rome, Pliny the Elder had no use for the radish, sneering that it was "a vulgar article of the diet . . . showing a . . . remarkable power of causing flatulence and eructation."

By the mid-1500s, radishes had found their way into English gardens. John Gerard named four different types as well as a wild radish in his 1597 *Herball*. He suggested consuming the roots to ward off colds and coughs but otherwise saw no reason to eat them except "to procure appetite."

While some heirloom flowers and vegetables have completely disappeared, there are still many old-fashioned radishes available. Try a zesty, crunchy type in your favorite Oriental recipe, or a use a radish with a spicy, mustard bite for mouthwatering pickles.

PHILADELPHIA WHITE BOX

Landreth and Sons introduced these mild, crisp radishes in the 1880s. The small, turnip-shaped roots are pure white and produce short tops. They're fine for growing in cold frames.

Philadelphia White Box. (Courtesy of Seed Savers Exchange)

PLUM PURPLE

For a tasty side dish, braise these big, magenta roots with butter, garlic, and thyme and then add salt and pepper to taste. Ready in 25 days, this French heirloom stays sweet and crisp and resists turning pithy throughout the season.

Plum Purple. (Courtesy of Seed Savers Exchange)

FRENCH BREAKFAST

Dating from 1879, this scarlet-topped beauty is among the earliest radishes, maturing in 24 days. Child's 1899 garden catalog called it "a grand little
table sort" with a "delicately flavored flesh, free from coarseness or any biting
quality." Serve the roots in the French fashion: dip them in butter and kosher
salt and eat them with buttered bread for breakfast. The crisp flesh is white
and mild.

BLACK SPANISH

Popular in Spain throughout the Middle Ages, the Black Spanish is late to
mature, needing about 60 days in the ground. But it is also hardy, so it can be
sown in late summer for a fall and winter harvest. Underneath the rough, deep
purple to blackish skin, the flesh is white. The Round Black Spanish radish,
which dates to at least 1824, forms large, turnip-shaped globes with a medium
hot to hot flavor. They keep well and can be eaten raw or boiled.

Crunchy Icicle radishes.
(Courtesy of David Cavagnaro)

WHITE ICICLE, also known as Lady Finger

These all-white roots mature in around 30 days. They grow 4 to 6 inches long and taper at the tips like an icicle or carrot. Skip this sweet-fleshed variety if you have heavy soil, which causes the roots to become stunted. Otherwise, add sand or other amendments to your garden to make them easier to cultivate. White Icicle, which is tolerant of hot weather, dates back to at least 1896.

VIOLET DE GOURNAY

The French seed company of Vilmorin-Andrieux listed this old variety prior to 1885. It's noteworthy for its unusual purple skin and sweet, white flesh. A winter radish, it takes its name from the French town of Gournay and can tolerate some hard frost without splitting. Give it 65 to 70 days to mature.

GERMAN BEER, also known as Munchen Bier

Large, tapered roots and a pungent flavor distinguish this antique German radish. They are delicious when sliced and eaten on black bread or sprinkled with salt or sugar and served with ice-cold beer. Wesley Greene, garden historian for the Colonial Williamsburg Foundation, reports that it is "an excellent winter radish for us and similar to the eighteenth century turnip radish. I sow it in September for a fiery treat in January and February."

RAT'S TAIL—*R. SATIVUS* VAR. *CAUDATUS*, also known as Rat-Tailed Radish and Purple-Podded Radish

Introduced to America in the early 1860s, this Japanese native was not a big hit, as you might guess from its unappealing name. Instead of forming a bulbous root, the plants produce long, purple seed pods. Some cooks boil or stir-fry the pods, while others chop them for salads or salt them and eat them

A novelty radish, Rat's Tail. (Courtesy of Seed Savers Exchange)

like peanuts. But the pods must be picked when they're still small and tender. Left to mature, they turn tough and fibrous, fit only for the compost heap.

According to heirloom gardener and author William Woys Weaver, Pennsylvania Dutch housewives often put the pods in vinegar, which turned them green. The resulting brine was then used to make colorful pickles. Because the pods have a spicy horseradish flavor, they yield pickles that can bite back.

Growing Tips

Radish seeds are easy and fun to grow. Because they sprout in about 3 days, they can be used to mark the rows of other, slower-germinating crops. Fast-maturing radishes also help loosen the surrounding soil when you pull them up. You can harvest them, of course, while other vegetables are left to grow around them.

Although any root crop grows better in well-tilled soil, radish seeds can break through ground that would defeat lesser veggies. Cover them about ½ inch deep in the garden, leaving 1 to 2 inches between small varieties and up to 6 inches between the larger types. Radishes do not like transplanting, so sow where you want them to grow. When the seeds sprout, thin the seedlings to 2 inches apart and save the green tops to flavor salads or soups.

Radishes prefer cool temperatures, so start them in early spring or late fall. The seeds germinate best when the soil warms to at least 45°F. Give the plants a sunny spot, and don't let them dry out. Radishes that get thirsty become woody, peppery hot, and unpalatable.

If you find you've harvested more radishes than you can possibly use, store them in the refrigerator, or cover them in layers of damp sawdust or sand and stash them in a cool place. Under ideal conditions, they'll keep for 1 to 2 weeks. You can avoid the problem altogether by staggering your plantings, sowing a few radish seeds every 10 to 15 days throughout the season.

If you're saving seeds, be aware that radishes cross easily, so grow only one variety at a time, or harvest one type before you plant another. Simply wait until the radish pods are dry before you harvest them. Then drop the pods into a paper bag and let them rest in a cool, dark room for about a month. They'll be sharp and hard to open, but after they become brittle, you can winnow out the seeds by shaking them in a sieve or rolling them between your gloved fingers. The seeds should stay viable for about 5 years.

SNAPDRAGON—*Antirrhinum*

If you have any kids following in your muddy footsteps through the garden, why not encourage their budding hobby? Lots of plants are simple and fun for the younger set to grow.

Sunflowers are good for beginners, with large seeds that are easy for small fingers to poke into the ground. Pole beans that shimmy up bamboo stakes make great living teepees for summer play. Radish seeds sprout fast, very satisfying for the "Are-we-there-yet?" crowd.

Snapdragons aren't to be missed, either. They are arguably the best toys in the yard, with bright blossoms that really do snap open like little jaws when you pinch them.

Botanists think that snaps are native to southwestern Europe and the Mediterranean area. Romans probably introduced the earliest flowers, the purple *A. majus*, to Britain, and by the Elizabethan age, snaps were also available in rose, white, crimson with bright yellow veins, and red with canary throats.

Jefferson once remarked that he'd admired snapdragons growing around Shadwell, his childhood home. In 1771, he added them to his "shrubbery" at Monticello, in an experiment to see if the plants would naturalize there. While the variety Jefferson planted is no longer available, you can still see the cultivar that replaced it when you visit.

Modern snapdragons aren't usually grown for their scent, although some do smell slightly spicy. But in 1932, garden writer Louise Beebe Wilder complained that the snaps of her era had an overpowering, sweet, "stuffing" fragrance. At least, she conceded, snaps had the good manners not to choke the air all around them. You had to stick your nose directly into a blossom, she admitted, to catch its odor.

Wilder must have had a keen sense of smell, because many other gardeners report that early snapdragons were largely scentless. The first truly fragrant snap was bred in 1963, and this represented a real about-face in the world of heirloom flowers. Most old plants have lost their perfumes through years of development for other characteristics, such as bloom size or color.

Snapdragons take their name from the shape of their blossoms, which open

> "The flower bears a perfect resemblance to the snout or nose of some animal. . . . The flowers grow at the top of the stalkes, of a purple color, fashioned like a frog's mouth, or rather a dragon's mouth, from whence the women have taken the name Snap-Dragon."
>
> Joseph Breck,
> The Flower-Garden
> *(1851)*

from the top to the bottom of sturdy spikes. Early *Antirrhinums* reminded people of animals' faces, with a snout and mouth on each floret. Even the Latin name for these plants comes from the Greek *anti*, for "like," and *rhinos*, for "snout." In parts of Scotland, the flowers were traditionally known as Mappie Mous, or rabbit mouths.

You can also see a face in snapdragons' seed capsules, although they tend to look more like creepy skulls than pleasant countenances. Gerard noticed the similarities: "The seed is black, contained in round husks fashioned like a calves snout . . . or in my opinion it is more like unto the bones of a sheeps head." Other nicknames for the seed pods have included "head of dog" and "head of calf."

Do be aware that snapdragon blossoms come in different shapes. If you're planting them for children, especially little girls who want to wear the colorful blooms like clip-on earrings, choose a variety that has the characteristic snap. Some modern snaps, like the Butterfly strains, have fixed, open-faced flowers. No matter how hard you pinch, they won't pop.

BLACK PRINCE

Several sources indicate that Black Prince first appeared in a Burpee's catalog in 1923, while at least one traces it back to 1912. The flowers are actually deep crimson or maroon, with heavily bronzed foliage. This one falls into the intermediate height range for snapdragons, reaching 18 inches tall.

TOM THUMB

This first dwarf strain of snaps, developed in the 1880s, provides some colorful "shoes" when planted at the "feet" of taller flowers. The seeds are often sold in a mix of bicolors, including white, rose, bright yellow, tropical orange, and deep red. Expect these diminutive beauties to mature at 8 to 9 inches in height.

NIGHT & DAY

Give them a little squeeze, and the burgundy dragons of this 1889 Victorian favorite will "yawn," opening to reveal silvery white throats. Try combining the velvety blossoms with white larkspur for contrast. The plants reach 1½ feet tall, with dark green to lightly bronzed foliage.

Black Prince snaps. (Courtesy of David Cavagnaro)

BRIGHTON ROCK, also known as Picturatum and Candyman

Popular in the 1800s, these snaps look like candy canes with multicolored stripes and swirls. But seed growers, take note: you may get some solid-colored flowers that lack the splashy markings. Look for mixes of pastels or bold colors in this variety: lemon yellow flowers streaked with violet, white dappled with pink or yellow, and sunny yellow streaked with rust or shrimp pink.

Growing Tips

Snaps love cool weather, so start their seeds indoors 8 to 12 weeks before the last spring frost. You can also sow the seeds directly in the garden after the last frost in spring. These plants are considered tender perennials or half-hardy annuals, so even if you misjudge the weather, they should survive a touch of frost. (Many cultivars can overwinter in garden zones 8 through 11, although you'll want to mulch them during any hard freeze.)

Snapdragon seeds need light to germinate, so sprinkle them lightly over a planting medium. If you're starting them indoors, cover them with clear plastic until the seedlings appear.

Once the baby snaps have their first true leaves, they can be hardened off and transplanted. Allow the plants to become 4 inches tall before you pinch the growing tips to encourage branching.

Full sun is best, but snapdragons will bloom, although not as prolifically, in light shade. Give them well-drained, moist soil, and they'll perform throughout the spring.

Don't feel bad about tossing your snaps onto the compost pile when the heat arrives and the plants stop blooming. You can try cutting back the stalks for more flowers, but southern gardeners probably won't have much luck. Snaps just do not thrive in the heat, and any repeat blossoms are often small. It's better for gardeners in hot climates to sow fresh seeds in late summer. By the following spring, fall-planted snaps should bloom nicely.

Since snapdragons open early in the growing season, they make great companions for pansies, flowering kale, and violas. If they succumb to the heat, try plugging sun-loving annuals like marigolds or petunias into their garden spot until temperatures drop and the plants perk back up again. Snapdragons are widely available in every color except blue, and they've earned a reputation as some of the brightest plants in the garden.

If you plan to save snapdragon seeds, remember that insects pollinate the flowers, so grow only one variety at a time to ensure seed purity.

Wilder liked *Antirrhinums* because they self-sowed freely when left to mature, and she recommended using them in rock gardens. As for attracting wildlife, "bees fancy [snapdragons]," she added.

To save their seeds, stop deadheading your plants in late summer and watch for the pods to form. The pods tend to crack open when you're not looking, but you can catch the ripened seeds whenever they are ready if you place paper bags over the flower heads and tie them with string. Stored properly in a cool, dark place, snapdragon seeds should be viable for up to 4 years.

In the 1950s, snapdragons ranked as one of the top five flowers for American cutting gardens.

SPINACH—*Spinacia oleracea*

It's strange but true: the green paint used to illustrate many of the exquisite manuscripts of the Middle Ages was derived from ordinary spinach. Spinach, a cool-weather crop whose name comes from the Persian word for "green hand," contains one of nature's few harmless green pigments (it's even reportedly safe to use as a body paint—if you're so inclined). Of course, spinach loses much of its bright color when it's cooked and turns a drab gray-green, because heat releases certain acids that react with its chlorophyll.

Botanists are not sure where spinach originated, although Asia is a good guess. The leafy plants were probably cultivated more than 2,000 years ago in what we now know as Iran. In Latin, the plants were *spanachia*, which morphed into the English "spinage" and "spinach." The scientific name *Spinacia* means "spine," while *oleracea* refers to an edible plant.

The Arabs adored this member of the goosefoot family, crowning it the "prince of vegetables." Moors carried spinach with them into Spain in the 1100s, and by the 1400s, the greens had spread throughout Europe. Colonists introduced spinach to America, where the seeds began appearing in American catalogs around 1806.

BLOOMSDALE, also known as Bloomsdale Long Standing

In 1826, the D. Landreth Seed Company introduced a new spinach that was eventually marketed as Bloomsdale. The name comes from the Pennsylvania farm where the company located its headquarters in 1847. This variety produces dark green leaves that don't taste bitter whether cooked or eaten fresh. It is a good choice for gardeners whose summers heat up quickly, as it is slow to bolt and lasts about 2 weeks longer in the garden than other crumpled-leaf types. The plants are ready in about 47 days from sowing. Because they're held erect, the leaves tend to stay clean even when rain splashes into the soil around them.

AMERICA

An All-American Selections winner from 1952, this Bloomsdale type spinach is slow to bolt and tolerates hot, dry weather. The crumpled, dark green leaves have a sweet yet peppery flavor. Give the plants 50 days to maturity, and then use the 8-inch leaves for eating fresh or freezing. This variety does not overwinter well, so plant it in spring or early fall.

America. (Courtesy of Seed Savers Exchange)

VIROFLAY

This is it—the "monster spinach" of France, listed by seed seller Vilmorin-Andrieux as Monstreux de Viroflay in 1885. The vigorous, spreading plants reach up to 2 feet in diameter in 50 days from sowing. It's good for the market or the backyard, but start your seeds early, as the plants bolt once the temperature approaches 75°F. The smooth, dark green leaves are oval shaped and grow to 10 inches long. Because they are low in acid, they have a sweet flavor. You can start harvesting in about 21 days from planting, but the leaves will remain tender and succulent even when large. Viroflay is the ancestor of several modern spinach hybrids. Space the plants 10 inches apart in the garden.

Giant Viroflay. (Courtesy of David Cavagnaro)

NEW ZEALAND—*TETRAGONIA EXPANSA*

A European favorite since the 1770s, this is not a true spinach, although it tastes a lot like it. Southern gardeners are especially fond of New Zealand because it performs well in hot climates and resists bolting or turning bitter. The small, pointed leaves are ready for harvest in 50 to 55 days from sowing. Try them raw or cook them instead of spinach when that cool-weather crop gives out. For faster germination, soak the prickly seeds for 24 hours before planting. The plants are frost sensitive, so pick them before the temperature plummets.

STRAWBERRY—*CHENOPODIUM CAPITATUM*,
also known as Strawberry Blite

Europeans have grown these compact plants, which are related to spinach, since the 1600s. This unusual, annual variety is hard to find, but once you get it going, it reseeds readily. In fact, use it carefully or it may become invasive. Its scarlet fruit clusters, which look like mulberries, can be tossed into salads or used for making dye. Some gardeners grow it strictly as an ornamental.

Growing Tips

If you've ever been disappointed with your spinach crop, it's probably because you planted in the spring. In most parts of the country, spinach quickly bolts as the days get longer and the temperature rises. And after spinach sends up a central flower stalk, it's downhill all the way. The leaves lose their juicy, tender flavor, and the plants become spindly and weak.

The solution is easy. Simply plant spinach in the fall, when the temperature is cooling down instead of heating up. If you must sow in the spring, start the seeds as soon as the ground can be worked. Spinach does not germinate well above 75°F. Southerners may want to give their plants some light shade.

For a jump start on the season, you can also start spinach seeds indoors in flats or pots. It's just as easy, though, to sow them directly in the garden.

Drop your seeds into soil that has been loosened or tilled 18 inches deep and enriched with organic materials. Plant them ½ inch deep and 2 inches apart, in rows spaced a foot apart. When the seedlings appear, in 7 to 10 days, thin them to every 6 inches. You can also cultivate spinach in large containers that have adequate drainage.

New Zealand.
(Courtesy of David Cavagnaro)

Keep your plants watered regularly and deeply, and add mulch to shade the soil and help delay bolting. For best flavor, pick the leaves when they're young, tearing off the outer ones first. If you prefer, you can cut off all the leaves at once with a sharp knife and allow the plants to grow another set.

To extend your harvest, plant more spinach at 2-week intervals. During the hottest part of the summer, try substituting New Zealand or another warm-weather green.

If you're saving seeds, plant only one variety of spinach at a time. Start your plants extra early in the growing season, because the seeds need another 4 to 6 weeks to ripen after you pick the leaves for eating. You don't have to worry about pollinating your spinach; the wind will do it for you. Just leave some of the plants in the ground until they bolt. The seeds are almost mature when the plants turn yellow. Once the seeds ripen, strip them from the plants, or pull up the plants and thresh them over a fine screen. Spinach seeds may be round and smooth or spiny and prickly, depending on the variety. To save your fingers, wear gloves when you clean the chaff from the prickly types. Store your spinach seeds in labeled containers in a cool, dry place. Under the right conditions, they should stay viable for 3 to 5 years.

An old French proverb says, "Spinach is the broom of the stomach." Some gardeners claim that the greens aid digestion, and it is thought that the plants have been consumed since ancient times as a natural laxative.

Besides its "cleansing" effect, spinach is quite nutritious. It contains iron, calcium, and potassium as well as vitamins A and C, folate, riboflavin, magnesium, and more. Unfortunately, it also contains oxalic acid, which can block the body's ability to absorb calcium and iron—so Popeye, the cartoon sailor who downed cans of spinach for strong muscles, wasn't really pumping up as much as he thought.

Spinach leaves cook down a lot. If you're cooking it for dinner, buy a pound of raw leaves for every cup of prepared leaves you plan to serve.

SWEET PEA—*Lathyrus odoratus*, also known as the Lady Pea

*"Here are sweet-peas, on tip-toe for a flight
With wings of gentle flush o'er delicate white
And taper fingers catching at all things,
To bind them all about with tiny rings."
English poet John Keats (1795–1821)*

Old-fashioned sweet peas, with their deliriously sweet perfume, simply can't be ignored. Perhaps it was their scent that first caught the attention of a Franciscan monk who saw them growing in their native Sicily.

In 1699, Father Franciscus Cupani collected seeds from the deep blue and purple blossoms and shared them with two friends: Dr. Robert Uvedale, a schoolmaster in England, and Dr. Casper Commelin, a botanist in Holland. The flowers that the men cultivated were widely admired, and by 1724, sweet peas were for sale on the commercial market.

Oddly, breeders generally ignored these cool-weather annuals until the 1800s, when work began to develop a palette of lovely solid, striped, and marbled colors. By the 1870s, Scottish hybridizer Henry Eckford added a grandiflora class of sweet peas with big, billowy blooms.

One of his varieties, Prima Donna, mutated to produce frilled petals held on long stems. This Spencer strain was named in honor of the Earl and Countess Spencer, on whose estate the flowers were found.

Unfortunately, sweet peas began to lose their rich, natural fragrance as breeders tinkered with other characteristics. By 1907, a single catalog listed some 461 varieties available for purchase from the Royal Seed Establishment of Reading, England.

America. (Courtesy of David Cavagnaro)

Thanks to the Spencer strain, sweet peas became some of the most widely grown and best-loved annuals by 1910. Today developers are working to restore the flowers' heavy perfume in modern forms.

JEWELS OF ALBION

This heirloom mix combines heat-tolerant varieties such as pale blue Flora Norton and the mauve Captain of the Blues. All are vigorous climbers with a strong fragrance.

CUPANI, also known as Cupani's Original

This is Father Cupani's wild species from 1699. With its violet and deep bluish-purple flowers, Cupani is the first bicolor. A bushy annual, it grows to 5 feet, with small but richly scented blossoms.

PERFUME DELIGHT

This collection of heat-tolerant heirlooms is a fine choice for gardeners whose summers are long and hot. The plants climb to 6 feet and bear flow-

Cupani. (Courtesy of David Cavagnaro)

ers that range from pale pink to deep red, and from lavender to dark purple. Mixes usually include whites and bicolors. Bury your nose in the blossoms for a whiff of honey and oranges.

LORD NELSON

Originally offered by Burpee's as Brilliant Blue, these navy-blue sweet peas came to America after winning an Award of Merit in the United Kingdom in 1907. One of the best to cultivate for scent, Lord Nelson grows to 6 feet tall.

notes

....
....
....
....
....
....
....
....
....
....
....
....
....
....
....
....
....
....
....
....
....
....
....
....
....
....
....
....

MISS WILLMOTT

Henry Eckford developed these orange-pink to salmon flowers in 1901 and named them for a renowned Victorian garden writer. The annual plants mature at 5 to 6 feet and bloom nicely even if started somewhat late in the season.

LADY GRISEL HAMILTON

Bred by Eckford in 1895, this grandiflora variety has muted heliotrope or lavender petals. Once widely popular, it was nudged out of the spotlight by the acclaimed Spencer strain. Garden author Louise Beebe Wilder loved this one, claiming that lavender, purple, and mauve flowers were the most fragrant, while white and pale pink blossoms offered only a "transparent" scent.

PAINTED LADY

Southern gardeners like this vigorous charmer, which keeps producing pink and pale rose flowers even as the temperature rises. From 1730, it originated as a sport of Cupani. The Spencer strain nearly caused this sweet pea to disappear, too, but the Lady was saved by an Australian family who kept it under cultivation for generations. The seeds are once again available on the commercial market. Sometimes you may find this one referred to as Old Spice.

HENRY ECKFORD

Breeder Eckford, of Shropshire, became known all over the world for his efforts to improve sweet peas. The stunning, clear orange variety that bears his name dates to about 1904.

BLACK KNIGHT

From 1898, this is another Eckford introduction with large, very fragrant flowers. The blooms may be dark purple or deep violet, or crimson black to deep maroon. Sweet pea fans consider it one of the best grandifloras.

DOROTHY ECKFORD

Named for the granddaughter of Henry Eckford, this pure white flower debuted in 1903. A grandiflora that grows to 5 feet, it was voted the best white variety of 1907 by the English National Sweet Pea Society.

Janet Scott.

(Courtesy of David Cavagnaro)

JANET SCOTT

Introduced by C. C. Morse and Company and Burpee's in 1903, these shell pink flowers are carried three or four to a stem on plants that grow to 6 feet.

FLORA NORTON

This 1904 offering from Morse-Vaughan is a clean, bright blue. It matures at 5 to 6 feet and has a sweet, potent scent.

Jewels of Albion and Perfume
Delight sweet pea seeds.
(Courtesy of Renee's Garden)

CAPTAIN OF THE BLUES

This Eckford sweet pea from the 1890s is one of the best of the blue flowers—even though the color is actually a deep mauve-blue.

COUNTESS CADOGAN

From 1899, this regal bicolor produces violet and bright blue blossoms on 4- to 5-foot plants.

MRS. COLLIER

James Dobbie, of Dobbies Garden Centres in Scotland, introduced these creamy white blossoms in the early 1900s. Considered one of the best grandifloras, Mrs. Collier won a Royal Horticultural Society Award of Garden Merit in 1906.

COUNTESS SPENCER

These wavy pink blossoms are said to have been discovered by Silas Cole, a gardener at the Spencer family's Althorp estate. Named for an ancestor of the late Princess Diana, the Countess was the first in the Spencer strain. It set the standard for the sweet peas that grow in most of today's gardens.

Growing Tips

Like garden peas, sweet peas need cool temperatures to keep them happy, so start the seeds very early in the spring, as soon as the ground can be worked. Gardeners whose winters are mild can plant their seeds in cool autumn weather for blooms in the following spring. For best results, dig a bed for your seeds at least 1 foot deep and add well-rotted manure or compost.

Sweet peas take about 14 days to germinate, but they'll sprout faster if you nick the seed coats with a knife or soak the seeds in tepid water the night before planting.

Start your seeds indoors in peat pots from mid- to late winter, and harden off the seedlings before moving them outside. Then plant the seedlings, pots and all, to avoid disturbing their roots. Alternately, sow the seeds ½ to 1 inch deep, and 1 inch apart, directly in the garden. When the plants emerge, thin them to every 18 to 24 inches and pinch out the growing tips to encourage branching. Sweet peas like "their heads in the sun and their feet in the shade," as old-timey gardeners say, so give them lots of sun on their leaves and keep their roots well mulched and watered.

These vigorous, floriferous climbers need support with fences, trellises, or netting as they grow. You can make wigwams for them by tying slender poles together and planting the seeds in a circle at the base of each pole. Some gardeners simply push strong branches into the ground around their seeds or seedlings and let the plants curl their tendrils around them as they grow.

The Garden in Summer

As spring drifts into summer, the real work of the garden begins. Too bad you can't just set out your heirloom seeds and leave them alone! Despite all the tilling and hoeing you've already done, and all the bags of manure and bundles of peat you've hauled and spread around the flower beds and vegetable patch, there is still more work to do.

Spring, for the most part, is about the preliminary stuff: preparing the soil, marking off rows, stringing supports for beans and peas, and tucking your carefully chosen heirlooms into hills and drills and rows. Now we have to tend what we've sown, and maybe resow as fast-maturing crops are harvested, leaving gaps in the garden.

As the heat and humidity climb, it is important to be vigilant. After all, it's much easier to prevent a problem than to fix one, and far better to keep weeds and diseases and bugs from gaining a foothold in the first place.

For combating diseases, most gardeners know that keeping the garden clean and orderly is a big help. Remove and replace any mulch as soon as you spot trouble brewing, and if your plants are still fairly small, encourage good air circulation by thinning to the recommended distance between each variety.

If your housekeeping attempts don't help, you may eventually have to pull up and destroy badly infected plants. If your community allows you to burn plant debris, and you can do so safely, go ahead and burn promptly. (Always follow local safety regulations, obtain any required burning permits, and never burn under windy or dry conditions.) Do not toss any diseased plants onto the compost heap. That's asking for trouble, as the warmth and moisture of the decomposing materials may spread the disease even further.

Be especially careful around any bean or pea plants, and don't wander among the rows when their foliage is wet from rain or dew. Many an unsuspecting gardener has brushed against bushes or vines suffering from bacterial blight and inadvertently transferred it throughout the patch.

"What a man needs in gardening is a cast-iron back with a hinge in it."
Charles Dudley Warner,
My Summer in a Garden
(1870)

Of course, diseases are not the only things that plague the summer garden. Insects can also be a nightmare, riddling the leaves of eggplants and cabbages with lacey holes or gnawing at sunflowers and morning glories. Sadly, many of the sprays and powders sold to combat them wind up injuring or killing some beneficial insects, too. The damage works its way up the food chain if any of those insects are eaten by birds and other creatures.

To avoid harming innocent bystanders, first try a nontoxic approach to insect control. Instead of dousing your plants with poisons, try knocking off any bugs with a stick or a gentle stream of water from the garden hose. You can even handpick bigger pests, like snails and slugs. Just be careful about what you touch, as some creatures are equipped to fight back. Green and brown saddleback caterpillars, for example, are almost invisible as they crawl along the stems of tomato plants. But they're studded with small, stinging spines that can irritate your skin, and grabbing one by mistake feels like getting stung by a bee. When you remove pests by hand, it's generally a good idea to wear protective gloves.

Remember, too, that your allies in your organic battle are all around you in the summer garden. Birds are some of the creatures whose aid you will want to enlist, as many feast on harmful crickets, moths, beetles, and caterpillars. If you have not done so yet, you may still have time to nail up some inviting birdhouses. You can also clean out nests from boxes whose occupants have already flown, in hopes of attracting a second set of residents.

To encourage the birds to stick around in your yard, offer them plenty of fresh water for drinking and bathing. Provide water in a pedestal bath as well as in a shallow container perched on a stump or placed directly on the ground, since some birds don't like to feed or drink from heights. Be sure your low bowls and feeders are away from dense vegetation that might conceal cats and other predators.

With luck, you'll attract gentle bluebirds to snatch up ravenous moths in midflight. Warblers may stop by to gobble fat caterpillars, mosquitoes, and beetles. Many other birds, including finches, juncos, sparrows, and thrushes, eat undesirable insects too.

Don't be afraid to try a bat box, either. Just one hungry bat can suck down about 500 mosquitoes and other small garden pests each hour. Despite bats' unsavory reputation about flying into your hair, their powerful sonar actually lets them give you a wide berth when you are outside. To lure them to your yard, plant heirloom blossoms such as jasmine, heliotrope, nicotiana, and four o'clocks. Bats help your summer garden by snacking on bugs, pollinating your plants, and even dispersing seeds in their droppings.

If insects continue to plague you, you can experiment with an old-timey gardener's trick: designate some of your heavily infested plants to serve as traps. Simply let the bugs have their way with a few sacrificial green victims to distract them from chomping on your healthier flowers and vegetables. Some gardeners swear that turning chickens loose in their yards has vanquished entire bug populations overnight. Chickens are probably in short supply if you're a city dweller, but leaving some plants unsprayed really can draw bugs away from their sprayed neighbors. Ultimately you may be able to avoid using chemicals at all, or at least use less of them.

The good news is that heirloom gardeners won't have to reach for the poisonous stuff nearly as often as everybody else. After all, we've started out with seeds that nature has primed to prevail. Every snapdragon or watermelon that thrives in an heirloom garden is already a survivor, a variety that has endured generations of problems and extremes of weather.

Over the centuries, gardeners have done their part to keep old varieties going by selecting seeds from the strongest, most delicious, or loveliest plants. As the summer progresses, tag or mark your favorites in the garden so you collect their ripened seeds as the year winds down. By doing this, you will help determine whether the heliotropes that flower a couple of seasons down the road will smell of almonds or vanilla, or whether the next generation of muskmelons will taste sweeter and juicier than the last.

The nice thing about heirloom gardening is that you can think about these things—genetics and plant characteristics—as much or as little as you like. If you select plants for specific traits like productivity or bloom size, you may get some interesting results worth sharing. If you're simply looking for bragging rights for the meatiest tomato on your block, that's fine, too.

In a sense, there is nothing special about heirlooms. Since they've adapted to whatever time and nature has thrown at them, most are remarkably easy to grow. They won't require anything other than the usual weeding, watering, and fertilizing you'd provide for modern plants.

Then again, heirlooms are very special. Look around a garden center and you'll see the difference. All the common, ordinary marigolds and vincas you'll find there are attractive and undemanding. But that's the problem, too—they're common and ordinary. Many gardeners choose heirlooms because we don't want to grow what everybody else is growing. We yearn for a different kind of flower or unusual vegetable that makes the neighbors stroll over to ask what it is and where we got it.

Heirlooms provide that kind of energy for the garden. Just remember to stop and enjoy your plants at the end of each summer day. Sit on the porch or stretch out in a hammock for awhile and admire your ripening corn and jewel-colored zinnias. Take a break. You've earned it.

AMARANTH—*Amaranthus*, also known as Love-Lies-Bleeding, Velvet Flower, Tassel Flower

"A popular plant in eighteenth century Virginia that usually requires support to best show the long, red blooms. One year I planted some next to a bed of cucumbers and discovered that the cucumber beetles so adored the Love-Lies-Bleeding, they never bothered the cucumbers!"
Wesley Greene,
Garden Historian,
Colonial Williamsburg
Foundation

English botanist John Gerard called it the "great purple flower-gentle," and the amaranth really is the giant of the garden. This native of Peru, Africa, and India towers over most other plants, with some forms reaching up to 12 feet tall. Admittedly, some amaranths are weedy looking and wouldn't draw a second glance from flower fans. But whether you admire them or not, you can't ignore amaranths' chenille-soft flower plumes, which come in eye-popping shades of magenta, reddish purple, and chartreuse.

Since ancient times, amaranths have served as edibles and ornamentals. Partially eaten seeds dating back 10,000 years have been discovered in Mexican caves, and grain types, such as *A. cruentus*, were a food staple for the Incas.

Amaranths were also eaten by the Aztec priests, who mixed them with honey and molded them into figures of the gods. They instructed worshipers to eat the idols, too, explaining that the crimson flowers and stems were the deities' flesh and bones. Catholics who witnessed these ceremonies condemned them as a kind of false communion and tried to stop the cultivation of amaranths by threatening to execute anyone who grew them. But some species escaped from cultivation and managed to naturalize in the wild. Eventually amaranths made their way to Europe, where they were embraced as garden novelties. Today there are about sixty known species still in existence.

Grain amaranths, which have a high protein content, make nutritious

A. *caudatus* bears soft, wine-red tassels.
(Courtesy of Renee's Garden)

breads and cakes. The fresh seeds, which are sometimes sold at health food stores, are good for dry-roasting, or they can be popped like popcorn kernels for a nutty snack.

Other kinds of amaranths are good for eating as greens for the table. For centuries, Asians and Third World natives cooked *A. tricolor*, also known as Tampala, as a substitute for spinach.

Of course, throughout time, the plants have been prized simply for their exotic looks. Amaranths symbolized immortality to the ancient Greeks, who decorated their tombs and temples with images of the long, drooping flowers. Even the plants' name comes from the Greek *amarantos*, meaning "unwithering" or "never waxing old."

In the Elizabethan age, amaranths were appreciated for their vivid colors and strange flower forms. Victorians loved them, too, often dosing them with manure until the plants' stems formed arches over the heads of passersby. Ladies and gentlemen could then stroll through these living tunnels and stroke the dangling tassels.

But flowers go in and out of style, and when garden designer Gertrude Jekyll pronounced purple a difficult color to work with, many amaranth fans turned against the gaudy plants, abandoning them for more conservative blossoms. By the 1900s, amaranths had largely disappeared from the landscape.

Luckily, renewed interest in heirlooms has drawn fresh attention to these stunning—some would say bizarre—plants, although nowadays we grow them more for flowers than baking flour.

LOVE-LIES-BLEEDING—*A. CAUDATUS*

This is probably the oldest ornamental type, first described in a sixteenth-century European herbal and offered commercially in 1810. The spectacular plants grow 3 to 5 feet tall with drooping ropes of blood or wine red flowers. Use them with other large plants that can hold their own in the garden, such as cannas, or let them clash exuberantly with purple verbenas and hot pink dahlias. This one flowers 60 to 70 days after sowing.

PONYTAILS

Topping out at 3 feet, Ponytails makes a good choice for urns or other large containers. The dark raspberry blooms look more like fuzzy balls or pom-poms than a horse's tail.

VIRIDIS

Everything about this amaranth is green, from its chartreuse flower clusters to its lime green stems and leaves. Combine it with sunny blossoms to bring out its softer side. It matures at 3 to 5 feet.

HOT BISCUITS—*A. CRUENTUS*

Even the seeds of this old beauty are an attractive golden brown. Some gardeners say the flowers are the color of cinnamon or wheat, while others think they look like fresh-baked biscuits. Even the plants' leaves are veined with gold or bronze. Also known as Prince's Feather, this amaranth hails from

Love-Lies-Bleeding.
(Courtesy of Renee's Garden)

South America, where it's grown as an ornamental and a food source. Start the seeds extra early, as the flowers need 12 weeks to develop atop the 6-foot-tall plants.

POLISH

Another stately amaranth, Polish grows to 7 feet tall. It's heavily branched, with red-tinged foliage and handsome burgundy flowers.

HOPI RED DYE—*A. CRUENTUS* X *A. POWELLI*

Hopi Indians traditionally ground the seeds of these amaranths to make flour for red cornbread. The young leaves can be tossed raw into salads or steamed and eaten as greens.

ELEPHANT'S HEAD—*A. GANGETICUS*

German immigrants helped save this rare strain, which boasts upright blooms that look like an elephant's raised trunk. Expect the maroon to deep purple blossoms to appear 70 to 80 days after sowing. This amaranth, which self-sows freely, is nice for a cutting garden and matures at 3 to 5 feet tall.

Growing Tips

Amaranths are easy to grow. Start the seeds indoors about 8 weeks before the last frost, and barely cover them with soil, as they need light to germinate. In a warm room, the seeds should sprout in 3 to 5 days. Within 2 weeks, the seedlings will be ready to transplant. Wait until all danger of frost has passed and the nighttime temperature remains reliably above 50°F before moving the seedlings outdoors. Space the young plants 10 to 12 inches apart in the garden. If you live where the summers are long and warm, you can sow amaranth seeds directly outside.

Amaranths are carefree annuals that thrive in full sun and hot weather, and they dislike excessive humidity and soggy soil. Victorian gardeners nurtured their plants with water mixed with pigeon dung; but amaranths are actually drought tolerant, and most only need an extra drink during dry spells. (You don't have to worry about cultivating them with pigeon droppings, either; too much fertilizer makes the plants lanky. Since amaranths are native to temperate and tropical regions, they'll do fine in average to poor soils.)

Your amaranths should begin flowering in midsummer and continue until frost. Mulch the plants deeply to keep them clean, as rain often splashes dirt onto their woolly tassels and makes them look bedraggled.

If you live in northern areas, your growing season may be too short for grain amaranths. Ornamental types should perform well in most of the country.

Amaranth seed heads mature gradually from the bottom to the top of the stalks. To collect the seeds, cut the heads before they turn completely dry and brittle, and beat or thrash them together, letting the seeds fall out over a large cloth. You can also gather the seeds by shaking the flower heads inside a paper bag when they are almost fully mature.

Allow your amaranth seeds to dry for a week after harvesting them. The chaff can be prickly, so wear gloves if you clean the seeds by rubbing them between your fingers. Finish the job by sifting the seeds in a sieve or over a piece of fine screen, and store them in a dry, airtight container away from light and heat. You'll have plenty for the next season. Amaranths are as prolific as poppies, with a single plant able to produce many thousands of seeds.

Love-Lies-Bleeding seeds.
(Courtesy of Renee's Garden)

CARROT—*Daucus carota* var. *sativus*

Describing someone as a "carrot-top" usually means he or she has brightly colored hair. But people have literally worn carrot tops on their heads throughout history. In the Middle Ages, French women cut the feathery greens from carrots to adorn their hats and hairstyles, as did the ladies of Queen Elizabeth's court.

The earliest carrots weren't red or even orange. Food historians believe that the plants started out as thickened purple or yellow roots that grew in

"Sow Carrets in your Gardens, and humbly praise God for them, as for a singular and great blessing."

Richard Gardiner,
Profitable Instructions
for the Manuring,
Sowing, and Planting
of Kitchen Gardens
(1599)

Afghanistan and probably developed from a mutation of the Queen Anne's Lace wildflower. Sometime between A.D. 900 and 1000, the plants spread into the eastern Mediterranean area, and by the 1300s, carrots were on the menu in Western Europe and China.

In the 1600s, settlers introduced carrots to the New World, where families traditionally whipped up a batch of sweet carrot pies at the end of each growing season. They knew the vegetables would get caught by an unexpected freeze in the field as winter arrived and would rot if left too long in storage.

By the 1700s, white carrots were known in Europe, where Dutch breeders began working to develop the orange, carotene-rich roots we know today.

If you've never seen carrot seeds on carrot plants, that's because we usually pull the plants before they can produce them. Carrots are biennials, so they don't set seeds until their second year.

ROYAL CHANTENAY

This crisp carrot, which comes from the Chantenay region in France, is known for its attractive color and sweet taste. Burpee's praised it in an early catalog: "Our trials of this new carrot the past season (1887) were very satisfactory, and we do not hesitate to recommend it as one of the best varieties. [It is] of more than usual merit as a table carrot. The flesh is of a beautiful rich orange color and of the very finest quality. The roots are very smooth, fine in texture, and easily dug." Give it 70 days to mature.

OXHEART

A rare and sometimes hard-to-find heirloom, this French carrot dates to 1884. The thick, blocky roots, ready in 65 to 75 days, have a rough heart shape. They grow 4 to 5 inches long yet can weigh up to a pound, so they're fine for gardeners with shallow soils.

GOLDINHART

Golden orange in color, tender and sweet in taste, Goldinhart was introduced by Burpee's in 1929. It is a half long variety, which means that its roots are shorter than usual, so it's a good choice for soils that are not deeply tilled. Burpee's still recommends it as "probably the best all-around carrot." It's a good keeper, and many cooks claim that it sweetens in storage.

CARROTS AND PEAS
OF RECOGNIZED MERIT

7

THOMAS
LAXTON

CHANTENAY

Chantenay carrots as pictured
in Ferry's 1923 seed catalog.

Antique carrots come in a rainbow of colors. (Courtesy of David Cavagnaro)

DANVERS

The crisp roots of this tasty heirloom can reach 9 inches long. Nice, strong tops make them easy to pull at harvesttime. The carrots have broad shoulders and taper toward the tip. This variety probably originated in Danvers, Massachusetts, in the 1870s.

TOUCHON

Many gourmets say this is the carrot to choose for eating out of hand. Touchon is an old French favorite with a sweet, nearly coreless flesh. It's quick to mature, needing about 65 days to produce deep orange roots that measure 6 inches long.

VIOLET

Historians believe that soldiers under Alexander the Great brought this carrot back from their journeys through India and Persia. The red-colored oddities were once valued for both the table and medicinal purposes. American colonists served them like beets, and modern chefs still shred or slice them into salads. One note: when cooked, violet carrots turn an unappetizing brown. According to heirloom gardener and author William Woys Weaver, there are basically two kinds of violet carrots that have been crossed with yellow carrots to produce our modern orange roots.

Growing Tips

"The Carrot wants rich, sandy loam, deeply tilled," explained a 1908 catalog. "Sow quite early in spring in drills 14 inches apart, and keep as free from weeds as possible." That's still good advice.

Carrot seeds are very fine, so mix them with a little sand or put them in a shaker to make them easier to handle. They can be sown directly in the garden in early spring. Resow every 2 weeks for a steady supply of carrots. Southerners can sow until midsummer for a fall crop.

An old trick calls for mixing carrot and radish seeds together and then sprinkling both over the ground at the same time. The quick-sprouting radishes appear first, helping mark the rows until the carrots appear 6 to 18 days later.

Plant your carrots in raised beds to promote long, smooth roots, or sow them in wide rows spaced 18 inches apart. Cover the seeds very lightly with soil, sand, or vermiculite, and keep them well watered.

When the seedlings emerge, thin them with scissors, so you don't disturb any neighboring roots, and weed often.

Carrots are ready to pick when their colors become deep and bright. You don't have to harvest all of them at once. After the tops die, leave some roots in

CARROTS.

In comparing our prices, please remember that we send the **seeds postpaid, by mail.** *If ordered by express or freight, 8 cts. per pound may be deducted from prices.*

SHORT HORN, OR EARLY SCARLET HORN CARROT.

OX-HEART CARROT.

SHORT HORN, or EARLY SCARLET HORN. One of the most popular; deep orange; flesh fine grained and of agreeable flavor; top small; grows well in shallow soil. Per pkt. 5 cts.; oz. 10 cts.; ¼ ℔ 25 cts.; per ℔ 75 cts.

EARLY VERY SHORT SCARLET, or GOLDEN BALL (also called **Earliest Short Horn for forcing**). This is the earliest carrot in cultivation. The roots are as round as a turnip, of small size, very rich color, flavor excellent and melting. Early carrots pay. Per pkt. 5 cts.; oz. 10 cts.; ¼ ℔ 25 cts.; per ℔ 85 cts.

OX-HEART or GUERANDE. This new carrot comes from France and is a decided advance in shape, as shown in the illustration. It is intermediate as to length between the half long varieties (such as Danvers) and the Short Horn Carrot, but much thicker than the latter, attaining at the top from three to four inches in diameter. It is of very fine quality for table. Per pkt. 5 cts.; oz. 10 cts.; ¼ ℔ 25 cts.; per ℔. 85 cts.

Half Long Scarlet, Stump-rooted. Suitable for shallow soils; smooth in skin and rich in color. Per pkt. 5 cts.; oz. 10 cts.; ¼ ℔ 25 cts.; per ℔ 85 cts.

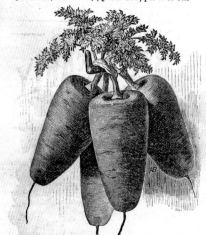

CHANTENAY OR MODEL CARROT.

DANVERS CARROT.

CHANTENAY or MODEL CARROT. For table use it is probably the best in shape and finest in quality of all. The carrots have attained such a uniformity that they are almost duplicates of each other. They are a little longer than the Short Horn, being thicker at the shoulder and hence more productive; always very smooth and fine in texture and easily dug; the flesh is of a beautiful, deep golden orange, tender. Per pkt. 5 cts.; oz. 10 cts.; ¼ ℔ 25 cts.; per ℔ 75 cts.

DANVERS HALF LONG ORANGE. This variety originated in Danvers, Mass., where the raising of carrots is made a special business, twenty to thirty tons per acre being no unusual crop. In form it is midway between the Long Orange and Short Horn. The root is of a rich, dark orange color, and grows very smooth. Per pkt. 5 cts.; oz. 10 cts.; ¼ ℔ 25 cts.; per ℔ 75 cts.

CORELESS LONG RED. A beautiful variety, growing twelve to sixteen inches long and two to three inches in diameter; stump-rooted, of rich color. Per pkt. 5 cts.; oz. 10 cts.; ¼ ℔ 25 cts.; per ℔ 85 cts.

LARGE WHITE VOSGES. This is a field carrot, and especially suitable for soils that are not very deep; it is productive, easily pulled and keeps well. It is

Burpee's 1891 assortment of delicious heirloom carrots.

the ground for a few more weeks. Some gardeners blanket their carrots with mulch until freezing weather threatens and then bring them in to store or use.

It is not easy to save seeds from carrots, but it can be done. You will need to start by selecting only healthy, vigorous plants. Then the roots have to be "vernalized," or exposed to enough cold to make them flower. There are two ways to do this.

If you live in a region that gets at least 10 weeks of cold, but not freezing, temperatures each year, you can mulch your carrots and leave them to overwinter in the ground. The following spring, remove the mulch and wait for leaves and seed stalks to appear. This method may sound easy, but the problem is that freezing temperatures sometimes kill the roots no matter what you try to do.

A second way to vernalize carrots is to harvest them as usual and then trim back the green tops. Store the plants in paper bags filled with wood shavings and enclose the paper bags in plastic bags. Refrigerate the bagged plants throughout the winter at between 36° and 41°F. Check the bags often and remove any condensation that forms inside.

The next spring, replant the saved roots at the same time you would plant fresh carrot seeds. Unfortunately, this exacting method isn't anymore foolproof than the first one. Diseases and pests can cause the replanted roots to fail, especially if your region is warm and humid. And no matter which seed-saving method you try, you will have to plant far away from wild carrots, as they'll cross-pollinate with your saved varieties.

But if you make it this far, seed stalks will eventually form on the carrot plants. When the seeds ripen and turn brown, they'll be ready to harvest and store. Or you can take the easy route—nothing wrong with that—and obtain fresh heirloom seeds each year. A 2-gram packet of carrot seeds contains approximately 1,200 seeds. That's enough to sow a 40-foot row.

A Rainbow of Carrots

Ever heard that carrots are good for your eyes? It's true that the vitamin A in orange carrots contributes to healthy peepers. Other carrots may provide health benefits, too. Researchers say the reds and yellows may help prevent cancer, while purple-skinned carrots with orange cores may stave off certain kinds of heart disease. And white carrots? They're colorless because they lack pigment, and scientists think they also lack medicinal value.

CORN—*Zea mays*

"Then plough deep while sluggards sleep, and you shall have corn to sell and to keep."
Benjamin Franklin, Poor Richard's Almanac

To the Iroquois and other tribes, corn, beans, and squash were the sacred Three Sisters, crops that nurtured the body and spirit. By tradition, they were planted together to help one another as they grew, like family members who work in harmony.

Native gardeners knew that their emerging beans and squash would latch onto nearby cornstalks for support. In return, the big squash leaves would shadow the corn roots and keep them moist and cool, while the beans would add valuable nitrogen to the soil.

Pumpkins and gourds were sometimes substituted for squash in Three Sisters' gardens, but corn, or maize, has always been vital to the Indian culture. Even before Columbus landed, native peoples were growing a grain they called *mahiz*. The pueblos of New Mexico still host annual dances to celebrate and honor corn.

Not surprisingly, corn was considered a gift from the gods. Although researchers have never pinned down an exact origin for the plants, they have found traces of corn meal dating back 7,000 years. From this evidence, they suspect that corn began as a wild grass in Mexico and Central America known as *teosinte*, or "God's corn."

Modern corn, of course, is much different from its early ancestors. Domesticated varieties can't even survive without human help, because their seeds—the kernels—cling stubbornly to the cobs instead of dropping off to self-sow.

Fortunately we can still cultivate many delicious heirloom corns. If you want corn for grinding into hominy or grits, choose a flint variety. If you're baking bread, pick a flour corn with softer seeds. Snackers can try popcorn varieties whose kernels explode when heated.

Dent corns have kernels with a distinctive wrinkled appearance. Sweet corn is the backyard gardener's favorite. Its milky kernels have a sugary taste when the fresh ears are rushed to the table.

BLOODY BUTCHER

This 1845 beauty produces towering stalks up to 12 feet tall. It's a dent corn, with unusual kernels that range in color from dark wine to blood red. Give it 120 days from sowing and expect to harvest two to four ears per stalk. Cooks can serve the ears fresh, if they're picked while they're small, or wait until the ears mature and grind the kernels into pink cornmeal. Many gardeners say this variety performs well even in poor soils and dry weather. Save a few ears for your fall decorations as the cobs are an attractive pinkish red.

Bloody Butcher. (Courtesy of Seed Savers Exchange)

COUNTRY GENTLEMAN, also known as Shoe-Peg

This old-timey white corn was introduced in 1891 by Peter Henderson & Company. Named for a popular nineteenth-century farm magazine, it's fine for canning, cooking, or freezing. The creamy white kernels form irregular rows on small cobs about 100 days after planting. The stalks grow to 8 feet tall and produce ears that are "tender and sweet; very desirable for the home garden," according to a Burbank's 1908 seed catalog.

Country Gentleman. (Courtesy of Seed Savers Exchange)

ANASAZI

Known to the Anasazi people since at least A.D. 100, this rare corn with red, yellow, and purple kernels is used primarily for making flour. Each stalk grows 6 to 9 feet tall and bears multiple ears in 90 to 120 days from sowing. This variety is believed to be the ancestor of many of the southwestern types; even its name comes from a Navaho word meaning "ancient ones."

BLACK MEXICAN, also known as Black Sweet, Mexican Sweet, and Black Iroquois

Rather than hailing from south of the border, this corn probably originated in upper New York State around 1864. Its sweet, white kernels turn purple to bluish black as they age. Don't be put off by the color; the ears are good for eating fresh as long as you pick them while the kernels are still white. If you harvest at a later stage, it's better to grind the kernels for blue cornmeal. Ready in about 80 days from planting, this one is a good choice for northern gardens and matures fast enough for a second crop in the South.

BURBANK'S EARLY MAINE

A 1908 catalog published by seedsman Seth Wyman Fife had high praise for this rare corn, which was named for the E. W. Burbank Seed Company. "The earliest and best Sweet Corn in cultivation. Has a pure white cob with a rich, cream white kernel, sweet and juicy. Looks nice on the table; has no objectionable look like the Cory and Marblehead corn with a red kernel and cob. Ears grow to be a good size, uniform in shape."

OAXACAN GREEN DENT

Commonly known and advertised as a dent corn used by Mexican Zapotecs to make green-flour tamales, this is most likely not a true variety. Perhaps the name arises from the use of immature maize as "green corn," like the use of the term "green apples." The stalks reach 6 to 7 feet tall in 75 to 100 days from sowing.

Oaxacan Green. (Courtesy of Seed Savers Exchange)

New Yellow California Pop Corn, sold by Burpee's in 1894.

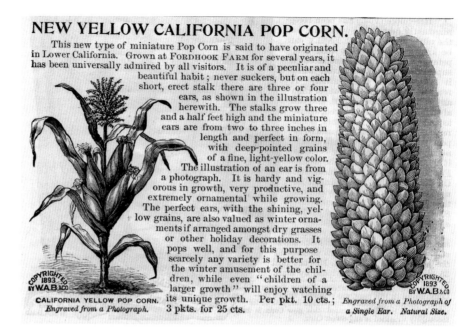

NEW YELLOW CALIFORNIA POP CORN.

This new type of miniature Pop Corn is said to have originated in Lower California. Grown at FORDHOOK FARM for several years, it has been universally admired by all visitors. It is of a peculiar and beautiful habit; never suckers, but on each short, erect stalk there are three or four ears, as shown in the illustration herewith. The stalks grow three and a half feet high and the miniature ears are from two to three inches in length and perfect in form, with deep-pointed grains of a fine, light-yellow color. The illustration of an ear is from a photograph. It is hardy and vigorous in growth, very productive, and extremely ornamental while growing. The perfect ears, with the shining, yellow grains, are also valued as winter ornaments if arranged amongst dry grasses or other holiday decorations. It pops well, and for this purpose scarcely any variety is better for the winter amusement of the children, while even "children of a larger growth" will enjoy watching its unique growth. Per pkt. 10 cts.; 3 pkts. for 25 cts.

CALIFORNIA YELLOW POP CORN.
Engraved from a Photograph.

Engraved from a Photograph of a Single Ear. Natural Size.

HOWLING MOB

Who could resist a corn with a name like this? Legend says that its developer, C. D. Keller, of Toledo, Ohio, was mobbed by buyers every time he brought the sweet, white ears to market. Give this variety, which dates to 1905, about 80 days to mature.

Growing Tips

Got plenty of sun in your garden spot? Corn can take all the heat that summer dishes out. Sow your seeds directly into the garden after all danger of frost has passed, planting 1 inch deep and 4 inches apart.

Since corn pollen travels on the wind from the tassels to the silks, you'll get better pollination if you plant in short blocks. Try making 4 or 5 short rows instead of long, single rows. Space the rows 3 feet apart, and thin the emerging seedlings to every 12 inches.

You can also plant corn in hills, alongside squash and pole beans, in the traditional Native American style. Simply choose tall varieties and start the corn 2 weeks before sowing the beans and squash. You may need to help the young squash and bean vines grab onto the stalks as they emerge.

Some varieties of corn take 100 to 120 days to mature, so be sure to choose early types if you live in a cold climate. If you need a jump on the weather, you can sow your seeds indoors and transplant after the last spring frost.

One warning: birds love corn seeds, so you may need to cover your rows with a special lightweight fabric that's designed to protect tender seedlings. Look for it at nurseries or garden centers.

Corn is ready to harvest when the silks turn dry and brown. Before you pick the ears, test them with your fingernail. Ripened kernels will burst and ooze a milky liquid when popped. If the liquid looks watery, don't pick yet—the ears are not ready. For grinding corn, wait until the kernels are completely dry before you harvest. If rainy weather sets in, you can bring the ears inside. They'll store for a short time.

Country Gentleman corn seeds.

Pick Quick, Heat and Eat

Heirloom corns are naturally sweet, but their sugars start turning to starch soon after the ears are picked. That's why many old recipes urge you to run to the cornfield, snatch up the corn, and race back to the kitchen to plop it in boiling water.

Modern varieties can hold their sugar content much longer, and some even taste sweeter for a few days after they are picked. That's fine if you need a product that will sit on supermarket shelves, but many gardeners prefer the true "corny" flavor of old types.

Be sure to allow extra cooking time when you're boiling heirloom ears. They're flavorful and nutritious but often not as tender as newer varieties.

CORNFLOWER—*Centaurea cyanus*

Of all the colors, blue is the rarest in the garden. Even the azure flowers promised on many seed packets turn out not to be true blue at all, but violet, purple, lavender, dark plum, bluish-black, or deep mauve. It's tricky to find blossoms that match the color of a summer sky.

Cornflowers come as close as any heirloom to putting blue on the garden palette. These shaggy beauties, introduced to America by the 1600s, have been grown throughout their native Europe and in Asia for centuries.

In Egypt, archaeologists discovered cornflowers buried with Tutankhamen, the young king who died around 1327 B.C. The plants, their thistlelike blossoms still intact, were woven into a wreath of olive leaves that adorned his sarcophagus.

Like asters, cornflowers belong to the *Compositae* family, although they have gone by many names. In the mid-1600s, herbalists knew them as "blew bottles," while in England they were bluets, and in Scotland, bluebonnets. The tattered and shredded look of their petals accounts for two more aliases, ragged sailor and ragged robin. Another common name, bachelor's buttons, may date to the Victorian era, when gentlemen wore the flowers in their buttonholes. Bachelor's buttons could also be a reference to the odd little circles of cloth that single men once sewed together. When stacked in rosettes, the bits of cloth made crude buttons for their coats.

Cornflowers were once a common sight in European fields, leading farmers to dub them "hurtsickles" because their wiry stems blunted the tools of anyone who tried to whack them down. The English botanist John Gerard complained that the plants "hindereth the reapers by dulling their sickles in the reaping of corn." Cornflowers aren't much of a problem anymore, though. Modern farming practices have largely eliminated them in the wild—a loss for those who love seeing wildflowers in their natural element.

These plants take their Latin name, *Centaurea cyanus*, from a Greek myth about a centaur called Chiron. According to legend, the half-horse, half-human creature healed himself with them after he was wounded by an enemy's arrow.

Aside from this story, cornflowers were largely ignored as medicinal plants until English herbalists in the mid-seventeenth century began recommending them to treat eye problems, probably for no other reason than their color. Cornflowers, of course, were blue, and many English people of that period had blue eyes.

Modern cornflowers are available in blue along with many other eye-pleasing colors, including pink, purple, wine, and white. Growers have bred them to produce full, lush blossoms, and their former weedy appearance has given way to a neater look with the introduction of shorter, more compact plants. Still, many gardeners prefer the heirloom types for their long, willowy stems and old-fashioned beauty.

Emperor William. (Courtesy of David Cavagnaro)

FLORENCE

Florence is a newer dwarf cornflower (the first dwarf was introduced in 1937). The thistle-shaped flower heads are densely packed with soft pink, white, blue, lavender, rose red, and violet petals. Like all cornflowers, this one is a fine choice for an authentic cottage garden.

Jubilee Gem.
(Courtesy of David Cavagnaro)

JUBILEE GEM

Large, double, bright blue blossoms make Jubilee Gem a standout. The bushy plants grow from 18 to 24 inches tall. Jubilee Gem is an All-American Selections winner from 1937.

BLUE BOY

Once cultivated by Thomas Jefferson at Monticello, Blue Boy arrived in America from Europe in the seventeenth century. The electric blue flowers grow 2 to 3 feet tall, so you may prefer to keep them toward the back of the border. With its sturdy silver stems, Blue Boy makes an excellent cut flower.

BLACK BOY

The blooms of this old charmer are actually deep maroon rather than black, making a striking contrast to its silvery leaves and stems. Try Black Boy alongside foliage plants that have a gray sheen, like Artemisia, Lamb's Ear, or Dusty Miller. Give this cornflower some support, as it matures around 2 feet tall. A few twiggy branches stuck into the ground nearby will make a natural, unobtrusive trellis.

Black Boy.
(Courtesy of David Cavagnaro)

Red Boy.

(Courtesy of David Cavagnaro)

RED BOY

This antique flower carries bunches of frilly red blooms above gray-green foliage. Topping out at 2 feet, it will also need staking or support. Red Boy, which reseeds nicely, has been traced to 1942.

EMPEROR WILLIAM

This tall, single cornflower closely resembles its wild ancestor. The dark marine blue blossoms are carried above gray-green foliage on 3-foot plants. Emperor William I of Germany choose a cornflower as his royal symbol. Legend says that he favored the plants because he found shelter in a field of cornflowers as a boy when pursued by Napoleon's troops.

Growing Tips

Cornflowers are hardy annuals that enjoy plenty of sun. They are easy to grow, as they dislike heavy feedings and tolerate both drought and poor soils.

Sow your cornflower seeds directly into the garden after the last heavy frost in spring. You can also start them indoors about a month before you want to move them outside, but it's not a good idea. Cornflowers are difficult to transplant.

Space the seeds 2 inches apart and cover them with a scant ¼ inch of soil. Alternately, you can scatter them by the handful over the ground or shake them into your palm and blow them lightly across the garden. If you do broadcast them this way, remember that cornflower seeds need darkness to germinate, so make sure they are lightly covered.

When the seedlings emerge, thin them to 6 to 12 inches apart. Taller varieties need staking when they're about a foot tall. Since cornflowers originated as weedy plants in grain fields, don't be dismayed if the old varieties start to look floppy late in the growing season. That's just their nature, and that wildflowery habit can be part of their appeal.

If you live where the winters are warm, cornflower seeds can be planted outdoors in early fall for blooms the next spring. Some gardeners even say that fall-sown plants are the most floriferous. In colder climates, wait until spring to sow.

Keep the blossoms deadheaded for continuous bloom, or let some of the seedheads dry on the plants for hungry birds. Because cornflowers self-sow easily, seed savers don't have much work to do. Unless you simply want to collect the seeds for later planting, you can allow the flowers to mature and release their own seeds.

Don't forget to clip a few faded blossoms for yourself. When they are thoroughly dried, cornflowers are lovely in everlasting arrangements.

Try sowing antique cornflowers throughout wildflower meadows or other informal plantings, or mix them into beds and borders. Red poppies, yellow and gold daylilies, and snowy Bishop's Lace make attractive companions for bright blue bachelor's buttons.

If cornflowers have one downside, it's that their foliage starts to look messy and unkempt as the season winds down. You can camouflage their fading

··
··
··
··
··
··
··
··
··
··
··
··
··
··
··
··
··
··
··
··
··
··
··
··
··
··
··

glory by tucking them between annuals and perennials that have more staying power, such as pink and ruby zinnias, tangerine-orange marigolds, or cheerful black-eyed Susans. Or copy Thomas Jefferson's planting scheme at Monticello, where cornflowers were encouraged to grow alongside calendulas, sweet peas, and yellow flag iris.

COSMOS—*Cosmos*

Cosmos could easily have disappeared soon after the plants were introduced to Britain from their native Mexico in 1799. It wasn't that these carefree annuals were hard to grow. Some gardeners just never got a chance to admire their silky, daisylike blooms, no matter how much effort they put into them. Cosmos are short-day plants, which means that they typically do not set buds or start to blossom until the days get shorter in autumn. Gardeners in northern areas routinely lost their cosmos to frost before seeing any flowers. That's why cosmos were not traditionally grown in cold regions—-why cultivate a plant whose flowers you can never enjoy?

Fortunately, enterprising breeders set out to solve this botanical dilemma. The first big improvements came in the 1890s with the introduction of brighter flower colors. Fuller, fancier blossoms were next on growers' agendas, and doubled types soon arrived.

Cosmos got their biggest boost in popularity, though, in 1930, with the debut of the Sensation strain. Finally even gardeners with relatively short growing seasons could enjoy these summer bloomers, which open about 56 days from sowing. Sensation cosmos are still widely available in white, crimson, bright pink, and deep rose.

The genus name, *Cosmos*, comes from the Greek word for "harmony" or "ordered universe," probably for the neat, regular arrangement of the plants' petals.

Our two most common species are *C. bipinnatus*, also known as the Mexican aster, and *C. sulphureus*, commonly called the orange or yellow cosmos.

C. bipinnatus is a native of the southwestern United States and of Mexico, where Spanish priests once raised the plants in mission gardens. Cosmos eventually made their way into European gardens, where they earned the nickname "peasant's flowers" because of their ability to thrive in the poor soils around humble cottages.

C. sulphureus is also a Mexican native. While both species are frost-tender annuals, it's easy to tell them apart. The yellow cosmos has rather coarse leaves that may remind you of a marigold's foliage, and its blossoms span a hot color spectrum from flame red to sunset orange to sunny yellow. *C. bipinnatus* has more finely cut, feathery foliage, and its blooms range from white to pink and purple.

C. sulphureus

DIABLO

These fiery flowers, whose name means "devil," were known in England by the late eighteenth century. The double blossoms sizzle in scarlet, molten orange, yellow, and gold. Stocky stems and slightly roughened foliage allow them to withstand more wind and rain than many other cosmos. The bushy plants mature at 2 to 3 feet tall. In 1974, Diablo was named an All-American

Diablo. (Courtesy of Seed Savers Exchange)

Selections winner. If its warm colors are too strong for you, water them down by adding some neighboring deep purple or blue blossoms.

LADYBIRD KLONDYKE

Short Ladybirds need a front-row seat in the garden, since they grow only 18 inches tall. Klondyke-type cosmos date to the early 1900s and bear glowing orange-yellow petals that shoot out in rays from the center of each bloom.

SUNSET

For awhile, growers seemed to lose interest in this 1890 introduction. But the 2- to 3-foot-tall plants with deep orange and bronze flowers have made a comeback, winning an All-American Selections honor in 1996. The ruffled, doubled blossoms open to 2 inches across. If Sunset seems too bright in your garden, quench it with silvery foliage like Artemisia or Dusty Miller.

C. bipinnatus

SEASHELLS MIXED

Rolled, fluted, and curved—how do you describe this flower's unusual petals? They really do curl in on themselves, like foxglove petals or seashells, producing a 3-D effect. The blossoms are studded with yellow buttons in the centers and rise above feathery green foliage on 3- to 4-foot plants. Mixed seed packages typically include white and watermelon pink, blush, rose, and red.

PSYCHE

These cosmos have a flirty, frilly look, thanks to an outer ring of long petals and an inner ring of shorter ones. Each bloom is punctuated with a golden eye. The plants grow 4 feet tall in colors that range from seashell pink to magenta.

SENSATION

This series took an All-American Selections medal in 1936. Try the daisylike flowers, which can reach 3 to 5 feet in height, with other stately annuals like cleome. Because these cosmos have a habit of toppling over occasionally, you may want to save them for a cutting garden so you'll regularly remove their

Seashells. (Courtesy of David Cavagnaro)

Sensation. (Courtesy of David Cavagnaro)

slender stems. Otherwise, they tend to flop over and lean on other plants as they mature.

DANCING PETTICOATS

This specialty mix is a combination of Seashells, Psyche, and Versailles, a cosmos favored by commercial florists. The plants mature at 3½ to 4 feet tall, and because they are so drought tolerant when mature, they are suitable for a xeriscape garden. Butterflies and bees will visit until the flowers fade; then hungry birds will nibble on the ripened seeds.

Dancing Petticoats. (Courtesy of Renee's Garden)

LADY LENOX OR LADY LENNOX

Described in a 1923 catalog as "one of our most superb fall flowers," this very tall, old cosmos was the typical late-blooming type, seldom flowering in northern regions before the first heavy frost. Some sources describe the big, pink blooms as "lighting up well at night." A Lady Lenox White was also once available, as was a Giant Lady Lenox with pink, white, and crimson flowers. All have been replaced by the Sensation series.

Growing Tips

Cosmos seeds are easy to grow and should germinate in 5 to 10 days. Sow them directly in the garden once all chance of frost is past. Or if you prefer, start the seeds indoors about 4 to 6 weeks before the last spring frost, using trays or containers filled with a good quality planting mix. Cover the seeds with ½ inch of soil and keep them moist. Cosmos seeds need some light to germinate, so provide indoor lamps or place them near a sunny window, but do not put them sit in direct sunlight. Intense light and heat will burn the emerging seedlings.

When the weather is reliably warm, harden off the plants and move them outdoors. Space your plants 8 inches apart in full sun. They will grow in partial shade, but at the expense of abundant flowers. Cosmos are undemanding about soil and will actually perform better when the ground is not overly fertile.

Pinch the young plants back early, near the base, to encourage side shoots that will bear more flowers. Alternately, you can wait until the plants are 18 inches tall and then cut them back by half. By mid- to late summer, cosmos have a tendency to become weedy-looking and lanky. Tall varieties may require staking, or you can prop their stems against other bushy plants.

Cosmos are generally disease-free, pest-free annuals that bloom throughout the summer. Some gardeners say they're the best annuals, bar none, for hot, dry conditions and poor soils.

For a continuous supply of flowers, sow more seeds every few weeks, counting backward from your first frost to make sure the variety you've chosen will have time to bloom. Keep the plants deadheaded to encourage reblooming.

Goldfinches and other small birds like cosmos seeds, so after you've collected as many seeds as you want, leave some dried flower heads for your feathered friends. Cosmos drop their seeds freely, so you can also allow them to self-sow.

Cosmos are nice for a child's garden, as they are so simple and fun to grow.

CUCUMBER—*Cucumis sativus*

Everyone, it seems, loves cucumbers, or at least the pickles we make from them. The Romans cultivated these ancient plants, which are native to India, in heated "greenhouses" built from sheets of mica, and it's said that Emperor Tiberius feasted on cucumbers every day of his life. Aristotle touted them as curatives around 850 B.C., while Cleopatra swore they enhanced her beauty.

Pickles are mentioned in Pliny's writings, in the Bible, and in Homer's *Odyssey*, where they are poetically dubbed "sailors' salty provisions."

Cucumbers initially seemed well suited for the climate that early colonists found in America. Unfortunately, they quickly fell victim to various New World wilts, bugs, and diseases, and today's gardeners usually resort to spraying to keep their plants healthy. Still, cucumbers are relatively easy to grow, and it's not hard to find a number of delicious heirlooms that have survived from the nineteenth-century seed trade.

LEMON

These small, round cukes with pale yellow skins do look a bit like lemons. Seed Savers Exchange credits Samuel Wilson of Mechanicsville, Pennsylvania, with introducing the variety in 1894. Crosby Seeds of New York and California also offered them some years later and instructed that they were "for pickling[,] or the seeds can be removed and then [the cucumbers can be] stuffed with a relish. This cucumber is a boon to those who are distressed after eating the common cucumber as this fruit can be easily digested." Lemon cukes have a sweet, juicy flesh and a mild, crunchy skin that tends to thicken with age. Pick these early and eat them out of hand like apples. The plants are well adapted across the United States to resist fungal diseases, but bugs love them, so you may want to sow extras. Plan to harvest in 60 to 70 days.

WHITE WONDER

This old southern favorite is ready 58 days after planting. Introduced by Burpee's in 1893, White Wonder was often advertised in Pennsylvania Dutch catalogs. It was welcomed below the Mason-Dixon Line, too, once gardeners realized how productive it was even after the temperature soared. The ivory-colored fruits have a crisp flesh and grow to about 7 inches long. They are delicious for pickling or slicing, but use them before they age, when they turn orange and form "warts."

SUYO LONG

Need a "burpless" cuke? Try this sweet variety from China, which is ready for harvest in 60 days. It tolerates heat and other adverse conditions, so it grows well across the country. Southeastern gardeners can sow throughout

Lemon and Armenian
heirloom cucumbers.
(Courtesy of Renee's Garden)

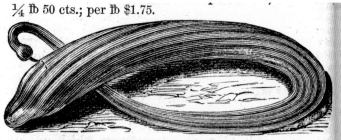

¼ ℔ 50 cts.; per ℔ $1.75.

SNAKE CUCUMBER.

SERPENT or SNAKE CUCUMBER. A remarkable
and very interesting curiosity. The cucumbers grow
curled up like a snake with the head protruding, and
sometimes are *six feet in length*. The illustration well
represents their shape, and, although they attain great
size, the quality is fair. Per pkt. 10 cts.

Burpee's said its Serpent or Snake cucumber, offered in the late 1800s, sometimes grew up to 6 feet long.

the season and harvest even in hot, humid weather. The spiny, ridged fruits have an excellent flavor, but keep the vines trellised, or the long, skinny fruits will become almost too twisted to use.

STRAIGHT EIGHT

An All-American Selections winner from 1938, this dark green variety with white spines is still very popular. As the name indicates, the fruits grow straight and are ready 58 days from planting. This is a standard slicing cuke; be sure to pick early, or when the fruits are about 8 inches long. They turn yellow when the seeds ripen and become bitter-tasting late in the season.

EARLY RUSSIAN

It's easy to imagine that this 1888 heirloom, which matures in 50 to 55 days, would thrive in a Russian gardener's short growing season. The plump cukes, which reach 3 to 5 inches long, have a mild flavor and are fine for eating fresh or pickling. Keep the prolific vines harvested or the fruits will go bitter.

RICHMOND GREEN APPLE

These Australian cucumbers have a pale green color and sweet, juicy flesh. Some people find the apple-sized fruits, which are low in acid, especially easy to digest. The plants are productive, bearing round or slightly oval cukes in 75 days.

VERT DE MASSY (MASSY'S GREEN)

French cooks pick these tangy novelty gherkins when they are no bigger than your little finger to make baby pickles. This 1800s variety is not a heavy yielder, but it is early, bearing slender fruits in 50 to 60 days. Let the cukes grow 4 inches long for salads, or preserve them with hot peppers and dill for spicy snacks.

EDMONSON

In 1987, Seed Savers Exchange reintroduced this heirloom, which had been grown by a Kansas family since 1913. The plants are extremely hardy, able to withstand bugs, drought, and disease, and bear greenish white fruits 70 days from sowing. Even when you're late harvesting these buttery-tasting cucumbers, they stay crisp and tender. Watch for the skins to darken and turn yellowish-orange as the seeds ripen.

JAPANESE CLIMBING

This Japanese favorite came into the American seed trade in 1892. Let the vigorous vines run up a fence or trellis and they'll reward you with crunchy, light green fruits in about 70 days from sowing. Keep picking and the plants will bear heavily.

WEST INDIA BURR GHERKIN—*C. ANGURIA,*
also known as Jerusalem Cucumber

Burr-shaped, spiny fruits distinguish this relative of the garden cucumber, which is native to Africa. The variety probably arrived in Jamaica via the slave trade in the seventeenth century, and the seeds were introduced to Virginia around 1793. Peel these hedgehogs before using them in salads, or pickle the gherkins whole, as recommended in recipes that date back to the Civil War. Not surprisingly, most bugs leave the prickly fruits alone. Once mature, the gherkins turn seedy and bitter, so harvest them before they exceed 1½ inches in length.

Old-fashioned cucumbers for pickling or eating fresh. (Courtesy of Renee's Garden)

Growing Tips

It's a good thing that cucumbers produce fast, because these tender annuals can't take any frost. They do need rich, well-drained soil and lots of sunshine.

Northerner gardeners with short summers can start their seeds indoors one month before the last expected frost. Hardened-off seedlings can be moved outdoors once all danger of frost is over.

Gardeners with long, warm summers can sow their cucumbers directly outside after the last frost. Plant your seeds ½ to 1 inch deep and 6 inches apart, in rows spaced 3 to 4 feet apart. Thin the emerging seedlings to every 2 feet. Alternately, plant 6 seeds to a hill, leaving 2 to 3 feet between hills, and thin to 3 plants per hill.

Vining cukes need trellises or other supports, or their fruits tend to curve and twist as they mature. Modern bush cultivars that produce straight fruits without trellising are also available.

Cucumbers have long taproots but shallower roots as well, so be sure to give them extra water and keep them mulched during dry spells.

You can harvest cukes at any size, but avoid letting them grow bigger than the size listed for each variety. Harvest often and the plants will continue to bear until late summer or the first frost.

Insects cross-pollinate cucumbers, so seed savers should plan to grow only one variety at a time. Choose your best vines and let their fruits continue to grow until they turn yellow. When they've ripened, cut them open and scoop out the seeds into a glass jar.

Add a little water to the jar and let the seeds and any pulp that clings to them sit for a few days. Stir occasionally when the goopy mixture starts to ferment. The seeds will "settle out," which means that any good seeds will drop to the bottom of the jar. Pour off the floating debris. Wash the good seeds until they are clean, and spread them to dry on paper towels or a piece of mesh. Label and store them in a cool, dark spot, and cucumber seeds may remain viable for as long as 5 years.

CUPHEA—*Cuphea*

Are there bats and firecrackers in your garden, or cigars and rabbits in your beds and borders? Tropical cupheas, members of the loosestrife family, inspire gardeners to see all sorts of images in their curiously shaped blossoms.

It's easy to understand how these relatives of crape myrtles get some of their common names. *Cuphea ignea*, also known as the cigar or firecracker plant, produces one-inch, tubular-shaped blossoms. With their fiery orange petals capped with purple black "ash" at the tips, you could almost mistake the blooms for stubby cigarettes.

Other cupheas remind us of animals. *C. llavea*, also known as St. Peter's plant, is sometimes sold commercially as the "bat-faced" plant. Its two elongated, scarlet red petals stand up like ears above the electric purple "face" of each flower. Other gardeners—the ones who don't like bats—simply say these strange blossoms look like the faces of tiny mice or rabbits.

Cupheas are native to the central regions of the Americas, especially Guatemala and Mexico. Only a few species are cultivated as ornamentals in these countries; the rest are grown primarily for their seeds, which can be made into oil.

"Cuphea" comes from the Greek word *kyphos*, meaning "curved," and refers to the plants' curved seed capsules. Not surprisingly, crape myrtles, which also belong to the *Lythraceae* family, sounded very similar when described in an 1798 issue of William Curtis's *Botanical Magazine*. The blossoms, the magazine reported, were "the size of the garden Clove. . . . very shewy, no wonder therefore that the natives should be in the practice of planting [crape myrtles] about their houses and their gardens. The petals are curiously crisped or curled, each petal resembling, in miniature, a leaf of some of our varieties of cabbage."

Although cupheas have a lot of ornamental value, growers made little effort to domesticate any of the approximately 260 known species until recently. One notable introduction has come from botanists at the University of California at Los Angeles (UCLA), who successfully crossed *C. ignea* with *C. micropetala*, also known as the giant cigar flower or the candy corn plant.

The result is David Verity, an exceptionally trouble-free cuphea that opens its attractive orange-red blossoms all summer long. The cigarette-shaped flowers are ideal for luring butterflies and hummingbirds. But if you try this modern cuphea, don't be disappointed if it seems slow to flower. Gardeners who have grown it report that the plants crave very hot weather and tend to perform better as the summer progresses.

Unfortunately, heirloom gardeners have very few cupheas to choose from, because the plants have never been widely used in America. Only about 10 species are recommended for our backyards or landscapes, and most cultivars, like David Verity, are fairly new.

At least a few heirloom cupheas are still around. Although the seeds are often rare and hard to find, they delight the gardeners who try them. Cupheas are typically easy-to-cultivate annuals or tender perennials that love summer heat and tolerate drought, producing flowers almost nonstop until frost. Unless they're grown indoors, the plants are seldom bothered by pests or diseases.

SUMMER MEDLEY—*C. MINIATA*

This rare charmer produces confetti-colored flowers that open at the tips of long, hairy stems. Its small, dark green leaves make a nice backdrop for the tube-shaped blossoms, which come in rose, scarlet, carmine, and violet. The plants grow 1 to 2 feet tall and attract butterflies from late spring until early fall. Although Summer Medley is an annual in most gardens, it may behave as a tender perennial if you live where the winters are mild.

BATFACE—*C. LLAVEA*

Keep your plants in a sheltered location, and this tender perennial cuphea, which is not old enough to classify as a true heirloom, may last until Halloween. Then you can weave the slender branches of tiny flowers around your grinning jack-o'-lanterns. The flowers really do look like diminutive bats with scarlet red "ears" and shocking purple faces. They are carried in clusters atop long, arching stems studded with dark green, lance-shaped leaves. Although the plants can grow to 2 feet, they have a cascading habit and can arch gracefully over a garden path or be coaxed to trail over the edge of window boxes. This one can handle full sun to light shade and is forgiving of heat and dry conditions.

FIREFLY—*C. LANCEOLATA*

In 1932, Louise Beebe Wilder, author of *The Fragrant Garden*, praised this Mexican annual for its intense perfume. The purplish flowers, which appeared on stems covered with sticky, lance-shaped leaves, were typically grown in greenhouses of that era. Firefly is a pretty, modern cultivar with deep violet and cerise-red petals. The plants can reach up to 4 feet tall. Flowers appear about 90 days after the seeds are planted.

DAVID VERITY—*C. IGNEA*

This ornamental cuphea was developed from the late 1970s into the early 1980s at the Mildred E. Mathias Botanical Garden at UCLA. Named in honor of the garden's curator, David Verity is vigorous and cold tolerant, bearing narrow, dark green leaves that make a nice foil for its bold, firecracker-colored flowers. Try it as a houseplant, or use it outside in beds or hanging baskets. These extremely drought-tolerant plants grow 2 to 3 feet tall and equally wide.

Growing Tips

Although their flowers are petite, cupheas are delightful plants, whether you grow them as a shrubby groundcover or use them in masses to lure colorful birds and pollinating insects. Because they are bushy and grow quickly, cupheas can form a small hedge in the landscape or fill in the bare spots under taller plants in beds and borders. You can even tuck these long-blooming plants into the nooks of a rock garden to help brighten a somber palette.

Since cupheas are native to tropical regions, they usually perform best during the hottest part of the summer. Be sure the weather has stabilized and your soil is dependably warm before starting your seeds outside.

Cuphea seeds can be difficult to find, but you may discover heirloom gardeners willing to trade their stock if you can't locate a commercial source. If you live in a cool climate, you will have to sow your cuphea seeds indoors in flats or pots, since they can take up to 12 weeks to flower. Otherwise, an early freeze might kill the plants before you get any blooms.

If you sow cupheas indoors, harden off the seedlings for at least two weeks before transplanting them to the garden. If you rush them outside, they may fail to thrive in chilly temperatures. Space the plants 12 to 14 inches apart and give them full sun to light shade and well-drained, average to rich garden soil. Mulch them well and feed them lightly with a slow-release fertilizer in mid-summer and again in early fall. Once cupheas are well established, they can tolerate periods of drought.

To keep the plants compact and loaded with blooms, pinch out the growing tips or lightly prune back the stems in July or August. Because of their rather sprawling growth habit, cupheas usually look better in informal settings. They are especially nice grown alongside cannas and elephant ears, which are exotic enough to hold their own with these tropical beauties.

Many cupheas will self-sow and return the following year. You can try to collect their seeds; but the capsules shatter easily, and you may miss them unless you watch the plants closely. A better bet is to search out the few seed vendors who offer these heirlooms or to contact fellow collectors who will trade their seeds.

EGGPLANT—*Solanum melongena*

If the only eggplants you know are the shiny purple fruits sold in American supermarkets, then you don't know eggplants. Not all of these Asian natives are shaped like giant pears or encased in tough skins. But don't worry. One trip to a gourmet grocery or ethnic foods store is enough to introduce you to a new world of eggplant tastes, sizes, and colors.

Eggplants have been on our plates for at least 2,000 years, when the first wild ancestors of these fruits were enjoyed in India. By the 1300s, eggplants had made their way into Italy and Africa. Spaniards carried them into the Americas, where European and New World gardeners initially disliked their strong flavors and grew them only as ornamentals. Eggplants finally moved into the kitchen garden in the 1900s, when developers produced a more palatable product.

Today, gardeners in Japan, India, Thailand, the Philippines, and China cultivate many different eggplants. There are elongated Oriental "eggs" with sweet, soft skins, and flattened African types with a bitter bite. Eggplants come with skins of brown, white, green, violet, dusky purple, near-black, stripes, and even tomato red. Some are as small as chicken eggs, while others are long and slender.

notes

Striped heirloom eggplants brighten a summer harvest. (Courtesy of David Cavagnaro)

Admittedly, eggplants can be a handful for even the greenest thumbs. The plants demand a long, hot growing season to set fruits, and they are susceptible to fungal diseases and insect pests. But if you're willing to experiment, you may discover more flavors and recipes than you'd ever imagined. A bowl of eggplant curry or ratatouille, a plate of moussaka, or some eggplant Szechuan dip can be a mouthwatering revelation.

LITTLE SPOOKY

Japanese gardeners on Hokkaido Island once believed this old variety could chase off evil spirits and guarantee a good harvest. The 3-foot-tall plants bear ghostly white fruits that grow to 7 inches long and 3 inches wide.

APPLEGREEN

Developed in 1964 by Professor Meader of the University of New Hampshire Experiment Station, this delicious American eggplant is dependable and productive. It also matures early, so it's suitable for northern gardens. The fruits are pale green, like Granny Smith apples. You won't need to peel the tender skins that cover the white, mild flesh. Seed savers should let the skins turn yellow before harvesting.

THAI GREEN

Gardeners with a short growing season appreciate this heirloom egg, which can often survive a light frost. The lime green fruits are elongated and grow to 12 inches. This is another variety with a tender, edible skin and a mild flesh. Give it 80 days to harvest.

BLACK BEAUTY

This old standard, dating to 1902, is probably our most commonly grown eggplant. The deep purple to nearly black fruits are large and flavorful with glossy skins. For the best taste, pick them when they're relatively small, about 74 days after sowing. The plants grow to 3 feet and perform well even up north, if the weather stays warm.

LOUISIANA LONG GREEN

Also known as Green Banana, these fruits look like unripe bananas or long, light green balloons. The bushy plants grow to 3 feet tall. When the fruits mature at about 8 inches long, they may need supports to keep them off the ground. The tender flesh has a sweet taste.

ROSA BIANCA

Italy is the homeland of this delicate gourmet favorite. The teardrop-shaped fruits have white skins streaked with rosy lavender or purple. Chefs praise the eggplants, which mature in 80 days from planting, for their creamy texture.

CASPER

Another good choice for cool climates, Casper starts bearing about 70 days from sowing. Under the ivory skins, the meat is snowy white and mild. These fruits are good for eating fresh, and you don't need to peel them if they're small. Some cooks say they have a mild mushroom flavor. The compact plants are suitable for container gardening.

DIAMOND

Seed Savers Exchange reintroduced this Ukrainian variety to the United States in 1993. Diamond produces clusters of deep purple fruits in 70 to 80 days. The elongated eggs grow up to 9 inches long on 2-foot plants and have a firm flesh.

WHITE EGG

Pick these white "eggs" when they are the size of a standard hen's egg. The fruits ripen and turn bright yellow in about 72 days. Cooks praise their old-fashioned eggplant flavor. The plants have been grown in England since the 1500s.

White Egg. (Courtesy of David Cavagnaro)

TURKISH ITALIAN ORANGE—*S. INTEGRIFOLIUM*

You could mistake these reddish-orange fruits for tomatoes, but they are actually a species of eggplant from Turkey. Southern Exposure Seed Exchange found the plants in Italy and reintroduced them to the United States in 1990. The spineless, 4-foot plants bear heavily, producing seedy fruits that have the best flavor if picked while green. Once the fruits turn red, the skins become bitter. If you prefer, try this one as an ornamental. The fruits are attractive as they mature from solid green to green with orange stripes to solid orange.

Growing Tips

Simply put, eggplants need heat. Gardeners with cool, short growing seasons should choose their varieties carefully. If your season is long and warm, you can plant both late- and early-maturing types to ensure a continuous supply for the table.

Give your eggplants a jump start by sowing the seeds indoors 10 to 12 weeks before the last spring frost. Cover them with $\frac{1}{4}$ inch of soil.

When the seedlings are 2 inches tall, pot them up into individual containers. Bump them up to bigger pots if they get too big before you can transplant.

After the last spring frost, harden off the seedlings. But wait another 2 to 3 weeks before you move them into the garden, to be sure the soil is warm enough. Set the young plants 12 inches apart in rows spaced 30 inches apart. It's helpful to mulch with black plastic, which warms the ground around their roots and encourages early fruiting.

You can harvest eggplants at any size, but pay attention to their appearance. The fruits are usually too old to use once the skins turn dull. It's easy to tell when the eggs are ready; simply press them gently with your thumb. If the skin bounces back, the fruits are ready to pick. If the skin stays indented, the fruits are probably tough and overripe. If the skin doesn't move, give your eggs more time to grow.

Cut, do not pull, your eggplants away from their stems. Pulling usually breaks the plants. Eat or process your eggplants quickly, as they do not keep well.

Eggplant seeds are easy to save. The plants usually self-pollinate, but you

Little Spooky eggplant seeds.

can isolate different varieties or grow only one variety at a time to ensure seed purity. Simply let some of the fruits turn dull and hard before harvesting them. Then cut them in half and scoop out the seeds. Don't forget to label them before storing.

Any Eggplant by Any Other Name

Europeans know eggplants as "aubergines," while Australian gardeners call them "eggfruits." If you're hungry for eggplant in West Africa, you'll ask for a "garden egg," but in the West Indies, you'll order "brown jolly."

Potatoes — Solanum tuberosum

We can't ignore delicious heirloom potatoes, even though they are seldom grown from seeds. They rate a mention in this book because, like eggplants, they belong to the nightshade family, but they are typically started from cut tubers that contain at least one "eye." The tubers should be planted in spring, as soon as you can work the soil, in trenches 6 inches wide by 6 inches deep. As they grow, they'll benefit from plenty of water and aged compost.

Don't miss Russian Banana, a yellow-fleshed fingerling that can grow as large as a banana. Another old favorite, Carola, is a heavy yielder that's ready to harvest midseason. Its creamy yellow flesh makes delicious scalloped potatoes, soups, or fries. If you're daring, try the late-season All Blue, which has unusual dark blue skin and flesh. Or stick to Yukon Gold, an early potato that has become both popular and widely available. It's great to bake and serve with a juicy grilled steak.

FOUR O'CLOCK — *Mirabilis*, also known as Marvel of Peru, Dwarf Morning Glory, Beauty-of-the-Night, Belle de Nuit, Morning Rose, and Noon-Sleep

The scent of four o'clocks, author Louise Beebe Wilder promised in 1932's *The Fragrant Garden*, would take you back to "your country-spent childhood," if you were lucky enough to have had one.

You can't really set your clock by these fragrant flowers, which typically open at dusk in North America, but Carl Linnaeus once did. In Sweden, the blossoms unfurl around 4:00 P.M., and the famous botanist, who had also noted the opening and closing times of many other plants and wildflowers, included *Mirabilis jalapa* when he designed a *horologium florae*, or flower clock, for his garden.

You can still plant these tender perennials for your own version of Linnaeus's living timepiece, but don't depend on them for staying on schedule. Four o'clocks actually bloom at various times of the day, depending on the climate and where they are located. And while the scented, fluted blooms usually unfold in the afternoon and stay open until the temperature rises the following day, they will sometimes pop open even when the sky is cloudy.

While the plants take their common name from Linnaeus, who described them in 1753, the first part of their scientific name, *Mirabilis*, comes from the Latin word meaning "wonderful." Linnaeus reportedly mistook their tuberous roots for the source of a drug called *jalapa*, which accounts for the species portion of their name. No doubt their old nickname, Marvel of Peru, refers to their marvelous colors and delicate, nocturnal fragrance.

Botanists think that four o'clocks were grown by the Aztecs long before the Spaniards arrived, and they trace their presence in Europe to some two centuries before Linnaeus wrote about them. In America, the plants were cultivated around 1767 by Thomas Jefferson, who deemed Linnaeus's flower clock "very clever."

Four o'clocks remained popular with American gardeners until the 1950s, when their bold blooms—at least one designer has mocked them as "clown-colored"—fell out of favor. Perhaps we lost interest in them because their flower show lasts for only a few hours each day. They also may have dropped out of use because their nocturnal blossoms made them wonderful plants for moon gardens, and nowadays, few people plant gardens they intend to visit only after dark. Still, we can hope for a revival. Flowers that don't mind wearing a Joseph's coat of many colors, along with an intense perfume, surely deserve some respect.

DON PEDROS

Southern Exposure Seed Exchange acquired this charming old variety, which tops out at 18 inches high, from a donor whose family lived in Spain. While Don Pedros comes in a mix of colors, you will get mostly yellow or ma-

"Several years ago a young visitor asked me about this plant and I told her the name came from the fact that they open at four o'clock. She was back at four to see them open and they never did. . . . I have some growing at home as well, and they finally opened about six. Makes me wonder if six o'clock Virginian time is equal to four o'clock Peruvian?"

Wesley Greene,
Garden Historian,
Colonial Williamsburg
Foundation

Four O'clocks Teatime Mix. (Courtesy of Renee's Garden)

genta flowers in commercial packets. Some blossoms may be striped, spotted, or variegated.

YELLOW TWILIGHT

This very rare heirloom dates back to 1890. It self-sows reliably and has sprung up for generations around a homestead in Lancaster County, Pennsylvania, an area known for its Dutch, German, Amish, and Mennonite settlements. The sunny yellow flowers, which carry an orange blush in their throats, may remind you of apple tree blossoms.

LIMELIGHT ROSE

Another hard-to-find antique, Limelight Rose is a knockout, studded with neon pink blooms that burst from its heart-shaped, chartreuse foliage. One source suggests that this one is a descendant of a variegated four o'clock lost sometime in the late nineteenth century. The bushy plants reach 3 to 4 feet in height and fill the night air with a jasmine fragrance. Limelight is a similar, modern introduction with shocking pink petals and yellow green leaves, some of which are variegated. It sounds similar to a *Mirabilis jalapa* described in an 1889 seed catalog, a plant that had "leaves light green, marbled; very ornamental."

BROKEN COLORS

Remember tie-dyed T-shirts? This rare charmer looks as if it's been dipped, streaked, sponged, striped, spotted, and splashed with color. Expect rose, mauve, magenta, gold, canary yellow, pink, and fuchsia blossoms amid the dark green leaves. "Broken" refers to the striped effect of the colors.

ALBA

This selection of white four o'clocks brings a citrus scent, like orange blossoms, to the garden. The fluted flowers are borne in clusters on 2-foot plants. If you're using these in a night-blooming garden, they will help attract fascinating nocturnal pollinators like hawk moths and sphinx moths. Like other four o'clocks, Alba also draws butterflies and hummingbirds when the blossoms open during daylight hours.

TEATIME

Butterflies and hummingbirds adore these iridescent, 2-inch blooms. Teatime is a blend that typically includes soft pink, pure white, bright yellow, rose, lavender rose, and purple-red flowers. You may also find Tea Time [*sic*] sold in single-color packets. The plants grow 2 to 3 feet tall with multiple branches and form a low hedge when grouped close together.

Four O'clocks Alba.
(Courtesy of Select Seeds)

These antique flowers
fill summer afternoons
with the scent of jasmine.
(Courtesy of Renee's Garden)

Growing Tips

Time is not a problem for these sweetly scented, tender perennials. They grow quickly, so only gardeners who live where the summers are quite short need to sow their seeds indoors.

But if you really want to give your four o'clocks a head start, plant the seeds indoors in flats or trays 4 to 6 weeks before the last expected spring frost. Bury them ½ inch deep, and keep the seeds moist until they sprout, which is usually in 5 to 10 days. Thin the seedlings to every 2 inches.

When all danger of frost has passed, harden off the seedlings. They will be ready to transplant into well-worked, ordinary garden soil when they're about 2 inches tall. Space the young plants 12 to 14 inches apart in the garden.

Four o'clocks also grow well when they're seeded directly into the garden after the last spring frost. The plants will thrive in full sun, blooming from summer until frost. Although each flowers lasts only a few days, you'll have plenty of blooms, as the bushes are prolific.

Four o'clocks can tolerate some shade, but they may become lanky and require cutting back. You'll seldom have to worry about heat or drought, as the plants are able to withstand both extremes.

Most gardeners will need to treat four o'clocks as annuals, replanting yearly. In warmer areas, the plants form black, fleshy, carrot-shaped roots that can grow quite large. In fact, in tropical areas that mimic the plants' native Peru, tubers weighing up to 40 pounds have been recorded. Although these tubers can become a nuisance if left unchecked, they are easy to propagate. Simply dig them up before they become really large. Then store them over the winter and replant as desired the following spring.

But four o'clocks are very easy to grow from their seeds, which are oval and look like wrinkled grains of pepper. They self-sow readily, too. In fact, the seeds can become as much of a nuisance as the tubers if you don't keep them under control, so plan to till or hoe your soil frequently if you don't want volunteers popping up.

If you decide to collect your four o'clock seeds, be sure to keep them away from children and pets, as the seeds and plants themselves are highly poisonous. Before you plant the following spring, soak the hard-shelled seeds overnight in tepid water to encourage faster germination.

FOXGLOVE—*Digitalis*, also known as Fairy's-Cape, Gloves-of-Our-Lady, Fairy's-Thimbles, and more

Careful—don't sneeze when you're handling foxglove seeds. They are as fine as pepper and as easily scattered as dust. Just how tiny are they? One commercial seed company advertises a packet that contains approximately 283,000 seeds per ounce.

Still, these diminutive seeds pack a lot of garden punch. Foxgloves can grow to 6 feet tall, with stately flower spires that look elegant in back-of-the-border plantings or naturalized settings.

In Britain, *D. purpurea*, the so-called purple or common foxglove, is actually an old wildflower. These foxgloves were often tucked into cottage gardens during the Middle Ages, squeezed between vegetables for the table and herbs that were brewed into medicinal teas or made into poultices.

Other *Digitalis* species are native to Europe, northwest Africa, and parts of Asia, where they have been valued for centuries for their beauty as well as their healing properties.

Dioscorides, a first-century Greek physician who traveled with Nero's army, was among the first to suggest a medicinal use for foxgloves. He included them in *De Materia Medica*, a manuscript that served as an important pharmacological reference until the end of the fifteenth century.

In his 1597 *Herball*, John Gerard recommended using foxgloves to heal bruises suffered by "those who have fallen from high places." Nicholas Culpepper, a seventeenth-century herbalist, employed a helpful salve made from the plants: "My self am confident that an Oyntment of it is one of the best Remedies for a Scabby Head that is."

But English doctor William Withering is usually credited for discovering that digitalin, a stimulant derived from foxgloves, could be used to treat ailing hearts. Withering probably also introduced purple foxgloves to America when he sent some seeds to a colleague in New Hampshire in 1789. He urged his friend to experiment with the plants, employing them both as a drug and a "beautiful flower in the garden."

Always use care when handling foxgloves. All parts of the plants—leaves, seeds, and foliage—are poisonous, which makes them undesirable for gar-

Foxglove Apricot Faerie Queen.
(Courtesy of Renee's Garden)

dens frequented by children or pets. Culpepper, writing again about the plants, warned, "The operation of this herb, internally taken, is often violent, even in small doses. It is best therefore not to meddle with it, lest the cure should end in the churchyard."

This dangerous reputation, along with the flowers' tubular shape, undoubtedly earned them some of their menacing nicknames, which include dead man's thimbles, dragon's mouths, dead-men's-bells, witches'-gloves, and bloody fingers.

Still, foxgloves have their charms, and their name may simply come from the German word for "finger-hat" or "thimble," which refers to the shape of the blossoms. Early Britons believed that fairies roamed the forest thickets where the flowers grew.

In Norway, the plant was known as *Revbielde*, or foxbell. According to legend, foxes wore the flowers like socks on their toes so they could prowl quietly among the henhouses.

SUTTON'S APRICOT

This gorgeous, apricot pink strain was selected from foxgloves sold by the House of Sutton, an English seed company founded in 1806. In 1858, Queen Victoria made the firm the official seed supplier for her royal household. Sutton's Apricot, which many gardeners consider one of the most desirable foxgloves, sends up 3- to 6-foot-tall stalks from a dense rosette of dark, hairy leaves.

GIANT SPOTTED FOXGLOVE

This one is also a product of the Sutton seed company. Its creamy white and pink hanging bells are splashed with dark purple blotches in their throats, luring hummingbird moths to visit the 5- to 6-foot flower stalks. According to some old sources, the finest spotted foxgloves were originally sold by Webbs, an English seed company that served every monarch from Queen Victoria to Queen Elizabeth II.

ALBA

White to greenish-white bells that lack the usual spotted throats distinguish this old foxglove. Offered by seedsman Bernard McMahon in 1804 and by Joseph Breck in 1838, Alba grows to 4 feet and yields wonderful cut flowers. Try it in a moon garden, where it almost glows in the darkness. Its classic form makes it a good companion for the blowsy blossoms of antique roses.

STRAWBERRY—*D. X MERTONENSIS*

This hybrid strain dates to approximately 1926, when it was developed at the John Innes Horticultural Institute in England. The plants are shorter than most foxgloves, maturing at 2 to 3 feet tall. Big, strawberry-colored blossoms stand out nicely against its deep green foliage. A Royal Horticultural Society Award Winner, this perennial sets fertile seeds that grow true to type.

Growing Tips

If you start your foxglove seeds outdoors, sow them in midsummer in an area of the garden that is sheltered from harsh weather. Simply toss the seeds

Strawberry.
(Courtesy of Select Seeds)

Classic foxgloves bloom in spring and summer.
(Courtesy of Renee's Garden)

over the ground and press them down lightly, but don't cover them, as foxgloves need light to germinate.

Keep the seeds moist until they sprout. In early autumn, when the seedlings are 3 to 4 inches tall, transplant them to a permanent location, spacing them 18 to 24 inches apart. The young plants will need moisture, but don't overdo it. Foxgloves have a tendency to rot during their dormant winter period if the ground stays too wet, and good drainage is a key to success with them.

If you prefer, foxglove seeds can be sprinkled over a growing medium in indoor pots or trays. Hardened-off seedlings will be ready to move into the garden by early fall.

Foxgloves are biennials, so they will produce mostly foliage in their first year. In their second year, they should bloom nicely. Keeping the stalks cut to the base after the flowers fade will encourage more flowering side shoots to grow.

There's a joke that foxgloves will make their own decisions about where to live, because they self-sow generously under the right conditions. If you don't mind letting Mother Nature choose their homes for you, allow some of the dried flowers to remain on the plants, and the ripened seeds will drop when they're ready. Otherwise, collect the tiny seeds in paper bags when the capsules split in late summer.

Foxgloves prefer rich soil and shade or dappled sunlight. They can take some sun if you live where summers are short and mild, but you'll need to provide adequate water during dry spells. Watch for the blossoms to open from spring into early summer.

Because they thrive in partial shade, foxgloves can be planted to make a natural transition between established gardens and cool, dark woodlands. For a traditional cottage garden look, try mingling them with Shirley poppies, bellflowers, hostas, ferns, peonies, sweet Williams, and bleeding hearts. Pastel-colored larkspurs and columbines also combine beautifully, as do many herbs.

Forgot What You Planted?

It's easy to do. You planted seeds, and now your first-year foxgloves are ready to move to a permanent spot in the garden. The problem is, you can't remember exactly which colors you set out, but you won't get any blooms until the following year. So while you're trying to move them around, you're clueless as to color. You can still coordinate your garden by looking at the foxgloves' leaf stem, or petiole. If it has a pink or purplish blush, it should produce pink or purple blooms. If the petiole is greenish-white, the foxglove lacks pigment and will bear white flowers.

"I've grown foxgloves head-high, but the biggest problem here is getting them to come back as biennials. One year I had a sea of them, and I pulled back the mulch to expose the ground so the dropped seeds could germinate. I even collected some of the seed pods, but I didn't get a single [seedling]. I gave some to a friend, and she got them everywhere. And she didn't even really try to grow them."

David Bradshaw,
Professor of Horticulture,
Clemson University

GARDEN BEAN—*Phaseolus vulgaris*

Wax beans, snaps, poles, kidneys, strings, pintos, black beans, field beans, navy beans, *haricots verts*—it's almost insulting to refer to all these delicious vegetables by their nickname, "common beans." They are certainly not common in the sense of being ordinary. Beans come in a dazzling assortment of tastes, colors, shapes, and sizes and have a variety of uses. Heirloom gardeners have hundreds to choose from, including varieties with such wonderfully evocative names as Fat Goose, Lazy Wife, Garden of Eden, Bacon, and Peanut Butter Bunch.

Our modern beans, which are also widely known as garden beans, are derived from plants that once grew wild in Central and South America. But we've been cultivating beans for ages, and archaeologists have found traces of domesticated types that date back more than 7,000 years.

Before the colonists settled in the New World, beans were grown by native peoples as often as maize. Although nowadays we assume that early Bostonians invented the recipe for baked beans, it's more likely that Indian women were already cooking the vegetables and taught Pilgrim women how to prepare them. Because chores—including preparing meals—were forbidden on Sundays, devout colonists put their beans on to cook the night before, and a custom of serving baked beans for Sunday breakfast was born.

Snap or String Beans

BLUE LAKE POLE

For more than a century, these delicious beans have been the standard for backyard gardeners and commercial growers. Developed in the Blue Lake area around Ukiah, California, Blue Lake Pole was the only variety grown for commercial canning in the early 1900s. Its white seeds form inside tender, stringless pods about 60 days from sowing. If you keep them picked, the prolific vines will grow to 6 or more feet and bear nicely until frost. Food historians think this bean was selected from Striped Creaseback, a variety dating to 1822. Many gardeners swear that it's still the best canning bean, but it's also good for eating fresh or freezing.

CHEROKEE TRAIL OF TEARS

Kent Whealy of Seed Savers Exchange reintroduced this heirloom after obtaining some seeds from the late Dr. John Wyche, a descendant of Cherokee Indians. According to legend, the Cherokees carried the beans with them in 1838 when they were forced to leave their Smoky Mountain homes and walk to Oklahoma. The vines climb to 8 feet and bear violet flowers. Inside the 6-inch pods, glossy black seeds form about 85 days after planting. The green-and-purple-streaked pods don't need stringing before they're snapped, or you can

Heirloom beans and tomatoes are summer's bounty. (Courtesy of David Cavagnaro)

shell the beans out and dry them. Save yourself some work and let the vigorous vines run up your sunflower stalks instead of staking them.

BLACK VALENTINE

Peter Henderson of New York developed this stringless variety in 1897. The jet black beans and pods can be harvested in 48 days for snapping, or they can

be dried after about 55 days for soups. Once they're cooked, the beans turn a purplish color and develop a meaty texture and a faint, nutty taste. The bushy plants are hardy and resist bean mosaic. Choose this one if you need an early bean, as the seeds germinate even in cool soil.

Shelling and Dry Beans

1500 YEAR OLD CAVE BEAN, also known as New Mexico Cave
These beans were discovered sealed in a clay pot in a cave in New Mexico, where they were probably stored by Anasazi Indians some 1,500 years earlier.

Black Turtle beans.

(Courtesy of David Cavagnaro)

It's been reported that some of the beans still germinated when planted. This bush bean produces big, flattened pods. Inside, the seeds are white mottled with brown or maroon.

VERMONT CRANBERRY

Known for holding its shape after cooking, this tasty bush bean is an eighteenth-century favorite. Originally from New England, it grows well across the United States, lending a nutty flavor to side dishes. The cranberry-colored beans are round and medium sized, ready for shelling in 75 to 85 days.

BLACK TURTLE, also known as Turtle Soup Beans

Native to South America, these small, ebony beans can be picked 90 to 100 days from sowing. After cooking, they become soft but hold their shape. The pods grow on semibushes, 3-foot-tall plants that produce better when they are staked or trellised. These inky beans taste similar to mushrooms, and they're delicious in frijoles, chili, salads, or rice dishes. Try spicing them up with a dash of cilantro or lime when adding them to salads. Introduced to American gardeners in the 1840s, the seeds probably take their name from their dark, shell-like appearance.

JACOB'S CATTLE, also known as Trout, Coach Dog, and Dalmatian Bean

Passamaquoddy Indians introduced these kidney-shaped beans to settlers in New England, where they performed nicely in that region's cool, short growing season. The beautiful, plump seeds are creamy white with maroon speckles, ready for harvest 85 to 95 days from sowing. Use them shelled or dried for an earthy, slightly sweet flavor. It's thought that the 2-foot-tall, bushy plants were developed by Jacob Trout of Virginia.

Growing Tips

Beans are warm-season crops that need full sun and rich, well-drained soil. Sow your seeds 1 inch deep outside after the soil is reliably warm, in late spring or early summer. Plant bush-type seeds 2 to 3 inches apart in rows spaced 18 inches apart. When seedlings appear, thin them to every 6 inches.

Vining or pole beans will need strong supports, so sow them every 2 inches around poles spaced 3 feet apart. Thin to 6 seedlings per pole. Alternately, sow the seeds every 2 inches near a trellis and thin to every 6 inches.

Keep your seeds watered until they sprout. After they're established, beans don't usually need extra water unless it's very dry.

Beans are easy to grow. For a fall crop, plant 10 to 12 weeks before the first expected frost in your area.

Snaps are ready for picking when the pods are firm but the seeds inside are still small. Harvest often and the plants should bear until frost.

Shell beans are ready to harvest when the pods are firm and filled out. Be sure to gather them before the seeds completely mature, or you'll have to save them for dried beans.

Saving beans for replanting is easy. The plants are self-pollinating; but bees sometimes mix things up, so to ensure that your seeds stay pure, grow only one variety at a time. If you do grow several varieties at once, heirloom gardening author William Woys Weaver recommends planting at least 20 feet apart.

To save seeds, allow some of the pods on your healthiest plants to dry. When you can shake the brown pods and hear the seeds rattle around inside, they

In 1887, Maule's advertised beans that produced "572 pods to the pole."

are ready to pick. This may be up to a month after you would usually harvest beans for the table.

Spread the pods over a screen and make sure they are completely dry before shelling them. If you prefer, you can save the unopened pods until you're ready to plant again. Label the pods or seeds before you store them in a cool, dry spot. The seeds generally remain viable for up to 5 years.

HELIOTROPE—*Heliotropium*

"We made nosegays for mamma's vases in our beautiful garden where the fuchsias and geraniums were 'hardy,' and the sweet-scented verbenas and heliotropes were great bushes, loading the air with perfume."

Juliana Horatia Ewing, Six to Sixteen, a Story for Girls *(1872)*

"... Through the open door A drowsy smell of flowers— gray heliotrope, And white sweet clover, and shy mignonette— Comes faintly in ..."

John Greenleaf Whittier, Among the Hills *(1869)*

Breathe deeply and describe the scent that lingers over a bed of heliotrope. Is it the fragrance of pure vanilla or a warm cherry pie? Baked apples or baby powder? Almonds or wine? Gardeners tend to disagree over this old-fashioned flower's perfume, which varies during the day. The aroma is often heightened or diluted by changes in the temperature, sunlight, and even the amount of wind blowing through the garden.

Heliotropes are not truly ancient plants. Their original name, *H. peruviana*, indicates that they are natives of Peru. In the 1700s, French botanist Joseph de Jussieu found heliotrope seeds that he forwarded from South America to Paris, where the plants were cultivated in the Jardin du Roi. It's said that de Jussieu swore he nearly became drunk on the flowers' perfume. French gardeners evidently agreed that heliotropes were intoxicating, as the plants were embraced and labeled *herbe d'amour*, or the flower of love.

By 1757, heliotropes had made their way into British gardens, where the tender blossoms were nurtured outdoors and transferred into conservatories or greenhouses when the temperature plummeted. Two prized varieties that emerged during the Victorian era were Miss Nightingale, a dwarf with dark lilac flowers, and Beauty of the Boudoir, a selection that seems to have vanished.

Thomas Jefferson collected heliotrope seeds while serving as Minister to France and sent them back to Monticello around 1786. He apparently was smitten with a wild heliotrope he spotted that boasted pretty blue blossoms. In a letter to a colleague, he mused that the plant was "to be sowed in spring. A delicious flower, but I suspect it must be planted in boxes & kept in the house in winter. The smell rewards the care." Other early heliotropes offered gardeners a choice of white, lavender, blue, or purple blossoms.

White Lady, a late bloomer with baby blue buds that opened to icy white, came onto the commercial market in the nineteenth century. Some growers think it still exists, perhaps now known as Alba.

Heliotrope has never been widely used for medicinal purposes, although *A Modern Herbal*, published in 1931 by Mrs. M. Grieve, touted a tincture made from fresh, whole plants. The plants were listed as remedies for "clergyman's sore throat and uterine displacement"—quite a strange combination.

Most old heliotropes have disappeared, although catalogs suggest that once we had about 10 common types. The flowers described ranged from lilac to blue, and lavender to dark amethyst, with medium green to dark green or variegated gold foliage. No doubt we have also lost some rich perfumes.

Still, the heliotropes available today can add an unrivaled sweetness to the garden. Plant them near porches, decks, or doors so you can enjoy their

Old heliotropes smell of violets and cherries. (Courtesy of Renee's Garden)

fragrance, or pot them and bring them indoors for short periods of time. Butterflies love their nectar, so they are great additions to naturalized areas or wildlife gardens.

The plants take their name from the Greek word *helios*, meaning "sun," and *trope*, meaning "to turn," possibly because early peoples thought heliotropes could track the sun across the sky. The flowers represented faithfulness to the Victorians, who gave them to their sweethearts to mean, "I am devoted to you."

FRAGRANT DELIGHT

This old-fashioned flower is known for its heavy perfume. The violet blossoms are highlighted with small, snowy centers, while the dark green leaves have a purple cast. The plants mature at 2 feet.

MARINE OR DEEP MARINE

Once popular in Victorian nosegays, Marine has a light scent that some gardeners describe as violets, while others insist it is closer to vanilla and cherries. The leaves are dark blue-green or dark green tinged with purple. The flower sprays range from dark or navy blue to deep violet and appear atop 18-inch plants.

ALBA

This honey-and-vanilla-scented hybrid is perfect for an all-white garden. It produces masses of big, snowy flowers and medium green foliage. Topping out at about 15 to 24 inches tall, the plants are a good choice for containers or the front of beds and borders. An 1892 catalog described a heliotrope of "purest white" with an almond aroma.

DWARF MARINE

Maturing at about 14 inches, this compact, bushy heliotrope works well in window boxes, so you can catch its perfume on breezy days. Butterflies are drawn to the velvety flowers, which range from royal purple to violet blue. With its dark green leaves, this one is pretty when cultivated alongside ruby red begonias or gold Rudbeckias.

Deep Marine. (Courtesy of Renee's Garden)

IOWA

While Iowa is a modern hybrid, it earns a mention here for its delightful scent. Some growers find it reminiscent of sweet wine, while others say it's a mixture of mulled cider and vanilla. The plants grow to 3 feet and produce deep purple panicles surrounded by purplish green leaves.

Growing Tips

With one or two exceptions, commercial sources for antique heliotropes are hard to find. Try searching for old varieties in farmers' market bulletins or at seed swaps.

Heliotrope seeds should be planted in ample sun and rich, well-drained soil. You can expect blooms about 4 months after germination, so start early to fill a summer garden with these fragrant flowers. One note: some gardeners complain that their heliotrope seeds germinate poorly. Until you have determined how they'll perform for you, sow extras to avoid disappointment. You can always thin the seedlings later, or share them with neighbors.

Start your seeds indoors about 6 to 8 weeks before the last frost. Press the seeds gently into a growing medium mixed with fine sand, or scatter them over the top. Don't bury them, as heliotropes need light to germinate.

Cover the seeds with clear plastic to retain moisture. At temperatures between 70° and 80°F, the seedlings should pop up in 2 weeks. Once they emerge, remove the plastic and keep them in bright, indirect light. After the last frost, harden off the seedlings and move them to their permanent location in the garden. Pinch the tips and the side shoots of the plants as they grow to keep them bushy and encourage more blooms.

If you prefer, you can sow heliotrope seeds directly outdoors after the last frost. To intensify their fragrance, locate the plants in a warm, sheltered, sunny spot.

Heliotropes are small, tender shrubs. Because they're hardy to only around 40°F, they're treated as annuals in most places. They are easy to grow as long as you provide adequate water during dry periods; otherwise, the plants may wilt or stop blooming. Don't let your heliotropes stand in water, though, as they dislike wet feet.

Gardeners in the Deep South may need to site their heliotropes in partial shade, since harsh sunlight may fade their colors and make them decline faster than usual. High humidity is another problem for heliotropes in the South, but there's not much anyone can do about that.

Heliotrope Companions

Heliotrope's blue and violet blossoms look pretty with yellow, pink, and white flowers. Try them alongside pale gauras, or mix them into beds and borders packed with pink petunias, golden marigolds, and apricot- or butter-colored antique roses. For contrast, try silvery or white flowers and foliage, especially with the deep purple varieties. If you're using containers or hanging baskets, don't forget to tuck in a couple of small plants of Dwarf Marine.

Garden author Louise Beebe Wilder, writing in 1932, insisted she'd never been able to detect heliotrope's legendary cherry pie scent. Nevertheless, she said they made excellent companions for her roses.

HOLLYHOCK—*Alcea rosea*

Heirloom plants have had to put up with a lot, including gardeners' fickle tastes and the demands of the marketplace. But old-fashioned hollyhocks nearly succumbed to just one obstacle: rust.

The disease is caused by a fungus that strikes almost everywhere. It hit the United States hard in the 1870s, disfiguring many plants and ruining entire nursery stocks. Nobody was much interested in growing hollyhocks after that, and only a few strains survived.

Fortunately, growers figured out how to combat the fungus. By 1894, they had begun burning infected hollyhocks, a practice we still imitate when we burn plant debris to clean up our gardens. But gardeners in humid climates will always have to watch for signs of infection, which include yellow spots on the tops of hollyhock leaves and orange-brown pustules underneath. At least we now have fungicides to combat the disease, and good garden hygiene can go a long way toward preventing its spread.

Hollyhocks, members of the mallow family, are indigenous to Turkey and the Middle East. Crusaders were largely responsible for spreading the original wild yellow and pink flowers throughout Europe and probably gave them their common name by adding "holy" to "hoc," the Anglo-Saxon word for "mallow."

Hollyhocks were immediately popular when they arrived in America around 1631. Double-flowering types showed up in 1677, and by 1823, striped varieties were available.

By the mid-nineteenth century, hollyhocks and dahlias were neck-and-neck rivals for popularity in American gardens. Growers found the tall plants useful for adding architectural interest along fences and bare walls or as lush backdrops for shorter plants. Hollyhocks still make good companions for low-growing daisies, phlox, and lilies. One note: bees find them attractive, so avoid using hollyhocks close to decks and porches if the insects annoy you.

> "Hollyhocks are among the most pictorial of plants, and it is very difficult to find anything else to take their place. I like best the single ones in pink and blackish crimson, pale yellow and pure white, but the double ones are very fine and opulent, and the lovely shades and tints to be had very numerous. One I had from England, called Prince of Orange, was a splendid orange-copper colour. . . . I have a fine group of salmon-pink Hollyhocks against a large tree of the Purple-leaved Plum, and another cherry-coloured group has as a fine background a pink Dorothy Perkins Rose which drapes the wall behind it. White Hollyhocks are fine with Tiger Lilies."
>
> Louise Beebe Wilder,
> My Garden *(1920)*

Nigra. (Courtesy of Select Seeds)

CHATER'S DOUBLE

This Victorian-era variety has ruffled, double flowers that look like peonies. The 3½-inch blooms are available in shades of yellow, pink, red, lavender, white, and apricot. Mature plants can grow to 7 feet tall.

PRISCILLA

The story behind this antique flower says that Bazil Silkwood, an Illinois businessman, met a 10-year-old slave named Priscilla while visiting a Georgia plantation. He didn't see her again for several years. After the plantation owner died, Priscilla, recently sold to a Cherokee chief, pocketed a few hollyhock seeds from the slave quarters to take to her new home. Silkwood met her again in 1838, when he encountered the Cherokees on their terrible march along the Trail of Tears.

This time, Silkwood purchased the girl's freedom and adopted her. Legend says he paid $1,000 in gold. Priscilla planted some of her hollyhocks at the Silkwood home, where she died in 1892. In 1950, her seeds were returned to Oklahoma, where the flowers are still grown around many Cherokee homes.

Priscilla bears dainty rose pink blossoms with maroon veins on 4- to 5-foot plants.

THE WATCHMAN

Grown by Jefferson at Monticello, The Watchman has satiny, single blooms. On cloudy days, the flowers look almost black, but the color is actually deep burgundy or chocolate-purple. The plants grow 5 to 8 feet tall.

NIGRA

John Parkinson was among the first to describe these black beauties in 1629, remarking that the flowers were "a darke red like black blood." When they are backlit by the setting sun, the large blooms look maroon or purplish-black. If you grow ebony-colored hollyhocks like Nigra, try to avoid placing them against a background of dark green vegetation or at the edge of deep shade. The flowers are hard to see in the shadows.

TRIUMPH

Originally offered in 1936, Triumph sports semidouble to double blossoms that resemble big, frilly carnations. The plants may reach 7 feet tall. Flower colors range from white to rose, salmon, lavender, purple, red, or yellow.

It's Behind the House

Poor hollyhocks! Iowa farmers have long grown these stately plants around their outbuildings, including humble outhouses. The plants were used to hide the family privy so often, visiting ladies fell into the habit of asking to "see the hollyhocks," a request deemed less embarrassing than asking directions to

what they really needed. An Outhouse Hollyhock that reaches 9 feet tall is still available, with white, pink, burgundy, or magenta flowers.

Growing Tips

Hollyhocks are classic summer plants. Remember that they're biennials, so when you're growing them from seeds, you'll get only leaves and stems the first year. The plants will flower and set seeds in their second year and then die back in most parts of the country. Lucky gardeners may find their hollyhocks behave like short-lived perennials, surviving for another year or two, but that depends on the variety you are growing and the gardening zone you're in.

To start hollyhocks indoors, soak the seeds overnight before planting and sow them in peat pots 8 weeks before the last spring frost. They need light to germinate, so press them gently into the growing medium. They'll sprout in

10 to 14 days. After the seedlings are up and hardened off and there's no danger of frost, it's safe to move them into the garden.

If you prefer, you can also sow the seeds outdoors in a cold frame from late summer to early fall. You'll need to do this at least 2 months before the first frost so the seedlings will have time to form some true leaves. Once the leaves appear, mulch the young plants to protect them.

The following spring, remove the mulch and transplant your hollyhocks to their permanent location. Flowering starts in the spring in warm-winter areas and midsummer elsewhere.

Hollyhocks enjoy full sun and rich soil, and once they're established, they can tolerate short droughts. They do need lots of room for their bushy foliage, so space them at least 3 feet apart. This also improves air circulation and helps prevent disease. Stake the plants when they are about 3 feet tall.

Holly flowers open from the bottom of their flower spikes and continue upward. Once a spike is finished, cut it off, and you may be rewarded with another set of smaller blooms. For indoor arrangements, snip the flowers before they're fully open.

A note to seed savers: hollyhocks cross-pollinate readily. If you want to keep your seeds true to type, limit yourself to one variety.

Hollyhock seed pods look like little bags tied at the neck with string. Inside the pods, the seeds are arranged in a circle, like tiny shrimp in a ring. The trick to seed saving is to gather the pods before they open. Don't pick the pods while they're white; that's the immature stage. Wait until they mature and turn brown. Then rub the papery shelled pods between your fingers and let the seeds fall into a paper bag. Allow them to dry for at least 2 weeks in a well-ventilated area before storing them in an airtight container.

If all this seed collecting sounds like too much trouble, you can simply let your hollyhocks self-sow. They have a charming habit of coming back in colorful clumps, or colonies, around the yard.

Black Watchman hollyhock seeds. (Courtesy of Renee's Garden)

KISS-ME-OVER-THE-GARDEN-GATE—*Polygonum orientale*, also known as Prince's Feather, Prince's Plume, Princess Feather, Ladyfingers, and Ragged Sailor

You don't see Kiss-Me-Over-the-Garden-Gate grown much anymore, and that's a shame. This old-fashioned annual adds a light fragrance and a blast of bright pink or purple color to the landscape.

It's hard to say why Kiss-Me hasn't enjoyed as much of a revival as many other antique flowers and vegetables. It may have to do with the plants' size. They grow to be quite tall, with some varieties topping out at 8 to 10 feet, and may spread to 3 or more feet in diameter.

Of course, *Polygonum orientale* may have also lost ground because of its classification as an invasive exotic in some parts of the country. In Tennessee, it is considered an invasive exotic pest, since it naturalizes freely in wetlands or dry soils. Birds also like to dine on Kiss-Me seeds, helping spread them through their droppings far beyond their usual boundaries. That's not to say these handsome plants with the beadlike flowers shouldn't be grown anywhere—only that it is wise to check a reliable source, like the U.S. Department of Agriculture plant database, at <http://plants.usda.gov>, if you have concerns about bringing any nonnative into your area.

Over time, Kiss-Me plants have been known by a variety of names. Their old Latin name, *Persicaria orientale*, indicates they were discovered in the Orient. Aside from Ladyfingers and other romantic-sounding monikers, they've also been classified by labels that reflect their Far Eastern homes, such as Tall Persicary, Garden Persicary, and Oriental Persicary.

Botanist John Gerard added to the confusion when he referred to the plants in 1633 as Spotted Arsmart and Water Pepper, names apparently inspired by what he described as the "hot and biting taste" of their seeds. In 1754, Philip Miller elaborated on "Eastern Arse-smart" in his *Gardeners Dictionary*, reporting that the plants first arrived from "the Eastern Country" to "the Royal Gardens at Paris." He continued, "This plant . . . doth grow to be ten or twelve Feet high, and divides into several Branches, each of which produces a beautiful Spike of purple Flowers at their Extremities in the Autumn."

Polygonum orientale also has a long history in colonial America. Sometime

Polygonum orientale was popular in the Victorian era. (Courtesy of David Cavagnaro)

between 1736 and 1737, British businessman Peter Collinson sent seeds from the plants to an acquaintance in Williamsburg. He also forwarded some to the Quaker botanist John Bartram in Philadelphia, writing, "Inclosed, is some seed of a noble annual,—grows six or seven feet high, and makes a beautiful show with its long bunches of red flowers. . . . It is called the great oriental Persicaria."

By 1792, a color illustration of *Polygonum orientale* appeared in William Curtis's *Botanical Magazine*. Described as the Tall Persicary, the plant was recommended for the "brilliancy of its flowers" and its size, which made it a "formidable rival to the gigantic sunflower." The writer added thoughtfully, "It produces abundance of seed, which, falling on the borders, generally comes up spontaneously. . . . But it is most commonly sown in the spring with other annuals. . . . Will bear the smoke of London better than many others."

By 1804, Bernard McMahon offered the seeds on his Philadelphia seed list. Burpee's sold them in a 1935 catalog, but few commercial sources carry them today.

VARIEGATED KISS-ME-OVER-THE-GARDEN GATE— SHIRO-GANE NISHIKI

First mentioned in a 1900 catalog, the heart-shaped leaves of this rare heirloom are spotted and splashed with creamy white. Pale pink flowers appear in fall on 8- to 10-foot-tall plants. This annual is bushier than other varieties, but it self-sows nicely. It received the Mailorder Gardening Association's Green Thumb Award in 2004.

Growing Tips

You'll need patience with Kiss-Me seeds, which take an erratic 7 to 28 days to germinate and much longer to flower. Start the seeds indoors in containers filled with a good quality potting mix about 14 to 16 weeks before the last frost. Cover them lightly with ¼ inch of soil and water gently. The seeds will sprout better if they are chilled, so place the containers inside plastic bags to retain moisture and store them in the refrigerator. Leave them to cool for about a month, then move them to an unheated location. As the weather warms up, periodically check to see if the seeds are sprouting.

Alternately, start your seeds in a cold frame, sowing them in early spring and potting them into individual containers after the seedlings emerge. You can plant them directly into the garden, spacing them 12 inches apart, when summer arrives.

Polygonum orientale prefers full sun and moist, well-drained earth. It will tolerate some shade and needs average to rich soil. The seeds may take up to 18 weeks to produce blossoms, which usually appear from August to October.

Prince's Feather is another name for this charming antique. (Courtesy of David Cavagnaro)

Kiss-Me flowers are available in a range of pinks, from fuchsia to blush to deep rose. As they grow, the plant's long stems can be allowed to drape over garden gates or fences, providing a curtain of color.

After the flowers fade, Kiss-Me seeds tumble freely onto the ground. It may take a little effort to find this old beauty, but once you've got it going in your garden, you shouldn't have to worry. It's vigorous and self-sows with abandon.

Other Plants for a Kissing Garden

RED VALERIAN—*CENTRANTHUS RUBER*, also known as Kiss-Me-Quick

It may not sound appealing, but you have to wonder if *Centranthus* earned its everyday name for its distinctive, pungent smell. A few gardeners profess to enjoy burying their noses in its large flower panicles, describing their scent as a mild honey fragrance. Others pinch their noses and walk away, complaining, as author Louise Beebe Wilder once did, that the bruised stems and the blossoms reek of perspiration or a strong "catty" odor. If *Centranthus* offends you, it's easy to understand its common name. You wouldn't want to linger for more than a fast kiss when you and your sweetheart are strolling by.

Red Valerian is a perennial subshrub that first appeared on botanist John Tradescant's plant list in 1634. It yields clusters of red, white, mauve, and crimson flowers from about June through September. This Mediterranean native self-sows easily and has naturalized all over Europe, thriving even in rocky soils and on coastal beaches. It has invaded parts of the west coast in the United States. Give it sun or partial shade and ordinary but well-drained soil.

Design Tips

Kiss-Me blossoms are rather delicate, since they're held atop cornlike stems that can be buffeted by strong winds. Protect the plants by locating them where there is some shelter from the weather, but don't wall them in. A light breeze makes the pink or purplish-pink flowers sway on their slender stems, and their movement adds beauty and interest to the garden.

Because butterflies and bees are drawn to this plant's hanging catkins, and birds like to feast on the ripened seeds, *Polygonum orientale* is a natural for wildlife gardens. Try planting it alongside other tall, warm-weather bloomers such as black-eyed Susans or lemony sunflowers.

Snip the flower heads of these plants before they are completely open, and the blooms will continue to unfold. The stems are nice to use in bouquets, or they can be dried and saved for long-lasting arrangements.

David Bradshaw, professor of horticulture at Clemson University, learned about Kiss-Me plants as a child, after his sharecropper father fenced off a flower bed to keep out the farm's wandering chickens, ducks, dogs, mules, guineas, sheep, and goats. Bradshaw started a collection of plants inside the safety of the fence. "The only things I grew outside the fence," he recalls, "were two deep purple clumps of 'Kiss-Me.' They became as big as bushel baskets, and little old ladies from church would come by and cut the flowers. Nothing would do, but they had to kiss me at the gate."

LIMA OR BUTTER BEAN—*Phaseolus lunatus*
RUNNER BEAN—*Phaseolus coccineus*

Surprisingly, humble lima beans were once reserved for society's high-class diners. Only the most important Incas were allowed to consume these legumes, which probably originated in Central America around 5,000 B.C. Everybody else had to be satisfied with filling up on ordinary garden beans. We're lucky not to have any restrictions on eating limas nowadays, because there are so many tasty, nutritious varieties available.

Limas take their name from Lima, the capital of Peru, although the pronunciation has changed over time. Easy-to-store limas, like many other large seeds, made their way across the globe in the packs and pockets of far-ranging explorers, slavers, traders, and soldiers.

Phaseolus lunatus first showed up in Europe around 1591, but these heat-loving vegetables did not thrive in the cool climate. Limas were not widely popular in America, either, until Henderson's Bush, introduced in 1889, paved the way for many new and easy-to-grow bush types.

Runner beans are also natives of Central America and Mexico, but they belong to the species *coccineus*. John Tradescant, gardener to Charles I, is credited for bringing the Scarlet Runner and Painted Lady varieties to the British Isles. Like limas, runner beans, which are primarily grown in the United States for their beautiful white or scarlet flowers, eventually made their way into New World gardens.

Scarlet runners make wonderful plants for wildlife gardens, where they entice hummingbirds to their nectar-bearing blossoms. But the first white runner types, in the 1750s, were traditionally prepared for European table use. If you decide to grow runners for eating, be sure to pick the pods while they're young and tender, or shell the beans out for the best flavor.

"Daily the beans saw me come to their rescue armed with a hoe, and thin the ranks of their enemies."
Henry David Thoreau,
Walden *(1854)*

Bush limas, offered by
Burpee's in 1891.

Runner beans take their botanical name from the Latin word *coccum*, an ancient dye made from the berries of scarlet oak trees. *Phaseolus* refers to a boat with a canoelike shape—like many bean pods.

Lima or Butter Beans

SNOW ON THE MOUNTAIN

Heirloom gardener John Coykendall of Knoxville, Tennessee, received these prolific beans from Washington Parish, Louisiana, where they had been raised since 1880 by generations of the same family. Their colors fade as the beans age, but they start out a handsome maroon with a dusting of "snow" around each eye.

CHRISTMAS LIMA, also known as Large Speckled Calico or Calico Lima Bean

What better dish to serve at Christmas than beans that taste like chestnuts? This 1840s heirloom is a heavy cropper, producing in 75 to 100 days. The cream-colored seeds have maroon swirls and speckles and grow as big as quarters. Count on these pole types to bear even when the weather turns hot and humid. The beans can be shelled for eating fresh or dried.

HENDERSON'S BUSH LIMA

One old story says that a working man found this bean growing alongside a road and sold it to the T. W. Woods & Sons seed company in 1885. It was later sold to seedsman Peter Henderson of New York, who named it after himself and put it on the market in 1887. Another story claims that the beans were discovered by a soldier returning home from the Civil War. Whatever the truth, there's no doubt this is one of the most popular beans for home or commercial growers. Each dark green pod holds 3 to 4 small, white seeds. The drought-tolerant bushes bear in 60 to 75 days. A 1908 Burbank seed catalog raved that it was "a very rich, luscious, Bean, that has the advantage of not requiring poles to run on while it comes earlier into bearing."

notes

HOPI ORANGE LIMA

Hopi Indians get credited for saving this rare, hard-to-find strain, which was discovered growing on Bourbon Island in the Indian Ocean in the eighteenth century. The seeds are mottled orange and black and may have originated in South America. The 6- to 8-foot-long vines produce in 75 to 80 days. The Hopis dry the beans or grind them to make flour.

Runner Beans

PAINTED LADY

Many gardeners use these pretty runner beans as a living screen, letting the greenery hide unsightly views. As the only runner bean with bicolored blossoms, this one is certainly worth growing for its showy scarlet and white flowers. The foot-long pods plump up with buff and brown seeds about 68 days after planting. First described in an 1827 study of the flora of Rio de Janeiro, Painted Lady was probably known in England by the early 1600s. It has a pole habit and requires trellising. In tropical climates, it behaves as a perennial.

Painted Lady runner beans. (Courtesy of Renee's Garden)

SCARLET RUNNER BEAN, also known as Scarlet Conqueror, Fire Bean, Mammoth, Giant Red, and White Dutch Runner

Like other runner beans, this variety is usually grown in the United States for its handsome dark green foliage and brilliant red flowers. The vigorous vines run up to 15 feet long and bear in 65 days from planting. The seeds, shaped like limas, range from glossy black to black-violet with dark red markings. This is not a great eating bean. Some people snap and cook the young pods, but most rate the taste only as fair and complain of the coarse texture. Grown in America since 1800, this is one of the oldest runners, first mentioned in 1750.

Red Saba and Snow on the Mountain bean seeds. (Courtesy of John Coykendall)

MAGIC BEANSTALK

These could be the beans Jack grew in the old fairytale. The 10- to 12-foot vines produce loads of showy scarlet flowers. When mature, the seeds are an attractive black with purple swirls. Both the seeds and the fat pods are edible.

PURPLE HYACINTH BEAN—*DOLICHOS LABLAB*

Botanically speaking, this is not a true runner bean. But it's included here because it has a running growth habit, and its swags of dark purple foliage and amethyst blossoms are gorgeous when trained along fences or trellises. Jefferson described the plants growing at Monticello in 1812: "Arbor beans, white, scarlet, crimson, purple . . . on the long walk of the garden." Although a French physician illustrated a white variety in 1591, the purple type probably wasn't sold in the United States until 1802. Heirloom gardening author William Woys Weaver warns not to eat the dried beans or let children handle them, as they contain possibly lethal toxins.

"One of the first New World beans described in Europe [scarlet runner bean] seems to be more popular there than in the colonies in the eighteenth century. They struggle in the heat of the coastal plain of Virginia but do remarkably well in the cooler climate at Monticello in the foothills of the Blue Ridge."

Wesley Greene, Garden Historian, Colonial Williamsburg Foundation

Growing Tips

Lima or butter beans should be sown directly in the garden after the last frost. They are particularly sensitive to cold weather and soil, so wait a couple of weeks after planting snap or shell types before you sow.

Cover your seeds with ½ inch of soil and space them 3 to 6 inches apart. The pods will be ready to pick when they feel plump and firm and turn bright green.

Plant runner beans 1 inch deep and 4 to 6 inches apart, in rows or hills

These vigorous vines produce handsome black and purple beans. (Courtesy of Renee's Garden)

☀ Renee's Garden ☀

Magic Beanstalk
Scarlet Runner Bean

"Flower treasures for the eye & heart"
—Renee Shepherd

spaced 2 feet apart. Other than their spacing, treat them like snaps and shells, but remember that these vigorous climbers need support. Because their foliage is thick, avoid growing them where strong winds may blow them down or where they will shade shorter, sun-loving plants.

To save limas or runners for seeds, let the pods dry on the vines before collecting them. Bean families usually do not cross; that is, you won't get a cross between a runner and a Lima. But varieties may cross within each family, so stick to growing one variety at a time to ensure seed purity. Alternately, you can research the types you're growing to find out how to isolate them so they don't cross. Lima and runner beans may remain viable for up to 3 years.

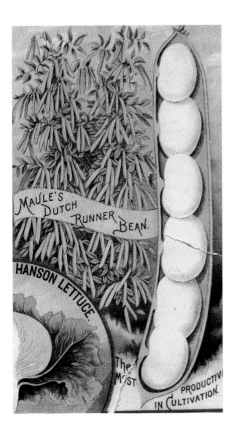

Prolific runner beans sold by the
W. Henry Maule Company, ca. 1887.

MELON—*Cucumis melo*

Let's clear things up right off the bat. There are two kinds of melons commonly grown in American gardens: muskmelons (*C. melo*, *reticulatus* group), and honeydews and casabas (*C. melo*, *inodorus* group). What we've been calling cantaloupes aren't really cantaloupes at all. They are muskmelons. But more on this shortly.

Whatever name they go by, melons are ancient plants. They have been depicted in Egyptian paintings that date back to biblical times, and historians think they may also have their roots in Iran and northwest India.

Archaeologists have uncovered melon drawings near Pompeii, in the ruins of another city buried by Mount Vesuvius's fiery blast. The Venetian merchant Marco Polo (b. ca. 1254) passed through Afghanistan, where he described finding "the best melons in the world in very great quantity." After sampling

*"Friends are like melons.
Shall I tell you why? To
find a good one, you must
a hundred try."*
*French poet
Claude Mermet
(b. ca. 1550)*

some melon strips he found drying in the sun, he pronounced them "sweeter than honey. And you must know that they are an article of commerce and find a ready sale through all the country around."

Columbus gets credit for introducing muskmelon seeds to Haiti. Eventually the plants made their way into Central and South America, and by the 1600s, they were known in North America. Cantaloupes—remember, we call them cantaloupes but they're actually muskmelons—became a major food crop in the United States after the Civil War.

In 1881, a French melon known as Netted Gem arrived on our shores and became widely popular. The French also introduced American gardeners to the White Antibes winter melon, also known as the honeydew melon, in 1900. We've been mixing up our melons ever since.

Real cantaloupes, *cantalupensis*, are small, round fruits with orange or green flesh and rough, warty rinds that lack netting. Common in Europe, they are seldom seen here. But it really doesn't matter if we go on calling our muskmelons cantaloupes. All that matters is that we enjoy their sweet, cool goodness every summer.

COLLECTIVE FARM WOMAN—*C. MELO* VAR. *INODORUS*

This hard little winter melon resembles a honeydew, although it isn't as heavily netted. It ripens early, in 80 to 85 days, making it a good choice for areas with short growing seasons. The flesh is yellowish white and sugary tasting. Some gardeners say they can detect its mild, flowery fragrance.

Like the Moon and Stars watermelon, this variety was rediscovered by Kent Whealy, who located it through Moscow's first privately owned seed company. Once feared lost, the plants had been kept under cultivation on a collective farm—hence the name. These melons hail from the Ukrainian Black Sea region and typically weigh about 2 pounds.

QUEEN ANNE'S POCKET MELON—*C. MELO* VAR. *DUDAIM*

This tiny treasure has been known for about a thousand years. Grow it as a novelty, because it doesn't really have much flavor; some gardeners even describe it as a bland-tasting honeydew. The little fruits have a musky perfume and irregular green, orange, and yellow markings.

According to legend, Queen Anne was in the habit of tucking a melon into

Collective Farm Woman.

(Courtesy of David Cavagnaro)

her pocket as a sachet. Victorian women carried them to mask body odors. Also known as the Plumgranny, this Persian native was once widely grown in the Ozarks. *Dudaim* is the fruit's Hebrew name.

C. melo *var.* reticulatus

HALE'S BEST

This early muskmelon was developed by a Japanese gardener around 1920. It has an excellent flavor and a sweet scent. The mottled golden skin is heavily netted, and the 2- to 3-pound fruits have a salmon-colored flesh. Heirloom gardeners often praise it for its good, old-fashioned taste. Give it approximately 75 to 80 days from sowing.

JENNY LIND

Named for the singer in P. T. Barnum's traveling show, this 1840s muskmelon has a light green flesh. Small, sweet fruits are ready for harvest in about 70 days. It's distinguished by a cap, or turban, on its netted skin.

Queen Anne's Pocket Melon. (Courtesy of Seed Savers Exchange)

EMERALD GEM

Once the most popular melon of the Gilded Age, this heirloom dates to 1886. It was developed by Burpee's from seeds provided by William Voorhees, a Michigan gardener. The green rinds have a light green ribbing, and the flesh is pale orange with a sweet, slightly spicy taste. The melons mature at 2 to 3 pounds each in 70 to 90 days.

Jenny Lind.
(Courtesy of Seed
Savers Exchange)

Emerald Gem.
(Courtesy of Seed
Savers Exchange)

MINNESOTA MIDGET

Bigger isn't always better. These diminutive fruits—for melons—grow to just 3 to 4 inches in diameter on vines that mature at about 3 feet in length. Introduced by the University of Minnesota in 1948, this is an extra early variety, ready in 60 to 75 from sowing. The gold flesh is thick and sweet, with lots of natural sugar.

Growing Tips

Melons need lots of heat and a long growing season. They also love rich earth, and you can hardly add too much organic material to their soil. (In fact, discarded melon seeds often erupt from the compost heap.) Be prepared to give them plenty of water, too, as the fruits develop.

The growing requirements for melons are basically the same as for watermelons. Start your seeds indoors 3 to 4 weeks before the last spring frost, but wait until the weather is reliably warm to harden off and transplant the seedlings. They'll rot if the ground is wet and cold, and they prefer air temperatures ranging from 65° to 75°F.

Alternately, sow melon seeds outdoors after the last frost. Plant them about ½ to ¾ inch deep. Thin the seedlings to every 18 to 24 inches in rows that are 6 to 8 feet apart. Proper spacing will help fresh air circulate around them and avoid disease.

Your muskmelons (or cantaloupes, for those of us who resist change) will be ready to harvest when they pull away easily from their stems and when they smell ripe and fruity. But it's best to pick them before they separate naturally, to avoid overripening. Test before you pick by pressing your thumb down gently near the stem. A table-ready melon should slip right off the vine.

Honeydews ripen a little later, and the slip test doesn't work for them. But you'll know they're ripe when their skins turn cream colored or pale yellow, and the blossom end of the fruits feels slightly soft.

Melons can cross-pollinate, so grow only one type to ensure pure seeds for saving. However, you may still get some cross-pollination if anyone else is growing melons within a half-mile of your patch. Watermelons belong to a different genera and species, *Citrullus lanatus*, so you don't have to worry about them crossing with your muskmelons, honeydews, casabas, and cantaloupes.

If you do grow different types of melons and then save their seeds, the next generation of plants you grow may show some undesirable traits. Of course, they may have some unexpectedly good characteristics, too. It's a bit of a gamble, and that's nothing to be afraid of, if you feel inclined to experiment. After all, nature does it all the time.

It's not hard to save melon seeds. All you need to do is scoop the seeds out of the ripened fruits, rinse them gently, and let them air-dry on paper plates or pie tins for a couple of weeks. Keep the seeds in a single layer, and stir them occasionally to speed things up. Don't try to save time by heating the seeds in the oven, though. A warm room is all you need. Label your seeds and store them in airtight containers in a cool, dry place. *C. melo* seeds may remain viable for up to 5 years.

Collective Farm Woman melon seeds.

MIGNONETTE—*Reseda odorata*, also known as Frenchman's Darling and Sweet-Scented Reseda

It's not difficult to imagine young Napoleon Bonaparte, only 29 when he conquered Egypt in 1798, pocketing a handful of seeds from some of the strange flowers he encountered there. No doubt the blossoms whose seeds he collected for the Empress Josephine caught his attention with their strong, sweet scent.

But the flowers themselves must not have been terribly attractive; at least one early botanist who saw them sniffed that they reminded him of a "fragrant weed." Pale and small, the blossoms grew along the sprawling branches of a shrubby-looking plant called *Reseda odorata*.

Reseda is actually an herb that was probably introduced to Egypt and northern Europe by first-century Romans, who took it along to use as a sedative. The scientific name comes from the Latin *resedare*, meaning "to calm, heal, assuage, or restore." Old English garden books make scant mention of these plants, and as author Louise Beebe Wilder once wrote, what was known about them would fit on a thumbnail.

Still, it's safe to assume that Josephine was intrigued with her seeds, as she sowed them throughout her gardens at Malmaison. She dubbed her plants mignonettes, which translates as "little darlings," and with her influence, the

"'There's a lot o' mignonette an' poppies,' he said. 'Mignonette's th' sweetest smellin' thing as grows, an' it'll grow wherever you cast it, same as poppies will. Them as'll come up an' bloom if you just whistle to 'em, them's th' nicest of all.'"
Frances Hodgson Burnett,
The Secret Garden
(1909)

"I like to place mignonette in a glass bowl, it is so cool and fresh in its green and gold and a spangling of silver and a ruby here and there that brightens it at close quarters."
E. A. Bowles,
My Garden in Summer
(1914)

flowers soon became popular throughout southern France. Fashionable ladies copied her habit of growing them in pots so one could enjoy their scent
without bending to the ground, while French perfumers set about capturing
their essence in bottles.

By the mid-eighteenth century, mignonettes were equally beloved in
England. London city dwellers grew them in profusion on balconies and in
window boxes, while wealthy Victorians kept them potted up in conservato-

ries and shuttled them in and out of their homes as needed for party decorations. By 1829, the scent of mignonettes had become so pervasive, one Londoner grumbled that entire city streets had become "oppressive with the odor." Apparently he was in the minority. Most early gardeners cherished mignonettes for their honey and raspberry scent.

Mignonettes made their first appearance in American literature around 1752, when Philip Miller described them in his *Gardeners Dictionary*. The blossoms, he noted, were "a dull colour" but noteworthy for their "high ambrosial scent."

Jefferson probably grew mignonette in his gardens at Monticello prior to 1803, as we can surmise from a letter written that year by his granddaughter, Anne Carey Randolph: "We were so unfortunate as to lose the Mignonett entirely although Mama divided it between Mrs. Lewis Aunt Jane & herself but none of it seeded."

Jefferson must have replaced the seeds, because he records planting the fragrant flowers near the northwest cistern in his garden in March 1811. But apparently the seeds were lost again. In 1812, he sent a message to Philadelphia nurseryman Bernard McMahon and mentioned mignonette seeds, "which I do not now possess."

William Curtis, a London pharmacist who began publishing the authoritative *Botanical Magazine* in 1787, eagerly told readers how to use the novel plants in their homes and gardens: "The luxury of the pleasure-garden is greatly heightened by the delightful odour which this plant diffuses; and as it is most readily cultivated in pots, its fragrance may be conveyed to the parlour of the recluse, or the chamber of the valetudinarian; its perfume, thought not so refreshing perhaps as that of the Sweet-Briar, is not apt to offend on continuance the most delicate olfactories."

MACHET

These fringed blossoms have been described as pale pink or salmon, peach, white tinged with scarlet, or white highlighted with reddish brown. Some growers find the fragrance fruity, like raspberries, while others describe it as spicy or a mixture of vanilla and raspberry. Machet plants grow 2 feet tall and are compact and vigorous, with broader leaves than their wild, twiggy ancestors.

MACHET GIANT

Breeders who developed the Machet Giant in the 1860s had aimed to produce longer flower spikes with hints of red and purple on the white blossoms. But their work was a trade-off, as the flowers lost some of their wonderful natural fragrance.

Other cultivars of mignonettes began appearing in seed catalogs in the 1930s. Flowers were single or double in colors that ranged from pure white to creamy yellow, or pale chartreuse to dark red. Seed sellers listed them under such names as Golden Machet, Machet Improved, Red Giant, White Pearl, Goliath, and Incomparable. Unfortunately, most have now disappeared from the commercial seed trade.

Mignonettes are excellent for a cutting garden, providing blossoms that may last up to a week in cool temperatures. But they fade fast in warm weather. In 1914, garden author E. A. Bowles described filling his home one sultry summer morning with bouquets of mignonettes, roses, and sweet peas. But, he added mournfully, the flowers "are really only good for two days."

Growing Tips

While mignonettes are perennials in their warm, southern Mediterranean homes, they're treated as hardy annuals here. They are not fond of transplanting, so it's best to sow them directly into your garden in rich, well-drained soil. Give the seeds an early start in spring or sow them in the fall for flowers the following year. Fall-sown plants are often more floriferous than those potted up in spring. Mignonette plants prefer full sun but will accept partial shade.

Once your seedlings are up, thin them to every 8 inches. Sow more seeds periodically throughout the growing season to ensure a steady supply of the racemes, or flower spikes. They'll open and begin to release their perfume in about 8 to 12 weeks from planting.

These charming plants do not have a long bloom period. Once the weather heats up, the seeds form fast. But you can prolong the flower show by watering the plants regularly and keeping them deadheaded.

Seed savers can either collect the seeds when they ripen on the plants or allow some of the blossoms to dry and drop their seeds naturally. Mignonettes self-sow freely, so you should have some volunteers.

If you find bees a nuisance, make sure to locate mignonettes, which lure these busy pollinators, away from your doors and decks. Otherwise, gardeners have traditionally planted mignonettes underneath their windowsills or beside their porches, where their fragrance can easily be enjoyed.

Since mignonettes have rather insignificant flowers, try growing them alongside bolder-colored blossoms that can echo their scarlet, peach, or chartreuse accents. Planting mignonettes in masses will also help them stand out in the landscape. If you do use them in large beds, you'll be prepared if you ever decide to test an old legend about these plants. It promised that any lover who rolled in mignonettes three times would meet with success in his or her endeavors.

Not all gardeners agree that mignonettes perform best in rich soil. Some heirloom growers insist that the plants actually put out a stronger, more intense perfume in gardens where the ground is poor, sandy, or even rocky. As one gardener told *Vick's Monthly Magazine* in 1886, "The reason that some Mignonette has scarcely any scent is, because the soil in which it is cultivated is too rich." Of course, many modern types simply don't have much scent because it has been lost during the years of breeding for other traits.

MORNING GLORY—*Ipomoea*

If just one plant could get the credit for reviving our interest in heirlooms, it would have to be the morning glory. Diane Whealy certainly recognized the value of old-timey plants when her grandfather, Baptist John Ott, gave her seeds of the royal purple flowers that had grown for years around his family home in Bavaria. Grandpa Ott's lovely morning glories are still the only type with that rich, deep purple color growing in the United States.

In other parts of the world, morning glories have been trailing and twining across the landscape for centuries. Seeds of *I. purpurea* from Italy and *I. tricolor* from Spain were known to the British in 1621. These early arrivals got a cool reception from early gardeners, though, probably because people were tired of clearing the choking vines of bindweed, the plants' close relative, from their vegetable patches. Unfortunately, the plants' blooms did not last long, either. Their glorious flowers remained open for only a few hours after

Grandpa Ott's morning glory helped launch the seed-saving movement. (Courtesy of Renee's Garden)

dawn and snapped shut whenever the sun disappeared behind the clouds. Morning glories didn't really catch on in Europe until the Victorians came along with their enthusiasm for new and exotic plants.

Back in America, morning glories made landfall around 1783. Once they arrived, the plants took root in many hearts about the same time that privies, those newfangled conveniences for rural homes, began popping up in backyards. Suddenly morning glories were both useful and popular. Their lush foliage, combined with the leaves of stately hollyhocks, made a great camouflage for the family outhouse.

Growers set to work improving morning glories in the 1940s and 1950s, but their breeding efforts slowed dramatically when word began to circulate that the plants' seeds caused hallucinations. People who consumed them for a cheap high were taking a terrible risk, as the seeds are toxic enough to cause death. But there is no reason that today's responsible gardeners can't enjoy these frost-tender plants for their irrepressible beauty, and modern seed savers are working to reintroduce some of the old types.

Morning glories have often been used in magic and religious practices. Monks drew them on the pages of manuscripts, letting the graceful vines illustrate their carefully copied text. Some witches were believed to use the flowers to cast spells. The plants were said to be especially powerful three days before the moon grew full.

Morning glories, with their twisting tendrils and vines, take their scientific name from the Greek words *ips* and *homoios*, meaning "wormlike."

GRANDPA OTT'S—*I. PURPUREA*

Each velvety, deep purple blossom of this old variety carries a rosy star in its pink throat. Train the tangled vines, which can grow 15 feet long, over trellises and arbors, or let them ramble across a fence. This one can handle the humidity in the Deep South.

SCARLETT O'HARA—*I. NIL*

An All-American Selections winner from 1939, Scarlett unfurls crimson or wine red blooms with pure white throats. Vines loaded with its trumpet-shaped flowers can reach 30 feet in areas where the growing season is long and warm.

CARDINAL CLIMBER—*IPOMOEA X MULTIFIDA*

Hummingbirds flocked to 1880s gardens filled with these cardinal red blooms. Also known as Hearts and Honey Vine, this climber can grow to 20 feet.

CYPRESS VINE—*I. QUAMOCLIT*

Don't confuse this one with Cardinal Climber. Although both have scarlet flowers, *I.* x *multifida* bears palm-shaped leaves, while cypress foliage looks ferny. Jefferson sent its seeds to Monticello in 1790, where his daughter Martha planted them "in boxes in the window." The vines are still grown there for visitors to enjoy. Victorian seed sellers described the blossoms, which stay open all day, as a "constellation of stars."

Each Grandpa Ott's flower has a starry throat. (Courtesy of Renee's Garden)

MOONFLOWER—*I. ALBA*

Victorian ladies filled their night-blooming gardens with these large, jasmine-scented flowers. The blossoms unfurl like white parasols at dusk or on overcast days. Plant them near porches or patios to enjoy their perfume. Originally listed in an 1884 catalog, the vines can stretch to 30 feet.

I. tricolor

FLYING SAUCERS

These 5-inch flowers, introduced by California seedsman Darold Decker in 1960, look like pinwheels with white and lilac or pale blue stripes. In 1962,

Scarlett O'Hara's crimson trumpets lure thirsty hummingbirds. (Courtesy of Renee's Garden)

Decker also debuted Wedding Bells, a rosy lavender morning glory with a yellow and cream throat.

PEARLY GATES

Gleaming white blossoms and Valentine heart leaves distinguish this All-American Selections winner from 1942.

HEAVENLY BLUE

These sky-colored flowers have white throats splashed with yellow. Originally known as Clarke's Early Heavenly Blue, after the gardener who discovered the plants in Colorado, the variety dates to 1931. Clarke, who realized he'd found a mutation with big, early blossoms, allowed Dutch wholesalers to

....

....

....

....

....

....

....

....

....

....

....

....

....

....

....

....

....

....

....

....

....

....

....

....

....

....

....

....

....

increase the seeds and put them into retailers' hands. Soon the rich blue blossoms were wildly popular. Somewhere along the way, Clarke's name has been dropped, but all the Heavenly Blue *Ipomoeas* on today's market come from his find.

Growing Tips

Morning glories are undemanding, frost-tender flowers that almost everyone can grow. In most of the country, they're treated as annuals and bloom heavily until frost. In areas that enjoy mild winters, they may behave like tender perennials.

Soak your morning glory seeds overnight, or nick them with a sharp knife to loosen their hard coats. Then let all chance of frost pass before you sow them outdoors. If there's any trick to growing these tropical natives, it's waiting to sow until the weather stays reliably warm. They will rot in cold, damp soil.

Alternately, you can start the seeds indoors 4 to 6 weeks before the last expected frost. It's not necessary, though, since the flowers won't bloom before midsummer. If you do start them inside, put the seeds into individual peat pots. Morning glories grow fast and generally dislike being transplanted.

Give these plants full sun and well-drained soil. True morning glories open at dawn and close around midday, unless it's cloudy. Avoid giving them rich soil, which produces lots of leaves but few flowers. The vines can be trained to climb strings, wires, and trellises. Try them in a hanging basket, also. They're lovely when you wind some of the vines through other upright flowers and allow the rest to swing gracefully over the basket's edge.

Morning glories will cross-pollinate, so you'll need to isolate them, or plant only one variety at a time, if you want to save seeds that grow true.

Be careful when using morning glories around children or pets. They self-sow prolifically, and the seeds are poisonous.

When Morning Glories Run Amok

More than one gardener has admired morning glories in their first growing season only to curse them ever after. "They're worse than weeds," is a common complaint. The problem is that the plants produce many seeds that grow practically anywhere they fall. Morning glories, it seems, are almost unstoppable.

Author Harriet Keeler turned her nose up at the morning glory in 1910, dis-

Pastel morning glories offered by D. M. Ferry & Company in 1923.

Grandpa Ott's and Scarlett O'Hara morning glory seeds. (Courtesy of Renee's Garden)

missing it as "somewhat of a rascal when given too free a hand in the garden. . . . It must be kept within bounds or kept not at all. . . . It will never be a favorite with the American people, and the morning-glory vine, despite all its virtues, will probably remain . . . a utility plant loved by a few, outlawed by others, tolerated by the many."

Of course, not everybody agrees with that stinging assessment. So what's the solution, if you love morning glories but don't want them to invade your yard? You can mulch them with thick layers of organic material so that any fallen seeds that sprout are easy to pull up. Or you can surround them with black plastic or layers of newspapers to discourage self-sowing altogether. Cultivating lightly with a hoe or tiller also works, if you leave sufficient room between the plants. Herbicides will kill emerging seedlings, but use chemicals responsibly, as they can harm other plants and wildlife.

NASTURTIUM—*Tropaeolum*

Glow-in-the-dark flowers? Incredible as it sounds, stories circulate that the Victorians once cultivated nasturtiums that flickered with light. That's according to Herman Bourne's 1833 *Florist's Manual*, one of the first horticultural works written for the average American gardener. Bourne described these pretty, edible flowers as "phosphorescent," or able to "[emit] light in the dark."

There's more evidence for the claim that nasturtiums once lit up the night: both the Swedish taxonomist Carl Linnaeus and his daughter apparently observed the phenomenon. George Nicholson's dictionary of gardening, published ca. 1887, also mentions the plants' ability to flash and emit electrical sparks under certain atmospheric conditions. Another early botanical writer noted, "The whole leaf seemed to twinkle with points of light."

Sadly, nasturtiums no longer sparkle, if, in fact, they ever really did. But years of selective breeding for characteristics like bloom size or color have altered many heirloom flowers, so it's possible that nasturtiums lost their twinkle.

At least modern gardeners can enjoy these cheerful plants for their attractive leaves, which look like miniature lily pads, and their bright mix of golden yellow, scarlet, and orange blossoms. New varieties have added cherry pink,

Golden Gleam.
(Courtesy of Select Seeds)

salmon, white, and mahogany to the palette, although a true purple, once listed in an 1889 seed catalog, is no longer available.

The nasturtium owes its Latin name to Pliny, who combined *narsus*, for "nose," with *tortus*, for "twisted." One whiff of their pungent smell and the reason is clear. Most of these flowers are not grown for their perfume.

The plants' other scientific name, *Tropaeolum*, comes from *tropaeum*, meaning trophy, and may refer to the shieldlike shape of the foliage. Spanish conquistadors who stumbled across the flowers in the Peruvian jungles some 300 years ago probably saw the dwarf or bush species, *T. minus*. A Dutch botanist introduced *T. majus*, a trailing nasturtium with larger blossoms, later in the seventeenth century.

After nasturtiums arrived in Spain with the returning conquistadors, they caught the eye of Nicholas Monardes, a local gardener and physician. Smitten by their charms, Monardes prevailed on sailors, traders, and traveling priests to bring him seeds from any other nasturtiums they could find. The doctor experimented with the plants and published his results between 1565 and 1571, helping spread the flowers into Portugal, France, and England.

By the 1700s, nasturtiums had made their way into colonial gardens. Jefferson is believed to have cultivated the trailing orange form around 1774.

Aside from their ornamental value, nasturtiums have a long culinary history. In the seventeenth and eighteenth centuries, they were commonly eaten as vegetables. European chefs chopped up the leaves and tossed the colorful blossoms with as many as 40 other "exotics," including rose petals, violets, and marigolds, and served them as salads to the royals.

Other early cooks pickled the pods as condiments and used the seeds in place of capers. Since fresh foods quickly spoiled on sea voyages, sailors once stowed barrels of pickled nasturtium seeds on their ships, hoping to ward off scurvy. Nasturtiums are indeed are rich in vitamin C, but you would have to eat a lot of them for any significant nutritional value.

During World War II, enterprising cooks coping with food shortages filled their pepper shakers with nasturtium seeds. (You can still make pepper by grinding the dried seeds and storing them in tightly capped bottles. Sprinkle in a little salt if desired.)

Nasturtium blossoms make a colorful garnish for cakes and baked goods, while the leaves form a tasty wrapping for scoops of softened cheese or other appetizer fillings. Tossed fresh into salads, nasturtiums lend a hot "bite" to the greens, thanks to the mustard oils in their leaves. That is probably why early English herbalists who sampled their strong flavor nicknamed them "Indian cress."

To keep nasturtiums from overpowering your salads, try combining them with a sweet, buttery lettuce, like Bibb. Although the plants are edible, don't use them if they have ever been treated with chemicals or pesticides. Avoid eating large quantities of the pickled flower buds, too, as they may contain potentially harmful amounts of oxalic acid.

EMPRESS OF INDIA

Burpee's offered this dwarf variety in 1884, praising it as "the most important annual in recent introduction." The Empress earns a crown for her bright vermilion flowers, which are carried over dark blue-green foliage. The long-spurred flowers attract hummingbirds.

Empress of India.
(Courtesy of Renee's Garden)

MOONLIGHT

These big, creamy yellow nasturtiums look delightfully pale on moonlit nights and may be as close as we can come to the legendary phosphorescent beauties. The seed was originally offered by Peter Henderson & Company of New York in 1910.

VESUVIUS

Dark blue-green leaves distinguish this dwarf nasturtium, which has been cultivated for over 80 years. While seed catalogs typically describe the flowers as salmon, many gardeners insist that they're orange, like lava from the volcano of the same name.

GOLDEN GLEAM

A semitrailer, this variety drapes nicely over sides of baskets and window boxes. The buttery gold flowers are semidouble and have a pleasant fragrance. It's said that one Golden Gleam seed sold for a hefty five cents during the Depression years.

SCARLET GLEAM

An All-American Selections winner from 1935, this nasturtium spreads moderately and produces lots of vibrant, orange-red flowers. The seeds for this series were reportedly discovered in 1928, in the garden of a Mexican convent.

Growing Tips

Nasturtiums are available in many forms, from dwarf, bushy plants that grow only 1 foot tall to semidwarf types that reach about 20 inches. Vining nasturtiums can climb over 6 feet.

You can try starting nasturtium seeds indoors for earlier blooms, but be forewarned: their long taproot makes them difficult to transplant. For best results, sow the seeds directly outdoors after all danger of frost has passed. Plant the seeds ½ inch deep and watch for sprouts to appear in about 9 to 12 days.

When the seedlings are about 4 inches tall, they can be thinned to every 12 inches. Keep their soil moist, but not soggy. The flower show generally begins in 10 to 12 weeks after planting.

Old-fashioned nasturtiums lend a spicy bite to salads. (Courtesy of Renee's Garden)

Your nasturtiums will be happy in poor but well-drained soil, as long as you give them plenty of sun. Soil that is too rich in nitrogen causes them to produce lots of foliage but very few flowers. You may have heard the old saying, "Be nasty to nasturtiums." That's a bit harsh; the seedlings do need regular watering until they're established. But after that, you can relax. Nasturtiums are undemanding and can survive without much attention.

Remember that nasturtiums prefer cool weather, so do not despair when flowering slows and the plants look rangy during the hottest part of the summer. A new flush of blossoms will usually appear as temperatures drop late in the season. Gardeners whose winter temperature stays above freezing can sow more seeds in September and October. Fall-planted nasturtiums should bloom early the following spring.

Rabbits don't seem to care for the taste of nasturtiums, but black aphids can be a real problem. Try insecticidal soap to control them, or simply plant some "sacrificial nasturtiums," as old-fashioned gardeners do, and allow the bugs to eat a few of your plants while you treat the rest as needed.

Nasturtiums are grown as annuals almost everywhere except the frost-free regions of the country. They'll self-sow freely when the seeds fall on un-mulched ground, but they are not aggressive and will not take over your yard.

If you're looking for a garden project for children, try nasturtiums. The wrinkled, pealike seeds are easy for small fingers to handle, and once established, the plants don't require much care.

NICOTIANA—*Nicotiana*, also known as Flowering Tobacco

"The perfume of the White Tobacco is very delicious at night and the tubular blossoms have a shimmering quality which makes them very charming in the moonlit garden."

Louise Beebe Wilder,
My Garden *(1920)*

French ambassador to Portugal Jean Nicot probably never imagined the controversy he would stir up when he came home with specimens of tobacco, a plant he had found growing in Lisbon. Tobacco, a Portuguese gardener assured him, had powerful healing properties, so in 1560, Nicot sent snuff made from the plants to his queen, Catherine de Medici, to ease her migraine headaches. It worked so well that Catherine dubbed tobacco *Herba Regina*, the "queen's herb." Two centuries later, Linnaeus honored Nicot for his find by naming the plants *Nicotiana tabacum*.

At first, everyone seemed to welcome the new plants. Monardes, the Spanish botanist and physician who worked extensively with nasturtiums, praised *N. tabacum* in his 1557 *Joyful Newes Oute of the Newe Founde Worlde*. It was, he declared, a treatment for intestinal worms, toothache, and other maladies. But by 1597, Gerard was becoming suspicious and warned that smoking "bringeth drowsiness, troubleth the sences, and maketh a man as it were drunke by taking the fume only."

Gerard was right in urging caution, of course. Eventually researchers would determine that pure nicotine is a deadly poison. By the 1880s, it was ranked as one of our three most potent insecticides, and gardeners have traditionally brewed a homemade nicotine tea to spray on their plants for pest control.

Tobacco had actually been used as a recreational drug and medicinal agent long before Nicot introduced the plants to the French court. Columbus, arriving in the West Indies in 1492, recorded that the natives met him carrying

Tobacco Jasmine.
(Courtesy of Select Seeds)

"fruit, wooden spears, and certain dried leaves which gave off a distinct fragrance." Native Americans were also known to "drink" smoke from the plants' burning leaves to stimulate their senses.

But smoking tobacco ignited controversy not long after it arrived in England. James, who despised the plants, slapped a 4,000 percent increase on tobacco import taxes. Then—in case anyone still doubted his opinion of the stuff—he pronounced smoking "a custom loathsome to the eye, hateful to the nose, harmful to the brain, dangerous to the lungs, and in the black stinking fume there of nearest resembling the horrible Stygian smoke of the pit that is bottomless."

Happily, the tobaccos in our ornamental gardens are not the ones so reviled by James. *N. alata*, or flowering tobacco, is an attractive species that has been known in America since the late 1800s. Another early ornamental was *N. longiflora*, sometimes called long-flowered tobacco or star petunia. Breck offered this Chilean native, which has a faint, sweet fragrance, in an early catalog. In England, delicate Victorian ladies chose the flowers for their moon gardens so they could enjoy the nocturnal blooms.

By 1916, breeders were crossing *N. alata* with other species to develop shorter, more compact forms. They succeeded in creating flowers that opened during the daytime, too, along with a broader color palette. Today the blossoms are available in white, red, scarlet, lime green, rose, and mauve. Unfortunately, many modern varieties have lost their old, rich perfumes.

N. alata, *also known as Winged Tobacco, Persian Tobacco, and Night-Scented Tobacco*

Although it's sometimes sold as a tender perennial, this species, introduced to England from Brazil in 1829, is easier to grow if it is treated like an annual in cold climates. The plants branch heavily, reaching up to 4 feet tall, and bear long, trumpet-shaped flowers. The creamy white blooms, which are held in sprays, open at night and close by noon the following day. When the temperature rises, watch for the flowers to drop their heads as if they are drowsy.

LIME GREEN

With its fuzzy, blue-green leaves and chartreuse blossoms, this nicotiana is a real eye-catcher. The plants grow to 4 feet in sun or shade, bearing 1-inch flowers for up to 3 months. Cut stems last a long time in vases. This one isn't

Jasmine Alata.
(Courtesy of Renee's Garden)

especially fragrant, although it draws attention for its unusual flower color, which has been described as acid green or lime sherbet. A Royal Horticultural Society Award of Merit winner, it dates back to least 1930.

CRIMSON KING

A white version of this velvet red beauty debuted in the 1930s. King Crimson grows to 15 inches and produces lipstick red blossoms. Give the plants full sun to partial shade.

SENSATION

These hybrids of *N. alata* and other species became available in the 1940s and 1950s. The starry flowers, available in a mix of colors including lavender, purple, rose, white, crimson, yellow, and cream, are hummingbird magnets. Gardeners like the plants, which grow 2 to 4 feet tall, because they don't sprawl as much as other earlier forms.

N. sylvestris, *also known as Woodland Tobacco and White Shooting Stars*

These statuesque plants with large, sticky leaves have been known to grow 5 or more feet in height, so give them room at the back of your border. The tubular flowers are long and skinny, flaring into little stars at the tips. The sweetly scented, pale green blossoms mature to snowy white. Discovered in Argentina around 1898, this tender perennial was once popular in moon gardens.

Growing Tips

Flowering tobaccos are content with average amounts of water and good soil. While the plants like full sun, they will tolerate shade.

Start your nicotiana seeds indoors about 8 weeks before the last expected frost, or wait until all frost danger has passed to sow them outside.

Mix the seeds, which are very fine, with sand for easier handling, and scatter or dust them over prepared soil or a good quality growing medium. Water them gently so they don't float away. If you're planting indoors, water your seed pots or trays from the bottom, letting the water wick up into the growing material. Don't cover the seeds, as they need light to germinate. You should see sprouts in 5 to 20 days.

notes

Renee's Garden

Scented Nicotiana
Jasmine Alata

"Flower treasures for the eye & heart"
—Renee Shepherd

This heavily perfumed nicotiana is native to South America. (Courtesy of Renee's Garden)

Transplant your seedlings when they are still quite small, preferably within a week after they've germinated, to avoid breaking the developing taproots. Space the young plants a foot apart in the garden.

Water regularly during dry spells, but don't let your plants stand in water. Deadheading will keep the flower show going.

Nicotiana self-seeds nicely, with the pods ripening gradually from the bottom of the stalks until they burst and spill the contents over the ground. If you collect the seeds, use tweezers to separate out the dried pods. Then label the seeds and store them in a cool, dark place. Remember that seeds from hybrid cultivars will not grow true to type.

Hummingbirds love these funnel-shaped flowers. Try growing them in masses near your door or around a garden bench, porch, or deck, so you can enjoy their fragrance. But be aware that the plants can look lethargic when the day warms up and the flowers droop and nod. The plants' leaves are also covered in sticky hairs that tend to catch dust, so nicotiana can start to look a little, well, dingy and frumpy. If that's the case in your garden, grow the plants in tubs or containers that can be rolled out of sight when they look shabby, or hide them at the back of the border, using shorter plants to conceal their foliage.

If you're tempted to make homemade nicotine spray, be forewarned. Even when diluted, nicotine is highly toxic and must be kept away from children and pets. Do not use it on edible plants, either, as it's absorbed by their leaves and lasts for a long time. Also avoid using nicotine spray on petunias or other members of the nightshade family, as it can spread the tobacco mosaic virus.

Jasmine Alata nicotiana seeds.
(Courtesy of Renee's Garden)

NIGELLA—*Nigella*, also known as Love-in-a-Mist, Lady-in-the-Bower, Devil-in-a-Bush, St. Katharine's Flower, Jack-in-Prison, Love-Entangle, and Love-in-a-Puzzle

Native to Damascus, northern Africa, and southern Europe, *Nigella damascena* is one of the most delicate flowers in the heirloom garden. The plants take their common name, Love-in-a-Mist, from their thin foliage, which surrounds the blossoms like a delicate net. When viewed from a distance, you can image the pink, blue, violet, and white blossoms floating in a "mist" of slender stems and leaves.

Nigellas are hardy annuals that lend an airy grace to the summer garden, where they bloom happily, if not for very long, even in poor soil. When they are green and immature, their seed capsules resemble little balloons, and many people dry them on their stems for everlasting arrangements.

Inside the capsules, the seeds look similar to onion seeds. You can eat the crunchy seeds or sprinkle them over foods as a seasoning. Some people say the seeds of *N. sativa* are the tastiest, variously describing the flavor as slightly bitter, peppery, or even resembling cumin.

Each nigella capsule is composed of several chambers that contain the matte black seeds. The botanical name for these plants, *Nigella*, comes from the Latin *niger*, referring to the dark seed color. Sixteenth-century girls who

"[Nigella] must be direct sown by seed. Transplanted plants never do well. I find this is also true of nasturtiums."
Wesley Greene,
Garden Historian,
Colonial Williamsburg
Foundation

bemoaned their freckled faces and arms sometimes crushed the seeds and slathered on the oil to lighten their skin.

To the Victorians, preoccupied with romance and love, giving someone a bouquet of nigella blossoms meant, "You puzzle me."

As members of the *Ranunculaceae* family, nigellas are related to buttercups. The double form of these flowers has been cultivated in England since at least 1597. The so-called Spanish fennel flower, *N. hispanica*, which hails from Spain and southern France, has been grown in England since about 1620.

MISS JEKYLL BLUE

Garden designer Gertrude Jekyll is said to have inspired the name for this variety. The 18-inch plants bear cornflower blue petals with finely cut edges. Ruffs of airy, emerald green leaves surround the blossoms. After the semi-double flowers fade, watch for puffy pods holding burgundy-striped seeds to form. This species dates back to at least 1810.

Miss Jekyll Blue. (Courtesy of David Cavagnaro)

Miss Jekyll Alba. (Courtesy of David Cavagnaro)

MISS JEKYLL ALBA

This pure white nigella is best used in masses so its pale color and feathery foliage don't get lost in the landscape. It's also nice to use in an all-white-and-green garden. Viewed after dark, the star-shaped flowers are almost luminescent in the moonlight. The double blossoms are made up of overlapping petals with serrated edges. At maturity, the plants reach 12 to 18 inches tall.

CAMBRIDGE BLUE

Dating to the late sixteenth century, this old charmer bears doubled, sapphire blue blooms that set dark seed pods. The foliage is soft and feathery, like fennel. Unfortunately, this attractive variety is rare and hard to find, and you're more likely to procure the seeds from other heirloom seed savers than from commercial sources. At one time, this antique nigella was grown at the Royal Botanic Gardens at Kew.

MISS JEKYLL ROSE

Rose-colored blooms appear above rings of lacy leaves on this variety, which grows 12 to 18 inches high. Sow the beige seeds, which are marked with deep rose stripes, in late fall or early spring.

TRANSFORMER—*N. ORIENTALIS*

If you're looking for a striking novelty plant, you'll want this unusual species, which is native to Asia Minor. Its blooms are composed of a single row of yellow or yellowish-green petals with tall, bright green stamens that shoot upward. After the flowers fade, you'll get seed pods that look like tiny, silvery umbrellas flipped inside out by the wind. They make striking dried arrangements. The 20- to 24-inch tall plants self-sow freely.

MIDNIGHT—*N. PAPILLOSA*

Commonly called the "fennel flower," this nigella species produces dark purple or violet-blue blooms followed by dark purple seed pods. The flowers lack the delicate netting of foliage found in most nigellas, so they don't appear to be enveloped by a green "mist." Still, the long stems, produced on plants that grow to 3 feet tall, are nice for cutting. Give this one 12 weeks after sowing to flower.

Growing Tips

Nigella plants are hard to find at garden centers, probably because they have a long taproot and don't transplant well. Fortunately, the seeds are easy to grow, content with average to poor garden soil, and tolerate both dry and wet conditions. They do require from 90 to 100 days to flower, however, so count backward from the first expected frost in your area and start your seeds very early in the spring. Nigella seeds can also be sown in the fall in most of the country. As long as you give them a slightly sheltered location, they should survive the winter, and you can expect flowers by the following spring or summer.

For best results, till or dig your garden soil deeply before planting, and rake until the dirt is fine and loose. Sow the small seeds in rows or beds, covering them ⅛ inch deep and spacing them 1 inch apart. These plants prefer full sun, and while they will tolerate light shade if that's all you can provide, you won't get as many flowers.

Water the seeds gently to settle them in, and be patient. They may take from 10 to 21 days or more to germinate. After the seedlings emerge and reach about 4 inches tall, thin them to every 9 to 12 inches.

This specialty seed mix includes *Nigella damascena* and other rare species. (Courtesy of Renee's Garden)

If your plants start to look floppy, usually when they're about 12 inches tall, go ahead and stake them. Once nigella is established, it's seldom troubled by pests or diseases. Hot weather may slow down or stop the flower production, but you can still enjoy the lacy green foliage, which makes a nice filler for gaps in your beds or borders.

For a longer harvest, make successive plantings of nigella seeds every 2 to 3 weeks. The plants appreciate deadheading, but don't forget to let some blossoms mature on their stems if you want to collect the seedpods for dried arrangements.

To save seeds for next year, allow some of the blossoms to dry in the garden, or pull the plants up by their roots when they start to turn brown. Tie the stems together and cover the flower heads with paper bags. Tie the bags with string and hang them upside down in a cool, dark location until the seed pods open and release their seeds. Finally, remove any chaff from the seeds and label them for storage.

Nigellas, with their bushy foliage and odd, spiky seed pods, add architectural interest to the garden. Try the white and blue varieties alongside scarlet red poppies for colorful contrast, or grow rose pink nigellas near the silvery foliage of Lamb's Ear, Dusty Miller, and Artemisia. For a unique favor at weddings, some brides give their guests small boxes or envelopes of Love-in-a-Mist seeds to toss instead of traditional rice.

David Bradshaw, professor of horticulture at Clemson University, grows heirloom nigella in pink, blue, white, and a dark rose pink to burgundy shade. "It's so light and delicate. I love it." He's allowed his plants to simply drop their seeds and naturalize for years, for a wildflower meadow effect. But as the flowers cross-pollinated, Bradshaw admits that the resulting colors became muddy. "Even the whites went dusty-grey. But you can grow nigella for a year or two and then start over from new seed. The seedlings are easy to pull out. I like the way the plants give a light airiness to the garden, like lace held together with spider webs."

Collector's Blend nigella seeds. (Courtesy of Renee's Garden)

ONION—*Allium*

The Bible tells the story of the how the Israelites complained bitterly about not having onions, among other favorite foods, to eat as Moses led them through the desert on their 40-year trek to the Promised Land. Who can blame them? It's hard to imagine life without the bite and spice of papery-shelled bulb onions, *Allium cepa*, or bunching types, *A. fistulosum*.

While onions are thought to have originated in central Asia—it's hard to pin them down, since their watery tissues quickly decompose and leave few archaeological traces—the vegetables certainly were popular in Egypt. As symbols of eternity, these root crops were entombed with the pharaohs, placed inside body cavities and eye sockets or attached to the deceased's legs and feet. Perhaps mourners believed that their sharp scent would cause the dead to gasp for breath again, or simply that onions, with their concentric layers, were a sign that life, too, would continue in an endless circle.

Onions have been dated as far back as 3500 B.C., and wild onions were probably one of the earliest cultivated crops. By the first century, the Greek physician Dioscorides was employing them for medicinal purposes. Early Greek athletes also valued them, eating pound after pound of the bulbs and drinking their juice to "lighten the blood" before competing in Olympic Games.

After the Greek conquest, Roman gladiators took up their practice of rubbing cut onions over their bodies, believing they enhanced muscle tone. Convinced that the crops were good for anything that ailed you—Pliny the Elder said onions could cure bad eyesight, heal dog bites, and relieve toothaches—the Romans made them a regular part of their diet and carried them along on forays into Germany and England.

By the Middle Ages, Europeans were primarily eating three main vegetables: beans, cabbages, and onions. Thin-skinned onions were even used at one time to pay for lodging and were given as presents to newly married couples.

Onions sailed into the New World on the Mayflower, but they were not new to the Native Americans, who had already been eating wild strains. Onions have held a place on our tables ever since, with the average American now consuming a surprising 18 pounds of onions each year.

AMERICAN GROWN
PRIZETAKER ONION.

COPYRIGHTED 1891 BY W. ATLEE BURPEE & CO.

THE PRIZE=TAKER ONION.

No further description of this fine onion is needed than to state that it is identically the same variety as the large, beautiful, straw-colored onions imported from Spain and offered for sale at the fruit stands in all our large cities every fall. Although of Spanish origin, this variety must not be confounded with the yellow onion named *Spanish King*, which is inferior in size and quality to the **American-grown PRIZE-TAKER.** The Prize-Taker Onion grows uniform in shape, of a nearly perfect globe, as shown in the illustration, with thin skin of a clean, bright straw color; it is of immense size, measuring from twelve to sixteen inches in circumference, while under special cultivation specimen bulbs have been raised to weigh from four to six pounds each. It ripens up hard and fine, and presents the handsomest possible appearance in market, while the pure white flesh is fine-grained, mild, and delicate in flavor.

Per pkt. 10 cts.; 3 pkts. 25 cts.; per oz. 30 cts.; 2 ozs. 50 cts.; per ¼ ℔ 85 cts.; per ℔ $3.00. By express, not prepaid, per ℔ $2.50; 5 lbs. or more at $2.25 per ℔.

Burpee's offered this straw-colored beauty in the late 1800s.

CIPPOLINI

These button-shaped beauties may look like baby onions, but they are really the bulbs of a flowering plant from the Italian Mediterranean. They're small, with rosy brown skins and a mild, sweet flesh. Gourmet cooks roast, grill, sauté, pickle, or shish-kebab them, but they're also delicious when eaten fresh and drizzled with olive oil. This one is a good choice for cool climates.

Cippolini. (Courtesy of Renee's Garden)

DANVERS YELLOW GLOBE

Danvers, Massachusetts, probably lent its name to this American variety, which predates 1850. The globes are slightly flattened, with golden brown skins and fine-grained white flesh. It's not recommended for fall sowing; but as a long-day onion, it has been bred especially for northern gardens.

AILSA CRAIG

With its mild flavor and hefty size—the globes can weigh up to 2 pounds—this one could be an exhibition variety. From Britain, Ailsa Craig was introduced in 1887 and named for the island of Ailsa, off the west coast of Scotland.

Gourmet cooks fancy these heirloom button onions. (Courtesy of Renee's Garden)

The onions have straw-colored skins and keep well in storage. They need about 120 days to mature.

SOUTHPORT RED GLOBE

This large, heavy yielder from 1873 has a pungent flavor. The glossy, purple-red skins cover a pink-tinged flesh. It's a good storage onion, and like Ailsa Craig, it will perform well in northern regions if planted in early spring. It needs 110 days from sowing.

Growing Tips

Some gardeners will only grow onions from seeds because they insist they have a sharper bite than onions grown from sets. That's just as well for heirlooms, because seeds for most old-fashioned types are easier to find than sets or plants.

notes

....
....
....
....
....
....
....
....
....
....
....
....
....
....
....
....
....
....
....
....
....
....
....
....
....
....

All onions crave cool weather and well-drained soil. Choose your varieties carefully, because day length triggers the formation of their bulbs. Short-day types "bulb up," or form bulbs, when the summer days are 10 to 12 hours long. Long-day types form bulbs when the days are 15 to 16 hours long. This means northern gardeners will be most successful with long-day onions, while southerners should grow the short-day kind. If you're buying onion seeds, check your package for details. If you get your seeds from a fellow gardener, he or she can tell you if they'll thrive in your area.

Start your onion seeds outdoors in well-tilled soil 4 to 6 weeks before the last spring frost. You can also start them indoors in late winter. Sow the seeds 3 inches apart in rows spaced 12 to 16 inches apart and cover them with a scant ¼ inch of soil.

If you're sowing outdoors, plant in wide rows, or simply scatter the seeds between other vegetables. When the seedlings emerge, thin them to every 3 inches.

Once the onions are established, cultivate around their shallow roots carefully. The bulbs suffer if weeds and grasses get the upper hand, so hoe around them often and lightly.

Onions appreciate good moisture and side dressing with fertilizer while they're actively growing. Be aware that your soil will affect the taste of your bulbs. Some types may taste hot in your region, while a gardener across the country complains that the same variety is too mild or bland for his palate. You may need to experiment to find what you like.

It's time to harvest the bulbs when your onion tops fall over in late summer or when the plants send up flower stalks. You can hurry up the process by knocking over the tops. Then pull the bulbs and leave them to dry in a shaded spot with good air circulation. While they're still green, the tops can be braided or tied together with string. For long-term storage, keep the onions indoors in a dry, cool room with good ventilation. Try not to knock off the papery shells, which will protect the bulbs until you're ready to use them. With any luck, your onions may last into the winter, but check them often and discard any that begin to soften or show signs of rot.

Because onions are biennials, you'll have to let the plants grow for two years if you want to save seeds. If your winters are mild, simply allow the bulbs to remain outside in the garden. Elsewhere, pull the bulbs and replant them

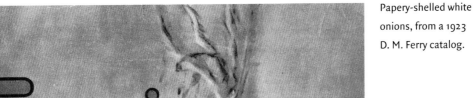

Papery-shelled white onions, from a 1923 D. M. Ferry catalog.

Cippolini Italian button onion seeds. (Courtesy of Renee's Garden)

the following spring. In their second year of growth, they'll produce seed stalks.

The seeds are ready to collect when the onion tops yellow. Simply rub the papery seedheads between your fingers and catch the black seeds in a bag or jar. Label them and store them in a dark, cool place until you're ready to plant again. Onions cross readily with each other, so you'll need to isolate them or grow only one variety at a time if you want seeds that grow true. Use the seeds soon; germination rates drop significantly after one year in storage.

While most horticulturists recommend rotating your crops, heirloom gardener and author William Woys Weaver argues for keeping a permanent onion bed in your garden. He cites the successful Wells Brothers of Wethersfield, Connecticut, who launched an onion business in 1788 and kept the plants growing in the same field for the next 80 years.

PEPPER—*Capsicum*

Gardeners have always been crazy for peppers. Traces of chilies have been found in Mexican ruins dating to 7000 B.C., and the Aztecs, who valued them highly, had at least seven words for these fiery fruits. We still can't get enough of them. Seed Savers Exchange of Decorah, Iowa, currently lists more than 800 kinds of peppers offered by its members, and entire websites, books, and magazines are devoted to their culture and use.

Maybe we love peppers because they are so versatile. There are blistering hot types for igniting stews and salsas, cayennes for grinding into colorful spice, mild- to medium-burn varieties for seasoning gumbos, and sweet bells for adding crunch to salads and slaws.

Food historians tell us that Columbus, while searching for a spice pepper, discovered what he called pimento peppers in the West Indies. He carried these fruits back to Spain, and they eventually spread throughout the world.

But it's much harder to trace other heirloom peppers, simply because the earliest gardeners did not record much information about the plants. Peppers are pretty lively, too, when it comes to cross-pollinating, so varieties have intermingled, muddling their names and characteristics. Still, modern botanists have managed to boil peppers down to five main groups.

Heirloom peppers yield a
red-hot harvest each fall.
(Courtesy of David Cavagnaro)

....

....

....

....

....

....

....

....

....

....

....

....

....

....

....

....

....

....

....

....

....

....

....

....

....

....

....

....

....

....

C. baccatum: These old Inca favorites come in various shapes and probably originated in Peru or Bolivia. Try the small yellow varieties, which have a wonderful lemony aroma.

C. annuum: In their tropical and subtropical homelands, these plants are perennials, not annuals. This group includes most of our common sweet and hot peppers, along with jalapeños and sweet bells.

C. pubescens: At 8,000 years old, this Bolivian species is one of the oldest domesticated plants. Unfortunately, the hairy-leaved plants seldom bear fruit in the United States because most gardeners can't provide their long growing season—120 days or longer.

C. frutescens: Most of our hot sauces come from the pods of these compact bushes. These peppers are hard to distinguish from *C. chinense*, and some experts would combine both into this species.

C. chinense: A Dutch physician collecting plants for Emperor Francis I named this species in 1776, but no one is quite sure why he named it for China. His journal noted, "I have taken the plant's name from its homeland," but surely he knew, since he found the plants, that they were native to South America and the Caribbean.

C. annuum

FISH PEPPER

As you'd guess from its name, this medium-hot pepper is widely used to spice up fish and shellfish dishes, but it makes salsa simmer, too. The fruits mature from creamy white with green stripes to orange and brown to solid red. Traditionally used in African American recipes, the fish pepper has been traced to the Philadelphia and Baltimore areas prior to 1870.

CORNO DI TORO RED

Having stuffed peppers for dinner? These sweet peppers, which grow 6 to 10 inches long and stand two inches across at the shoulders, can hold plenty of delicious cheese and spices. From Italy, this heirloom needs 75 to 90 days to ripen. Use it for grilling or sautéing, or save the curved fruits, which look like a bull's horns, for eating fresh.

BEAVER DAM

Named for Beaver Dam, Wisconsin, these hot peppers originally hail from Hungary. The conical fruits are ready in about 80 days, when they ripen from lime green to red. Slice them into rings to add mild to medium-hot flavor to sandwiches or salads. They've been known in the United States since 1929.

JIMMY NARDELLO'S ITALIAN

The Nardello family carried these seeds into America in 1887, when they emigrated from their small village of Ruoti, in southern Italy. Son Jimmy Nardello grew them in the Connecticut area for many years and passed them on to Seed Savers Exchange prior to his death in 1983. The 10- to 12-inch-long, banana-shaped fruits are excellent for frying or drying. They are among the most productive and disease-resistant heirloom peppers, producing reliably in northern and southern gardens.

HABANERO—*C. CHINENSE*

Don't be misled by the size of the fruits—this Caribbean staple is the hottest of the hot. Small, lantern-shaped pods start out green and mature to orange-red. They have a pungent aroma and more fire than jalapeños. Try them in hot sauces for a smoky accent.

TABASCO—*C. FRUTESCENS* VAR. *TABASCO*

Fiery Tabasco sauce was first brewed by the McIlhenny family of New Iberia, Louisiana. These torpedo-shaped fruits are held nearly erect on the plants and transform from yellowish-green to yellow and then from orange to red. The color change is a signal that they're ready to harvest.

Growing Tips

Start your pepper seeds indoors about 8 to 10 weeks before the last spring frost. Sow them 4 inches apart in shallow trays and cover them with ¼ inch of soil. Depending on the variety, the seeds may take 2 to 4 weeks to germinate. If your trays are heatproof, you can nudge the seeds along by providing gentle heat from the bottom.

When the seedlings' first true leaves appear, move them into individual 3-inch pots; move them up again if they get too big before you can transplant

An assortment of fiery antique peppers. (Courtesy of David Cavagnaro)

them. Once the weather is reliably warm, harden off the seedlings and put them in their permanent garden location. But don't push your peppers out the door in the springtime. They dislike wet, cool conditions and won't thrive until the soil averages 65°F or higher.

Space the young plants every 12 to 18 inches in the garden, in rows 2 feet apart. If you prefer, you can grow most varieties in large containers instead.

Peppers are thirsty plants, so give them plenty of water, especially during dry spells. Like tomatoes and eggplants, they are prone to diseases that build up in the soil, so avoid growing them in the same spot 2 years in a row. A paper collar around the stem of each young plant is cheap insurance against hungry cutworms. Tall varieties may need staking so they don't topple over.

Pick the pepper pods while they are still green, if you wish, or leave them to ripen; their color at maturity depends on which variety you're growing. Flavor generally increases as the fruits age, with sweeter types becoming sweeter and hotter ones, hotter. The fruits' vitamin C content, which is twice as high in orange or red peppers as in green ones, will also rise over time.

Keep picking and your plants should bear until frost. To string your peppers, leave a bit of stem on each fruit and let them dry them in a cool, dark place. Check them periodically and discard any that show signs of spoilage.

If you want to save pepper seeds, remember that peppers self-pollinate and cross-pollinate easily. To keep the seeds pure, grow only one variety at a time.

Be sure to wear gloves when you collect the seeds. To dry the seeds, scrape them onto a cookie sheet or piece of fine screen and keep them out of direct sunlight for about 2 weeks. Provide good air circulation to prevent mold. When the seeds are completely dry, store them in an airtight container. For best results, use the seeds within 3 years.

Gum Drop and Tabasco pepper seeds.

Too Hot to Handle

Seed savers and cooks, beware. Peppers contain varying amounts of a chemical compound called capsaicin, which comes from glands between the pods' outer skin and the white, inner ribs.

Pepper seeds usually get the blame—or praise, depending on how hot you like things—for the heat we feel in our mouths or on our fingers. But it's actually the capsaicin that causes the burn. Protect yourself from your peppers! Wear gloves to handle them, and keep a glass of soothing milk at hand when you nibble the hottest varieties.

PETUNIA—*Petunia*

When it comes to heirloom plants, petunias are practically newcomers. These frilly, sweetly scented flowers have been cozying up to our porches and spilling over window boxes for only two or three centuries. That's not long, compared with the columbines so beloved in seventeenth-century gardens or the ancient Italian asters known to Virgil.

But no matter; gardeners were quick to embrace the first petunias. A white flower, *Petunia axillaris*, was discovered in South America in 1823 and immediately caught on despite its small, unimpressive flowers and rangy stems. So did *P. integrifolia*, which was at least more interesting with its deep magenta blossoms and faint vanilla scent. Soon after this colorful little plant arrived from Brazil, breeders turned their attention to improving petunias' blossom size and color.

By 1880, gardeners had beds of doubles, semidoubles, and grandiflora petunias to choose from. By the 1930s, the bouncy blossoms were available in every imaginable shade. Sadly, the richest, heaviest perfumes faded along the way, as developers concentrated on creating petunias with ruffles, fringes, stripes, bicolors, waves, billows, and really, really big blooms.

Petunias are members of the nightshade, or *Solanaceae*, family, which makes them relatives of flowering tobacco. They take their name from the Brazilian word *petun*, which refers to a type of tobacco that is not used for smoking.

OLD-FASHIONED VINING—*P. MULTIFLORA*

You simply have to grow this heirloom charmer to appreciate the fragrance of the earliest forms. A century ago, the plants were common in Iowa gardens. They are noticeably hardier than modern types, with trailing, 3-foot stems. The single flowers have a fragrance that is similar to that of lily of the valley, and they're usually sold commercially in a blend of white, lavender, pink, and purple shades.

BALCONY—*P. PENDULA*

Evening brings out the sweet scent of this antique variety, described in 1934 as "The most showy of all petunias. . . . Plants are larger than bedding type and . . . of a rich velvety texture in clear bright colors, borne in unusual profusion all summer." The vigorous, cascading vines are excellent for hanging baskets. Balcony comes in a mixture of lavender, mauve, violet, white, pink, red, and royal purple blooms.

WILD PETUNIA—*P. INTEGRIFOLIA*

This old, original petunia is a charmer. The funnel-shaped magenta or rosy purple blossoms open to dark throats. At only 8 to 12 inches tall, the plants make a nice edging for flower beds, or you can allow them to trail gracefully

Balcony. (Courtesy of David Cavagnaro)

out of window boxes and hanging baskets. Nicknamed the "violet flower petunia," this one may perform as a perennial in zones 8 through 10 and as an annual elsewhere.

P. integrifolia Alba, introduced from Argentina to Glasgow Botanic Gardens in 1831, bears white or pale lavender blooms. The trumpet-shaped flowers are produced heavily throughout the growing season.

GIANTS OF CALIFORNIA—*P. SUPERBISSIMA*

We're not used to pampering petunias anymore, since modern varieties are so prolific and carefree, seldom troubled by pests or diseases. But if you grow this strain, developed more than a century ago by a California grower, you will need to give it some extra attention. The big, rangy plants need frequent pruning and pinching back. Still, the beautifully ruffled blossoms are worth your trouble. Look for the flowers, which are accented with dark veins, in white, rose, pale pink, and lavender.

Growing Tips

Beginning gardeners, don't say you weren't warned. Petunias are cheerful, colorful plants that dress up beds and borders throughout the spring and summer. But their seeds are tricky even for the most experienced green thumbs to

Old-fashioned vining petunias reseed generously. (Courtesy of David Cavagnaro)

handle because they're fine and very small. How small? A 1-ounce package can hold approximately 250,000 seeds.

Petunias also take a long time to flower from seed, as much as 8 to 12 weeks. In other words, more than one devoted heirloom gardener has dumped seed packets for bedding plants, seduced by all the modern, brightly colored flowers lining the shelves at garden centers.

But if you feel adventuresome, go ahead and give the seeds a try. You'll need to start them indoors 10 to 12 weeks before the last spring frost.

Mix the seeds with a little sand to ensure even sowing. Then sprinkle them over trays filled with milled sphagnum moss or a good quality growing medium. The seeds need light to germinate, so be careful not to bury them. Instead, use your fingers to gently press them down. Alternately, you can squirt the seeds with a fine mist of water until they make good contact with the growing medium or moss. Cover the trays with clear plastic and keep them in a brightly lit spot until the seedlings emerge. Temperatures of 70° to 80°F are ideal, but don't put the trays in direct sunlight, which can burn the emerging seedlings.

When the seedlings sprout, discard the plastic covering and transfer them to a cooler room. They still need bright light but not as much warmth at this stage of growth. Aim to keep them around 65°F during the day and 55° to 65°F at night.

To encourage the young plants to stay short and stocky, place them 4 to 6 inches below a fluorescent light and set a timer to keep it on from 16 to 18 hours each day. You may need to raise the fixture as the plants shoot up.

When the petunias put out their first set of true leaves, harden them off gradually. They can be transplanted into the garden after all chance of frost has passed and the soil stays reliably warm, or at least 60°F. Space grandiflora and multiflora types 1 foot apart. Millifloras can squeeze in at 4 to 6 inches apart.

These tender flowers grow happily in full sun and rich, well-drained soil. They'll tolerate some shade, but at the expense of lush blooms. Avoid wet areas, as petunias can't stand soggy roots.

Pinch the plants back when they are 6 inches tall to urge them to form side shoots that will yield more blooms. Spreading types are the exception; they don't need pinching. To keep the flower show going until frost, deadhead the plants as the blossoms fade. Of course, if you're growing masses of petunias, deadheading isn't really practical, so you may want to simply shear back a whole bed at once.

Petunias can handle hot weather but need extra water during dry spells. That's especially true for those grown in hanging baskets that are exposed to drying winds.

In midsummer, or when the petunias start to look leggy and weak, cut their stems back to 4 to 6 inches long. They should recover nicely in a few weeks and give you another flush or two of flowers until frost.

From Wild Petunias to Millifloras

Modern breeders have created hundreds of new petunias for gardeners to choose from, all of which descend from the two wild species originally found in South America. Most fall into one of five categories, depending on their flower size and growth habit. Whether you start with seeds, cuttings, or plants, it's nice to know which is which.

Grandiflora: These are our most popular and common petunias, with single or double blooms that measure up to 4 inches across. Some form mounds of flowers, while others have a pendulous growth habit.

Multiflora: Smaller than grandifloras, these petunias stay covered in blooms throughout the season. They can withstand rain and heat better than their bigger relatives.

Milliflora: Goldsmith Seeds introduced this petunia class in 1996. As the name suggests, they are miniature plants loaded with petite, early flowers. They don't require cutting back.

Spreading: Also called groundcover petunias, these plants develop flowers all along their stems. At 4 to 6 inches high, they'll blanket the garden with carpets of color.

Floribunda: These plants are essentially improved multifloras, with slightly bigger single or doubled blossoms.

SALVIA—*Salvia*

Whether you're looking for a plant to spice up a dish or one to brighten your garden, you'll find a salvia to suit your needs. These members of the *Lamiaceae*, or mint, family include about 900 species that grow all over the world.

Cooks and heirloom gardeners are probably most familiar with *Salvia officinalis*, the common garden sage. This evergreen subshrub from the Mediterranean is usually grown as a culinary herb. John Gerard cultivated various salvias or sages in his garden at Holborn in 1597, and French and German

Flower spikes of clary sage.
(Courtesy of David Cavagnaro)

chefs have been stirring its aromatic leaves into their sauces and sprinkling them over meats for centuries. Whether used dried or fresh, the leaves of sage also make a delicious seasoning for poultry, butters, stuffings, beans, breads, and gravies.

Garden sage is a fine ornamental, too, with long wands of soft purple flowers that bees find irresistible. Unfortunately, the plants tend to turn woody and decline after a few years. If grown where the winters are cold, the plants may die back completely, and you'll need to replace them annually.

But garden sage has not always been confined to the table. In ancient times, it was used to treat many illnesses. *Salvia*, the genus name, derives from the Latin word *salvere*, meaning "to be saved." In medieval Italy, medical students learned how to use the leaves to address a variety of complaints, and the German theologian Luther was said to believe in their curative powers. Legend says he once asked, *Cur moriatur homo cui Salvia crescit in horto?* or "Why should a man die whilst sage grows in his garden?"

While attractive, garden sage hardly ranks as the prettiest salvia. Many gardeners think *S. splendens*, or scarlet sage, is the showiest member of the family. First introduced to America in 1822, early plants grew 3 feet tall and boasted foot-long, brilliant red racemes.

To be fair, some people dislike scarlet sage, complaining that its bold blooms are too intense or that they clash with other flowers. In 1910, garden writer Harriet Keeler described the blood red blooms with a mixture of horror and partial admiration: "The mass of color of a well-grown bed defies description; it is magnificent, and it is barbaric." If scarlet sage is too overpowering for your tastes, too, try one of the modern salvia hybrids. They're widely available in cream, purple, pink, salmon, orange, and bicolor combinations. No matter which of these tropical beauties you grow in your landscape, you won't hear any gripes from hungry hummingbirds. They flock to the nectar packed in the tubular blooms.

S. patens

GENTIAN SAGE

Introduced to American gardens in the early nineteenth century, this frost-tender salvia hails from the mountains of Mexico. It carries whorls of true blue flowers on long stems from mid- to late summer. Unfortunately, it is not terribly showy, because the flower spikes can look rather sparse, but the charming, bright color is hard to find anywhere else in the garden. *S. patens* may return as a tender perennial for gardeners who enjoy mild winters.

CAMBRIDGE BLUE

This cultivar offers soft, sky blue flowers that appear from midsummer until frost, making them nice companions for late-blooming dahlias. The plants

Salvia Gentian Sage.
(Courtesy of Select Seeds)

grow to 2 feet tall and bear some of the largest blossoms of all the salvias. Try this one in a cutting garden, where it attracts butterflies and beneficial insects. Cambridge Blue has garnered a prestigious Award of Garden Merit from the Royal Horticultural Society.

CLARY SAGE—*S. SCLAREA*

All sages are salvias, although over time, sage has come to refer to herbs used for culinary or medical purposes, while we generally think of salvias as ornamentals. Native to southern and eastern Europe, these shrubby plants arrived in Britain around 1562, where the seeds were traditionally soaked in water to make a soothing eyewash. In fact, "clary" seems to come from the Latin word for clear or bright and may be a corruption of "clear eye." Clary sage did not show up in American catalogs until around 1827, but it has become a weedy invader in many parts of the country. It is seldom used for cooking nowadays, although John Parkinson once noted that the leaves could be "taken dry, and dipped into a batter made with the yolkes of eggs, flower and a

Pink clary sage. (Courtesy of Seed Savers Exchange)

little milke, and then fryed with butter until they be crispe." Today the leaves, which have a piney, slightly floral aroma, are used to make perfumes, cosmetics, and muscatel-type wines.

PAINTED SAGE—*S. VIRIDIS*, also known as Annual Clary or Bluebeard

Bees love this plant's colorful bracts, which come in creamy white, rose, blue, or purple. English growers knew it as purple-topped clary in the sixteenth century, a reference to the deep lavender bracts that surround the smaller, true flowers. You may see them in some reference books under their old scientific name, *S. horminum*. Cultivars are sold under such names as Oxford Blue, Pink Sundae, and Claryssa.

MEXICAN BUSH SAGE—*S. LEUCANTHA*

Spikes of soft, fuzzy, purple or purple and white flowers appear on this rugged salvia from August into October. Introduced from Mexico to England around 1847, the drought-tolerant plants are fine for xeriscaping. They are also useful for wildlife gardens, where their long stems can sprawl freely in all directions to entice hummingbirds. The plants grow as a perennial in zones 8 and up and perform better if cut back each spring, before new growth appears.

VICTORIA SERIES—*S. FARINACEA*

This classic salvia produces handfuls of lush, violet-blue flower spikes surrounded by gray-green foliage throughout the summer. It's nicknamed "mealycup sage" because the blossoms have a velvety look, as if they've been dusted with fine powder or flour. Another salvia in the series, Victoria White, bears soft white blooms. This herbaceous perennial, which is native to Texas and Mexico, grows to 3 feet in height. It may survive for several years if you live where the winters are mild.

BLUE BEDDER

At 18 inches tall, this cultivar is shorter than Victoria, but it's just as pretty. The violet-blue flowers appear on steel blue, squared stems that are characteristic of the mint family. Expect this annual to flower until the first hard frost.

Growing Tips

Although they're fine and sometimes tricky to handle, salvia seeds can be sown indoors. Mealycup sage, or *S. farinacea*, needs a long head start, so sow its seeds 10 weeks before the last spring frost in your area. You can wait until 8 weeks before the last frost to plant the seeds of *S. viridis* and *S. patens*. Alternately, you can sow salvias directly into the garden once the spring weather has become reliably warm. If you have a sheltered spot in your gar-

Blue Bedder.
(Courtesy of David Cavagnaro)

den, you can sow seeds in midsummer and transplant your seedlings in the fall or early the following spring.

Cover the seeds with as little soil as possible, and mist them gently with water to avoid dislodging them. Keep their growing medium moist, but not soggy, until the seeds sprout. Most salvias will take 2 to 4 weeks to germinate.

If you are planting inside, you may want to cover your pots or trays with clear plastic until the seedlings appear. Then remove the plastic and wait until a few true leaves appear before hardening off the young plants and moving them into the ground. Try spacing *S. splendens* or *S. farinacea* 10 to 12 inches apart so their colors pop out in the landscape.

Salvias are tolerant of most soils, but they prefer well-drained, rich ground. They'll do best in full sun, but most can tolerate light shade. Southerners may want to give salvias some shelter during the hottest part of the summer, when the intense light tends to fade their bright colors.

Deadhead your ornamental salvias often to keep the flowers coming, or prune shrubby culinary sages as needed to neaten them up.

Scarlet salvias can be difficult to work into a color scheme, so you may want to plant them by themselves, or use them where their crimson flowers will stand out against a backdrop of dark green foliage. Blue and violet-blue salvias make good companions for yellow blossoms; try them with Rudbeckia daises, melampodiums, or lemony yellow daylilies.

SCABIOSA—*Scabiosa*

Poor scabiosas. They take their name from scabies, an itchy skin disease— but don't hold their name against them. These willowy, graceful flowers do not cause itching. In fact, they were once thought to relieve irritated skin, although we no longer believe scabiosas offer any medicinal benefits.

These pretty plants go by many nicknames, and they're beloved for their soft colors and frilly single or doubled blossoms. The flower heads have a mounded shape, just like grandmother's old tomato red pincushion, and they're studded with stamens that stick up from the blossoms like tiny pins.

Scabiosa is a traditional cottage garden favorite, but here in America, we're most familiar with two species, *S. atropurpurea* and *S. caucasica*.

S. atropurpurea, from the Mediterranean region, bears rounded blossoms

"A garden favorite because of easy culture, extended period of bloom, and richness of color range."
Harriet Keeler,
Our Garden Flowers
(1910)

that come in shades of pink, blue, purple, red, and white. Although it is considered a hardy annual, this scabiosa may behave as a biennial in some parts of the country. Butterflies love its blossoms, which appear from midsummer until frost.

S. caucasica hails from Russia or southwest Asia. An herbaceous perennial, it was introduced to English gardens around 1803 and generally blooms from late spring through summer. Its scalloped flowers appear on slender stems above rosettes of gray-green foliage.

British botanist and author John Goodyer cultivated what he called Sweet Scabious in his English garden in 1621. The flowers he described were "of a delicate redd colour like to redd velvet."

Scabiosa was also known as Mournful Widow in seventeenth-century England. That melancholy name may be a reference to South American funeral wreaths that were sometimes made from the blossoms. To the Victorians, who often conveyed their unspoken feelings in the language of flowers, scabiosa signified loss, widowhood, and unfortunate love. By 1760, the plants had made their way into America.

While not as well known, another scabiosa species, *S. stellata*, is a lot of fun to grow. Sometimes called the starflower pincushion, it bears rounded heads that open to reveal a tiny star in the center of each fading flower. It is cultivated more for its seed pods, which turn bronze and papery when they're dry, than its small blossoms. The plants' long stems work well in everlasting arrangements.

Many wonderful old scabiosas have nearly disappeared, including Azure Fairy and King of the Blacks.

S. atropurpurea, *also known as Pincushion Flower, Sweet Scabiosa, Egyptian Rose, and Sweet Scabious*

BLACKAMOOR'S BEAUTY

Don't let this flower's sad nicknames, which include Mournful Bride, deter you from trying it in your garden. The ruffled, deep maroon blossoms are studded with white stamens that look like silvery pins on a field of deep red velvet. Some gardeners say they can detect a faint honey scent from the blooms. Bees and butterflies love the 2-foot-tall plants, which bloom about 16 weeks from

AN EFFECTIVE AND
EASILY GROWN ANNUAL.

EXCELLENT
FOR CUT FLOWERS.

MOURNING BRIDE

(Scabiosa or
Sweet Scabious)

These fragrant flowers were advertised in a 1923 D. M. Ferry catalog.

Blue Cockade. (Courtesy of David Cavagnaro)

sowing. After the petals drop, the attractive seed cones can be added to dried arrangements.

BLUE COCKADE

Large, mounded flower heads bob atop the graceful stems of this wonderful heirloom, first offered in a 1935 Burpee's catalog. The blooms are delicately scented on the 3-foot-tall plants. Despite its name, the blossoms usually look violet-blue or lavender. Expect this rare charmer to flower until fall.

GRANDMOTHER'S PINCUSHION

A Dutch selection of old-fashioned varieties, this scabiosa mix typically includes rose, deep red, salmon pink, white, and soft lilac shades. The frilly, heavily petaled flowers bloom from summer into late fall. You may need to stake these wildflowery plants, which range from 3 to 4 feet in height. The 2- to 3-inch blossoms have long stems and make charming arrangements in vases. Scabiosas like these were a favorite in colonial gardens.

Grandmother's Pincushion.
(Courtesy of Renee's Garden)

GIANT IMPERIAL MIX

Viewed from a distance, these flowers look like little powder puffs perched on swaying stems. The densely petaled blooms are fully doubled and measure 2 to 3 inches across, offering butterflies a secure place to land and feed. While this blend is often sold as a biennial mix, you'll probably have better luck if you simply consider the plants as annuals and resow each year. Commercial packages may include blue, red, white, salmon, lilac, pink, crimson, and lavender shades. The plants grow to 2 feet tall, with sturdy stems that are fine for cutting.

FIRE KING

Although this antique charmer can be hard to find, it's worth the trouble. The plants produce bright, fire red blossoms accented with ash white stamens, and they have a sweet scent that's irresistible to butterflies. Fire King is an annual that reaches about 30 inches tall. Give it partial shade if you live in a hot climate.

S. caucasica

CLIVE GREAVES

One of the first pincushion hybrids, and still one of the most widely grown, Clive Greaves made its debut in 1929. The large, ruffled flowers are a soft blue lavender and sometimes have cream- or light-colored centers. The blossoms are flatter and more open than usual, and they're produced on the 2-foot-tall plants for a longer period of time. This one received a Royal Horticultural Society Award of Garden Merit in 1993.

MISS WILLMOTT

British horticulturist Ellen Willmott, born in 1858, was known for the spectacular gardens she cultivated at Warley Place, her family home in Essex. She grew many different shrubs and flowers, which explains why you will also find roses, lilacs, and other plants named in her honor. The scabiosa that carries her name opens creamy white flowers atop 18-inch stems. Its blossoms, which sometimes have a tinge of cream or white, open until frost.

Frilly scabiosas attract summer butterflies.

(Courtesy of Renee's Garden)

Growing Tips

Both popular species of scabiosa need rich, well-drained soil and full sun. Once established, they are relatively easy to grow.

Scabiosa seeds are tiny, with an estimated 2,500 per ounce. They need about 12 to 16 weeks from sowing to come into bloom, so give your seeds a head start by planting them indoors in a good quality growing mix 4 to 6 weeks before the last spring frost. Space the seeds 1 to 2 inches apart and cover them only ⅛ inch deep. They should germinate in 8 to 15 days. Give the seedlings regular water and bright light until they're ready to move outside.

The seedlings can be hardened off and transplanted into their permanent garden location when they're 3 to 4 inches tall. Space them 12 to 18 inches apart.

Grandmother's Pincushion butterfly scabiosa. (Courtesy of Renee's Garden)

If you prefer, start the seeds outdoors instead, after the last heavy frost. Thin to every 12 inches after the seedlings emerge. Weed often but carefully, to avoid disturbing the plants' roots.

Although scabiosas bloom for a long time—sometimes right up to a killing frost—the plants aren't heavy bloomers, and you'll only get wisps of color if your flower beds are sparsely planted. Try using scabiosa in masses instead, and keep the faded flowers snipped to encourage repeat blooms. To make the delicate blues and pinks pop out in your landscape, grow them alongside pure white or silvery flowers and foliage.

Scabiosa is seldom bothered by pests or diseases, but if you notice powdery mildew on the leaves, your plants are probably suffering from poor air circulation. Long, skinny stems and few flowers can also signal that the plants are growing in too much shade. Scabiosas sometimes slow down when the temperature soars in mid- to late summer, but the plants should perk back up when cooler weather returns.

Butterfly Gardens

Scabiosas are among the best choices for butterfly habitats. Watch for Monarchs, Skippers, Fritillaries, and moths to visit the nectar-laden blooms.

SOUTHERN PEA—*Vigna unguiculata* subsp. *unguiculata*, also known as Black-eyed Pea, Cowpea, Crowder Pea, Purple Hull, or Field Pea

You might not guess that Master Gardener John Coykendall is an artist when you meet him as he's hoeing between rows of heirloom vegetables and flowers in the trial gardens at the University of Tennessee. But when he invites you into his home to admire his collection of multicolored peas and beans displayed in handsome wooden bowls, you realize he's more than an expert gardener. He has a keen eye for beauty.

While John originally trained as a landscape painter, he has been farming for about 40 years now, and he's made saving seeds his mission. Currently he keeps between 300 and 400 different varieties stored in big freezers in his home. Each year, he plants some seeds and gives some away. The Tennessee

Agricultural Museum in Nashville, Seed Savers Exchange in Iowa, and the historic gardens at Monticello are just a few of his beneficiaries. To John, heirloom seeds are worth preserving for their taste, history, and genetic diversity. They're just plain beautiful, too.

Today, gardeners have more than 1,000 different peas to choose from. The plants are classified according to whether they're tall or dwarf, early or late, or even better for snapping than shelling. Botanically speaking, southern peas are close relatives of the yard-long bean, a native of South America. That has never bothered southerners, who grow these vegetables more often than the rest of the country. That's probably because cowpeas, as they're also called, need long, warm nights to set their pods and do not perform as well where the growing season is cool and short.

African slaves probably introduced these plants to America around 1674, where they became a staple crop in the South. They were especially important during the Civil War, when the South was crippled by the loss of cash crops like cotton. Peas grew in almost any soil—they still do—so they helped many impoverished southerners survive Reconstruction.

"I've heard that 'Whippoorwill' peas got their name because they produce when the whippoorwills are singing. The only pea I like better is 'Piggott,' which comes from a parish in Louisiana. It's prolific, flavorful, and a little larger. Others I like are 'Turkey Crowder' and 'Paw's Old Gray,' both of which go back at least 100 years."

David Bradshaw, Professor of Horticulture, Clemson University

Left to right, Whippoorwill and Susanne cowpeas. (Courtesy of David Cavagnaro)

Southern peas fall into several categories. Many varieties are hard to identify correctly because names have gotten lost or mixed up over time. Crowders are the largest in the group and get their name because they "crowd up" against one another in their pods. They have a hearty flavor and produce a dark liquid when cooked. Blackeyes are white or cream-colored seeds with black or brown centers; hence the name.

Purple hulls may be purplish all over or only at the tip of the pods. Their seeds are usually white with tan, pink, or brown eyes. Pale cream peas have the mildest flavor of the southern types. You may see them sold as "zipper peas" because their shells are easy to open. After cooking, their broth is clear.

ZIPPER CREAM

Give these large, white peas 70 days to mature. The pods turn straw-colored when they dry on the bushy, disease-resistant plants. This heavy yielder shells out easily for eating fresh or processing and has a mild flavor.

WHIPPOORWILL

This old variety is dependable even in harsh weather or poor soils. The pods are ready to harvest in 70 days and contain speckled, tan peas. One story says the peas take their name from their markings, which resemble the colors of whippoorwills. You won't need to trellis the bushy plants. The peas, which pre-date 1850, make good soup, but many gardeners once used to grow the plants to build up their soil, or dried them as a winter hay for their farm animals.

CALICO CROWDER, also known as Polecat Pea or Hereford Pea

A good choice for mid-Atlantic gardens, these white and maroon peas also have a mild flavor and are ready in 70 days from sowing. They're good eaten fresh or dried. Give the plants some room, as the vines run to 10 feet. The pods are quite large, too, reaching 10 to 14 inches in length.

WASHDAY

Before the days of automatic washers, doing the family laundry was an all-day chore. It took hours to chop kindling to stack under a wash pot, bring water to a boil, and scrub clothes. Old-timey gardeners say you could get your wash done while you cooked these peas and made a pone of cornbread. This is

Mississippi Silver cowpeas.
(Courtesy of David Cavagnaro)

a half-runner variety that bears small, yellowish-tan seeds. Grown in Alabama since the 1920s, it dates to the 1800s.

RED RIPPER

John Coykendall says these peas are his favorites, with a taste that's closer to the flavor of shelled beans than peas. He received them from a man in Washington Parish, Louisiana, who had been farming for about 70 years.

Growing Tips

Southern peas like it a little warmer than garden and snow peas. Wait until after the last spring frost or until the soil is at least 70°F before sowing them. Then plant the seeds an inch deep and 4 inches apart. Old vining type peas need more room and should be sown 6 to 12 inches apart. Space their rows about 20 inches apart.

Southern peas don't need much water them once they are up. They'll also shade out most weedy competitors as they grow, so you won't have to do much weeding.

Your pods will be ready to harvest when the seeds inside begin to swell, but watch them carefully. The taste declines as the pods turn lighter and dry out. Like garden and snow peas, southern peas should be eaten or processed soon after they're picked.

Pump Up Your Peas

Like most legumes, peas grow better if certain bacteria, called rhizobium, are available in the soil. These bacteria help the plants convert nitrogen for their use while they're growing. Rhizobia occur naturally in the soil, so if you've previously cultivated peas in a certain area, they should already be there.

But if you're establishing a new garden, it's a good idea to add rhizobium to the soil. You can do this by coating your peas with an inoculant powder. It's easy to do; just dampen the seeds and dust them with the powder, sold at nurseries or through seed catalogs. Peas grown with inoculants are usually more vigorous and heavy yielding than those without.

If you're saving peas for next year, dry the seeds and then freeze them for at least 24 hours before storing them, to destroy any hidden weevils. In general, you can save southern peas for replanting in the same way you save beans.

Mendel's Peas

Most kids don't get through high school biology without learning about Gregor Mendel, the nineteenth-century monk who experimented with peas in his abbey garden. Mendel's work helped explain how members of the same species pass along certain characteristics and paved the way for modern geneticists. Plant breeders still use some of his methods to develop new flower and vegetable varieties.

Peas for Luck

According to southern tradition, you should serve certain foods on New Year's Day for good luck in the coming year. Eating peas is supposed to put coins in your pocket, while dining on a "mess" of collard greens ensures folding money, or dollar bills.

Some people eat their peas plain on the holiday, while others cook them up in "Hoppin' John," an African American dish made from black-eyed peas and rice and seasoned with ham, onions, hot pepper sauce, and a pinch of salt.

Red Ripper and Washday cowpeas. (Courtesy of John Coykendall)

SQUASH—*Cucurbita*

"Squash" once meant an unripe pea pod or a contemptible person. In Shakespeare's *A Winter's Tale*, a father tells his son, "How like, methought, I was then to this kernel, this squash, this gentleman."

How did things get so mixed up? What we refer to as cantaloupes are really muskmelons. Food historians say that some of the root crops we call turnips are actually rutabagas. Botanists admit to only slight differences between many collards and kales.

Squashes and pumpkins are also part of the great garden debate. Along with gourds and melons, they belong to the *Cucurbitaceae* family. But the biggest difference between the two plants is not botanical; instead, it's our habit of calling them one name or the other. Pumpkins are actually a kind of squash, although we use both words rather loosely when we're talking about the many different forms of winter and summer squash.

In general, you can think of summer squashes as having thin skins and soft flesh, and winter squashes as having harder skins and coarser flesh.

Like corn and beans, squashes have been around since ancient times. Some sources even put squash plants in the Gardens of Babylon. But it's likely that the vegetables derive their name from the Algonquin word *askutasquash*, which translates as "green things that may be eaten raw." The first bitter, wild squashes probably were eaten uncooked, while green and immature. But by

Heirloom summer squash. (Courtesy of David Cavagnaro)

1643, when squashes first appeared in American literature, they sounded more palatable, perhaps because the plants were already being selected for more desirable characteristics. Seventeenth-century author Roger Williams described them in *A Key into the Language of America*, his study of the Algonquian Indians in the New England area: "Askutasquash, their Vine apples, which the English from them call Squashes, about the bignesse of Apples, of several colours, sweet light, wholesome, refreshing."

Heirloom gardening author Amy Goldman sorts *Cucurbita* into four main species.

> *C. maxima*: These South American natives, introduced to the New World after 1492, have spiny vines and big leaves. They are known for their mild flavors and bright orange flesh.

C. moschata: From Central and South America, these plants have a
  sprawling growth habit and smooth stems.

C. pepo: Here's where we find our familiar jack-o'-lantern pumpkins;
  pattypans, also called scallops; summer crooknecks; "acorn" winter
  squash; and zucchinis. Native to Mexico and the United States, this
  species has spiny stems.

C. argyrosperma: According to Goldman, you won't find many commercial
  sources for the varieties in this species, which is native to Mexico. It
  includes the handsome Japanese Pie squash, with its dark green and
  orange rind, and the Green Striped Cushaw.

C. maxima

QUEENSLAND BLUE

This deeply ribbed, bluish-green squash is really native to Australia. Ready
in 110 days, the 8- to 15-pound fruits are round but somewhat flattened, with
a slight taper at the bottom. Under the thick skins, the moist, orange flesh is
nutty tasting. This is an excellent keeping variety that dates back to before the
1930s.

BOSTON MARROW, also known as Autumnal Marrow

This early winter squash (or late summer squash—take your pick) may have
originated with the Iroquois Indians. At least one source thinks that it is iden-
tical to a variety grown in Chile in the late 1700s. Heirloom gardening author
William Woys Weaver says the squash was put on display in 1834 as part of a
gardening exhibit in Boston's Faneuil Hall. Weaver suspects the skin was originally pink, selected toward today's reddish-orange. Inside, the flesh is carrot-
colored. It is ready for making delicious pies in about 95 days from sowing.

C. moschata

BUTTERNUT

You'll recognize these oblong squashes with tan or beige skins from the
supermarket. Goldman cites their origin with Boston's Joseph Breck and
Sons in the early 1930s. Their sweet, golden orange flesh makes them among

the most popular winter squashes. Give them 90 to 100 days from sowing. So many spices enhance their flavor; try them with allspice, cardamom, cloves, ginger, nutmeg, or a bit of brown sugar and butter.

NECK PUMPKIN

One look at these horseshoe-shaped fruits, and you can see how they got their name. You can hang them around your neck like a yoke when they're mature—a handy way to bring them in from the garden. Each squash has a bulbous base that can grow up to 8 inches in diameter. Heirloom gardener David Bradshaw, professor of horticulture at Clemson University, thinks this

A harvest of tasty winter squash. (Courtesy of David Cavagnaro)

squash arrived from Africa in the early 1800s. "You can cross cut it into sections to cook just one chunk at a time, and it will scab over to make its own seal," he says. Ready in 120 days from sowing, this squash is used by the Amish for making pies.

SEMINOLE PUMPKIN

Introduced to the United States in 1916, this variety is actually much older. "The 'Seminole' pumpkin is about the size of a volleyball and kind of flat at the top and bottom," David Bradshaw says. "The Seminoles refused to be rounded up when President Andrew Jackson tried to send them on the Trail of Tears, and took the pumpkin into the Everglades with them. It's evolved over the last 175 years, adapting to heat, humidity, insects, and diseases. It's not for carving, as the flesh is thick and sweet, with a spongy center, but it makes wonderful pies, soufflés, soups, and custards, and needs very little sweetening once you cook it. It keeps 15 to 18 months in common room storage." Give it 90 days to mature.

SUMMER CROOKNECK—C. PEPO

Jefferson grew many kinds of squash, pumpkins, and gourds at Monticello. This summertime favorite, he wrote around 1781, had been "found in Virginia when first visited by the English." But he concluded that the plants originated in "a more southern climate, and [were] handed along the continent by one nation to another of the savages." Summer Crookneck has a light yellow skin that becomes warty and orangish as it ages. The white flesh has a mild, delicate taste; it's good for baking, steaming, frying, or sautéing.

Growing Tips

Squash is easy to grow in full sun and well-drained soil that is rich in organic matter. If you're starting your seeds indoors, sow them in flats or pots 3 to 4 weeks before the last spring frost. Sow the seeds ½ to 1 inch deep in moist soil, and expect them to sprout in 5 to 10 days. After the seedlings emerge, don't rush them outside. These warm-weather crops need reliably warm soil and air temperatures.

After the seedlings have their first set of true leaves, harden them off and move them into their permanent garden spot. Most squashes are sprawling

Crooknecks and other antique squashes. (Courtesy of David Cavagnaro)

plants, so give them plenty of room in all directions. Check the variety you're growing for specifics, but in general, vining squashes need 6 to 8 feet between rows, while bush types need 3.

Alternately, you can sow squash seeds directly outside, planting 4 or 5 seeds to hills spaced 4 feet apart. When the seedlings emerge, thin to 2 or 3 per hill. For single plants, sow 2 or 3 seeds every 3 feet. Thin to 1 vigorous plant.

If your leaves wilt, it's probably because the plants are thirsty, so water regularly.

Squash blossoms are edible and delicious, especially when fried or stuffed with soft cheeses. Male flowers open first, followed by females that produce the baby squash. Be careful of using pesticides, which kill the bees that pollinate your flowers.

For best flavor, pick the squashes while they are small.

Grow only one variety at a time to ensure seed purity. But bees that zip over from neighboring gardens can still mix things up, so it's better to get new seed each year.

SUNFLOWER—*Helianthus*

The first sunflowers most likely made their homes in the southwestern parts of what is now the United States, where native peoples once made good use of these tall, sturdy, heat-loving annuals. Three thousand years ago, we might have seen their large seeds ground into flour for bread or pressed to make oil for cooking. Even the strong, thick stalks were set into the ground as a framework for simple dwellings.

Some archaeologists theorize that sunflowers have been around even longer than that famous staple of the Native American culture, corn.

Small wonder, then, that Spanish explorers and colonists sent the seeds of these useful plants back home in the early to mid-1500s. Sunflowers quickly spread into England and France, and by 1577, a mention of them popped up in a translation of *Joyful Newes Oute of the Newe Founde Worlde*, penned by the Spanish physician Monardes.

In 1597, Gerard decided to track the growth of these new plants: "The Indian Sun or golden floure of Peru is a plant of such stature and talnesse that in one Sommer being sowne of a seede in Aprill, it hath risen up to . . . fourteene foot in my garden, one floure was in weight three pound and two ounces." Gerard wasn't afraid to taste the buds, either, boiling them with butter, vinegar, and pepper for a snack. They went down easily, it seems, although they had an odd effect. He pronounced the seeds "exceeding pleasant meat, surpassing the Artichoke far in procuring bodily lust." Sunflowers even impressed King Louis XIV, who chose them as the symbol of his reign.

At one time, there were more than 2,000 named varieties of sunflowers, thanks largely to Russian breeders, who recognized their potential as a source of both oil and food. Most of these have now disappeared, although heirloom gardeners can still find many delightful choices available.

RUSSIAN MAMMOTH, also known as Russian Giant, Tall Russian, and Russian Greystripe

Peter the Great is credited with introducing sunflowers to Russia after seeing them in Holland. During the 1800s, more than 2 million acres of Russian farmland were devoted to the commercial production of oil from these sunny giants. This variety bears bright yellow heads atop 9- to 12-foot stalks. Breeders have improved its enormous blooms, each of which can produce up to 5,000 grayish-black seeds with white stripes. They are meaty and plump, ready for harvest in 80 days. You will need to thin this large variety, which is excellent if you're growing sunflowers for birdseed, to every 18 inches.

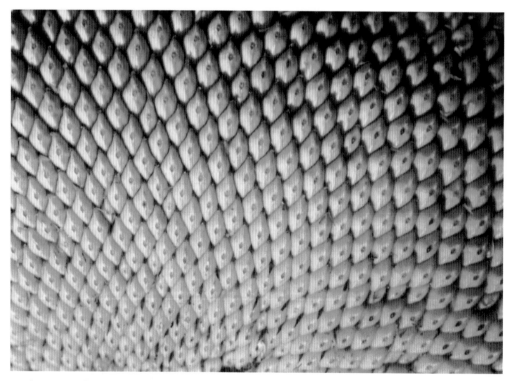

Tarahumara sunflower seeds. (Courtesy of David Cavagnaro)

TARAHUMARA

This rare beauty needs 85 to 100 days to form bright gold flowers with apple green centers. Each flower stalk bears a single bloom studded with large gray and white or ivory seeds. Tarahumara was probably introduced to Canada by Mennonite immigrants in the 1930s. Later, the variety was adopted by the Tarahumara Indians of Chihuahua, Mexico, a reclusive tribe that continues to follow the primitive lifestyle of their ancestors.

ARIKARA

When Lewis and Clark encountered the Arikara Indians of North Dakota in late 1804, they found only 2,000 survivors out of an original population of more than 30,000. The tribe had been decimated by recurring smallpox epidemics. While the orange-yellow sunflower that bears the tribal name is still available, it is increasingly hard to find. Arikara produces one or more flowers

Arikara. (Courtesy of David Cavagnaro)

per stalk about 100 days from planting. At maturity, the 12- to 16-inch blooms are packed with black, white, or streaked seeds.

Growing Tips

Don't be surprised if you see sunflowers listed under both ornamental and vegetable headings in old seed catalogs. These annuals brighten beds and borders as they turn their heads to track the sun's movement in the sky, but many gardeners have also grown them for their seeds, which make a nutritious snack for wildlife as well as humans.

There's no need to start sunflower seeds indoors, since they sprout quickly and easily. The plants dislike transplanting anyway, so plant your seeds directly in the garden after the last frost, and cover them with ½ inch of soil. Thin the emerging seedlings to every 2 feet, and resow more seeds every 2 weeks to keep your harvest coming. If a light frost hits your baby plants, don't panic. Sunflowers can usually tolerate a little chill in early spring.

Although these cheerful flowers are not temperamental about soil, they do demand full sun and a drink of water during dry periods. It's especially important to water them while the blossoms are forming.

A few of the taller varieties may need staking to help them withstand strong winds or rain. You can support them by inserting a stake or pole into the ground near each young plant. As the flower stalks grow, tie them gently to the poles about every 6 inches.

When the flowers begin to shed their petals, it's time to harvest the seeds. Tie a paper bag around each flower head to catch the seeds, or simply cut the entire head and store it, with the seeds intact, in a cool, dark place until you're ready to use it.

Sunflowers depend on insects for pollination, so if you are saving seeds to plant next year, keep different varieties isolated, or plant only one variety at a time to ensure purity. Make sure the seeds are completely dry before you label and store them. They may remain viable for up to 7 years.

As food sources dwindle during the winter months, hungry birds will appreciate any sunflower heads you leave to dry in the garden. When the birds have eaten their fill, cut the stalks to the ground or pull them up for the compost heap.

Be wary, though, of planting sunflowers too close to your vegetables. After

A Tarahumara flower head. (Courtesy of David Cavagnaro)

the birds, squirrels, and other creatures polish off the seeds, they'll often move right down the buffet line to your food crops. Many garden centers sell netting that can be used to protect the flower heads, but use it with caution. If birds or small animals become trapped in the nets, they may perish before you find and release them.

Sunflowers and Bouillabaisse

Dutch artist Vincent Van Gogh excelled at capturing the shaggy gold and yellow beauty of sunflowers on canvas. He considered them a symbol of gratitude and labored to create a series of paintings to show a visiting friend, fellow painter Paul Gauguin. Before Gauguin arrived, Van Gogh confided in a letter to his brother Theo, "I am working with the enthusiasm of a man from Marseilles eating bouillabaisse, which shouldn't come as a surprise to you because I am busy painting huge sunflowers."

Versatile Sunflower Seeds

Gardeners have found countless ways to use sunflowers. It's said that early Mormons, persecuted in Missouri for their religious beliefs, set out across the plains for Utah and scattered the seeds to mark a trail for others to follow.

Early American settlers made a crude soap from sunflower seed oil and boiled the shells as a substitute for coffee.

Buffalo Bird Woman, a Hidatsa Indian born around 1839 in what is now North Dakota, once recounted how her tribe used sunflowers to encourage their warriors. At the end of the growing season, the women harvested the flower heads and pounded the seeds into a fine meal. The meal was squeezed into lumps, wrapped in skins from buffalo hearts, and given to the men to eat when they grew tired.

Some folk medicine recipes call for browning sunflower seeds in an oven and then steeping them to make a soothing tea for whooping coughs and colds. The seeds have also been used as diuretics and expectorants. Early American settlers planted them around their cabins, believing the plants would ward off malaria when they emerged.

TOMATO—*Lycopersicon lycopersicum*

Every year, tomatoes top the list of favorite backyard vegetables. No store-bought pretender can match their home-ripened flavor, of course, but there's more to it. Growing them just seems to cause an outbreak of friendly "tomato-mania," with neighbors competing to harvest the first fruit of the season or tip the scales with record-breaking produce.

Tomatoes were not always popular. When these tropical natives arrived in Europe in the 1600s, nobody was interested in them until the French dubbed them *pomme d'amour*, or love apples. Italian cooks also welcomed them into the local cuisine.

In America, colonists were suspicious of the first tomatoes, perhaps because they belonged to the deadly nightshade family. The fruits finally took off in the 1830s and were widely enjoyed by the middle of the century.

Heirloom tomatoes are available in many wonderful varieties, so don't limit yourself to those boring, red globes. Look for old-fashioned colors like rosy pink, yellow, orange, and even brownish-purple. You can grow striped tomatoes, plum- or fig-shaped tomatoes, midget types, or meaty monsters. There are fruits shaped like ovals or hearts, tomatoes with smooth or ribbed skins, tomatoes that need two hands to hold, and grape types small enough to pop into your mouth.

Admittedly, these delicious heirlooms can have some problems. Many old types lack the disease resistance that has been developed in newer ones, allowing fusarium wilt to attack and kill the vines. To help prevent outbreaks, plant your tomatoes in a different spot every year. Heirloom vines can also grow quite large, even though they don't typically produce more tomatoes than modern plants. Keep their size in mind if your space is limited. But don't hesitate to try them. Old-timey tomatoes bring lots of color and flavor to the table.

MORTGAGE LIFTER

So many tomatoes have claimed to be the legendary Mortgage Lifter that it's difficult to know which one deserves the title. The variety is credited to M. C. Byles, or "Radiator Charlie," a 1930s radiator repairman from West Virginia.

Charlie, who lacked a formal education, created his large fruits by crossing six generations of tomatoes, including German Johnson and Beefsteak with English and Italian varieties. In the 1940s, he began selling his plants for one dollar each and earned enough over the next six years to pay off the mortgage on his farm. Soon other farmers were selling the fruits at roadside stands or out of the back of pickup trucks. Mortgage Lifter tomatoes can weigh up to 4 pounds each.

CHEROKEE PURPLE

It's believed that the Cherokees were growing this dark purple tomato with brick red flesh in Tennessee before 1890. The fruits have a smoky, sweet taste and are ready for harvest in about 82 days. Because they're soft and thin-skinned, they don't store well.

BLACK SEA MAN

This potato-leaf variety bears in 80 days from sowing. The name probably comes from the odd-looking veins that run underneath the mahogany brown skins. Some gardeners think the fruits, found in Russia by Seed Savers Exchange, have a slightly salty taste.

GOLDEN PEACH

This 100-year-old heirloom has a sweet flavor with a touch of tartness. The slightly fuzzy fruits are mature when they become pale yellow and show a pink blush. Good for slicing or eating fresh, they also keep well.

CZECH'S EXCELLENT YELLOW

Most yellow tomatoes don't have a lot of taste, but this variety has a good, strong flavor, although it is somewhat acidic. The vines are prolific, yielding 3-inch round fruits that make good sauces or salads. This heirloom owes it survival to the late Ben Quisenberry, who circulated it through his mail-order seed company, Big Tomato Gardens. Quisenberry ran his company out of an old Syracuse, New York, post office until he was 96 years old.

BRANDYWINE

One of the most popular heirlooms, Brandywine is a big, deep pink beefsteak tomato with a rich taste. Believed to be an Amish variety from 1885, Brandywine may actually have been introduced to America by Johnson & Stokes Seeds. Its name probably comes from Brandywine Creek, which runs through Pennsylvania's Chester County. Ben Quisenberry also helped preserve this tomato and passed its seeds along to Seed Savers Exchange before his death in 1986. Brandywine is thin-skinned and produces better in cool temperatures.

WHITE BEAUTY, also known as Snowball

This rare, creamy white beefsteak tomato has a sweet, mild flavor. Heirloom gardening author Benjamin Watson says it may have come from a pre-1860s variety known as White Apple. The fruits contain a lot of sugar and about as

Rainbow's End tomatoes.
(Courtesy of Renee's Garden)

much acid as red tomatoes. Ready in about 80 days, this heirloom does not produce many seeds.

Growing Tips

Start your tomato seeds indoors in pots 6 to 8 weeks before the last spring frost, covering them ¼ inch deep. For maximum germination, keep the soil between 75° and 90°F. Once the seedlings appear, they will need plenty of light and warm temperatures. If you start them in trays, move the seedlings into individual pots after their first true leaves appear. This will encourage them to form deeper roots.

Harden off your seedlings before moving them outdoors, and space them 12 to 24 inches apart in the garden. Set the plants a little deeper in the ground than they were in their pots, to encourage additional roots to form along the buried stems.

Determinate-type tomatoes will stop growing at a certain height, so you won't need to worry about supporting them with stakes or cages. Indeterminate types, which keep climbing and producing throughout the season, should be planted 24 to 36 inches apart.

Young tomato plants are often damaged by sun, frost, or even birds, so you

Philadelphia seedsman Henry Maule tempted gardeners in the late 1880s with his large, juicy tomatoes.

may want to protect them for a few days with a milk jug that's cut open at both ends.

Tomatoes need regular water and fertilizer. Keep the roots mulched to conserve moisture and prevent weeds, and pick the tomatoes when they are ripe or almost ripe. They will continue to ripen indoors.

Tomato seeds are actually quite hardy. As any gardener who has dumped tomato scraps into a compost heap can tell you, they often sprout unaided. But if you want to save seeds for later, there's a trick to getting good results. First, pick some tomatoes from your healthiest, most disease-free specimens. Cut the fruits in half and squeeze them over a clean glass jar. Add some water to the resulting goop and stir gently.

Next, let the jar sit for a couple of days, or until the pulpy mixture ferments. Add more water and stir again. Soon the good seeds should sink while the undesirable ones float. Carefully pour off the water and repeat, rinsing until only good seeds remain.

A mix of Brandywine, Marvel Stripe, and Green Zebra tomatoes. (Courtesy of Renee's Garden)

Dump the good seeds into a strainer and rinse once more under running water. At last they're ready to spread onto a cookie sheet to dry (they'll stick to paper plates or towels).

Label your dried seeds and store them in a cool, dark place. One ripe tomato yields about 50 to 100 good seeds. Most commercial seed packets contain 20 to 30, which should provide enough fresh tomatoes for the average family. Heirloom gardeners are never average, of course, so if you're going to process the fruits, you'll need more.

Rainbow's End tomato seeds. (Courtesy of Renee's Garden)

The Great Tomato Controversy

Are tomatoes fruits or vegetables? Botanically speaking, they are considered fruits, but that doesn't stop most people from calling them vegetables. I've used both terms here without worrying about it.

But believe it or not, the United States government has worried about it. In 1893, the Supreme Court ruled that the tomato is a vegetable. This was in response to an importer who had argued that tomatoes were fruits and thus should be duty-free. Tomatoes, the Court pronounced solemnly, are served alongside the main course at meals; therefore, they are vegetables.

WATERMELON—*Citrullus lanatus*

No Fourth of July party feels complete without a luscious watermelon, iced down and sliced into juicy chunks for sharing. Ironically, watermelons, which are about 90 percent water, may have evolved from wild vines that scramble over Africa's Kalahari Desert and store scarce rainfall inside their thick-skinned fruits.

But some botanists think these members of the *Cucurbitaceae* family hail from India, where their wild ancestor may have grown around 2000 B.C. Archaeologists are hard pressed to pin down the watermelon's origins because the ancient seeds they have found look as much like those of the cucumber as of the watermelon. Certainly, watermelons are antique plants. Their seeds were buried with the Egyptian king Tutankhamen (or were those cucumbers, too?), and what appears to be a watermelon harvest has been discovered in 5,000-year-old hieroglyphics.

If these heat-loving annuals did make their first home on the African continent, they probably left there in the tenth century and made their way into China via merchant ships. From there, thirteenth-century Moorish traders carried them into Europe.

The plants came into the New World with Spanish and Portuguese explorers, as well as with early European settlers and slaves from Africa. Records show that the plants were being cultivated in Massachusetts around 1629. In 1754, Philip Miller, author of *The Gardeners Dictionary*, raved over their "wholsome cooling Quality."

Across the ocean, watermelons were earning a reputation as difficult to grow in English gardens. In 1845, Jane Loudon, Victorian author of *The Lady's Country Companion*, warned her readers that the plants were finicky and ill suited to cool climes. "I would not advise you to grow cucumbers or melons; but, should you feel inclined to try your skill, you have only to have a hotbed."

By 1894, American humorist Mark Twain was singing their praises in his book *Pudd'nhead Wilson*: "[The watermelon] is chief of this world's luxuries, king by the grace of God over all the fruits of the earth. When one has tasted it, he knows what the angels eat. It was not a Southern watermelon that Eve took; we know it because she repented."

Although modern gardeners usually think of watermelons as dark green cannonballs for summer picnics, there are more than 1,200 varieties of watermelons around the world. Their juicy flesh comes in a rainbow of colors, from pale pink to scarlet, apricot to deep orange, yellow, and creamy white.

MOON AND STARS

For years, this variety was more legend than fact. Originally introduced by Peter Henderson & Company of New York around 1926, Moon and Stars simply disappeared somewhere along the line. Although Mennonite immigrants from Russia had introduced the variety to America, the seeds apparently were dropped by many commercial sellers because the roly-poly melons didn't stack and ship well. Still, heirloom gardeners continued to swap stories about a beautiful, dark green melon speckled with buttery yellow "stars" and a larger yellow "moon." It was said to have a sugary sweet, red flesh sprinkled with small, brown seeds.

Kent Whealy, of the Iowa-based Seed Savers Exchange, had been looking for Moon and Stars for years and mentioned it while filming a television interview.

DELICIOUS HOME GARDEN
WATER MELON
AND
CANTALOUPES

MONTE
CRISTO

TIP TOP

EMERALD GEM

D. M. Ferry featured Monte Cristo watermelon seeds in 1923.

The legendary Moon and Stars watermelon. (Courtesy of Seed Savers Exchange)

Merle Van Doren, a gardener in Macon, Missouri, saw the program and came to the rescue. "He gave us about 10 watermelons," says Diane Whealy, Kent's wife. "We . . . saved the seed to send to members [of Seed Savers Exchange]. They increased it in their gardens and then we were able to offer it to others."

Today, the seeds are widely available and rank among the most popular heirloom watermelons. Even the fuzzy vines, spotted with sunny yellow freckles that mimic the stars on the rinds, are a pleasure to grow.

RATTLESNAKE, also known as Southern Rattlesnake and Gypsy Oblong

Southerners sometimes refer to a watermelon patch as snaky, meaning both that the vines twist across the ground like writhing snakes and that the

Rattlesnake.

(Courtesy of David Cavagnaro)

tangle of vegetation in the garden is a cozy hiding place for snakes. While some snakes do curl up in overgrown gardens, Rattlesnake, which you may find offered as Georgia Rattlesnake, actually takes its name from the dark green markings that wiggle across its lighter rind. Some growers call these tiger stripes; others say they resemble the pattern on a timber rattler.

Rattlesnake is thought to have been developed in Georgia in the 1830s. Because its long, narrow shape made the melons easy to stack and ship, and its rind is relatively tough, this variety became a favorite even in northern markets. The sweet melons average between 25 and 45 pounds and mature in 90 days from sowing.

CUBAN QUEEN

W. Atlee Burpee gets the credit for introducing this exotic melon in 1881. The Queen really is majestic, bearing sweet, red-fleshed fruits that can grow to 70 or more pounds. The rind is striped with dark and light green. Like any monarch, the Queen likes to extend her reach into the lands around her, and these plants produce long, rambling vines.

ICE CREAM

Slice open this nineteenth-century melon and you'll reveal a white-seeded, white flesh that looks as cool and refreshing as vanilla ice cream. The plants perform well even in northern climates, producing round melons with pale green skin in about 82 days from sowing. While the true heirloom Ice Cream has become rare and hard to find, a black-seeded variety with pink flesh has been popular since it was served at the U.S. centennial celebration in 1876.

Growing Tips

Summer works a special magic on melon seeds, which crave the hot, sunny growing conditions of their tropical origins. If your growing period is short, choose small, round varieties to avoid disappointment.

For a jump start on the season, sow your watermelon seeds indoors 3 to 4 weeks before the last spring frost, placing them in individual pots. They need soil temperatures of 75° to 85°F to germinate, so supply very gentle heat to the bottom of the pots if necessary.

Once your seedlings are up and show their true leaves, and all danger of frost has passed, harden them off and move them into the garden. If your summers are cool, you may want to mulch the ground around the roots with sheets of black plastic. It will soak up the sun's rays and help warm the soil.

Southern gardeners with long growing seasons can simply start their watermelon seeds directly in the garden after the last spring frost, or about the same time that they plant corn and beans. Tuck the seeds an inch deep into hills of light, sandy soil, leaving 4 to 6 feet between each hill. Thin to two plants per hill.

Most watermelon vines run like mad, so they will need lots of room and ample water. When baby melons appear, be merciless and thin them down to 3 or 4 per vine to produce bigger, sweeter fruits.

Keep an eye on the watermelons that form closest to the base of your plants, as they will be the first to mature. Although many people swear by thumping the melons to listen for a dull plunk, you can also tell they're ripe if you gently roll them over and see a white or pale yellow spot forming on the underside.

Melons grow exuberantly, but even if your space is limited, do not despair. Small melons can be trained to grow up a fence or trellis instead of along the ground. Simply guide the plants in the direction you want them to go, until the emerging tendrils catch hold of the support. As the melons mature, tie slings of sturdy cloth or old nylon hose to the support and rest the fruits in them. They will enjoy the time they spend in their airy hammocks, just as anyone would after a long, hot day in the garden.

If you're saving seeds, grow only one variety of watermelon at a time to ensure seed purity.

ZINNIA—*Zinnia*, also known as Youth and Old Age, Medicine Hat, Brazilian Marigold, Garden Zinnia, and Old Maids

It's hard to imagine that anyone got excited when the first zinnias arrived in Britain by way of Paris in 1753. *Zinnia peruviana* had a messy growth habit and lanky branches. Its flowers looked like small marigolds, but their colors were not much to rave about. They were boring—mustard yellow and terracotta—and the blossoms became even more muted and drab as they aged. Even colonial Spaniards who had seen the plants growing wild in their native Mexico thought they were ugly and dubbed them *mal de ojos*, which means "evil eye" or "sickness of the eye."

These first zinnias were closer to weeds or wildflowers than today's big, carnival-colored beauties, but they were all we had until 1796, when another species, *Z. elegans*, was also introduced from Mexico.

These plants were much nicer. Although they also grew about 3 feet tall, they bore slightly larger flowers, with petals that flared out like rays around a center cone. (Those raised centers may have inspired one of the flowers' early nicknames, Medicine Hat.) Some sources describe the blossoms as scarlet or crimson, although William Curtis's eighteenth-century *Botanical Magazine* illustrated *Z. elegans* with dreary lavender blooms.

Still, these new flowers attracted interest. Breeders began experimenting with the plants, and by 1856, the first doubled types were known in French gardens. A few years later, double forms showed up in America, and by 1864, zinnias were available in purple, orange, red, and salmon.

Z. haageana, a dwarf species also native to Mexico, arrived on the gardening scene in 1861. The Philadelphia seed company of Henry A. Dreer listed it for

Granny's Bouquet.
(Courtesy of Renee's Garden)

sale in 1876, describing it as "a double variety of *Zinnia mexicana*; flowers deep orange, margined in bright yellow."

It wasn't long before developers made serious attempts to increase the size of zinnia blossoms. A mammoth strain soon came onto the market with a name nearly as long as the 40-inch plants were tall: *Z. elegans robusta grandiflora plenissima*. Giant Dahlia, introduced by Bodger Seeds in 1920, caught gardeners' fancies with its huge, dahlia-like flowers and went on to win a Royal Horticultural Society award. The big, slightly flattened flowers were available in a range of colors, and gardeners snapped them up. Burpee's released a zinnia that resembled a cactus dahlia in the same year, heightening interest in the plants.

At the other end of the size scale, new dwarf zinnias were popping up. These Lilliputian and Tom Thumb types ranged from 3 to 12 inches tall.

Zinnias take their name from Johann Gottfried Zinn, an eighteenth-century German botanist and physics professor. The professor penned the first scientific description of the unremarkable wildflowers that have evolved into our modern zinnia hybrids. Today, the flowers are available in every color except blue, with single or doubled flower forms that look like buttons, beehives, chrysanthemums, and dahlias.

notes

Z. elegans

BENARY'S GIANT

The Benary seed company, founded in Erfurt, Germany, in 1843, lent its name to these jewel-colored flowers. The rounded blooms are densely petaled, like dahlias, and open up to 6 inches across. Extra-long stems on the 3-foot plants make this variety an excellent choice for cutting gardens. Look for the cheerful blossoms in clear pink, yellow, red, orange, purple, and white. Zinnias often succumb to powdery mildew, but Benary's Giant is exceptionally disease resistant and stands up well to rain or heat.

LILLIPUT

At just 18 inches tall, these zinnias are ideal for window boxes and borders. The pom-pom blooms come in a mix of colors and open to 1½ inches across. Early designers used short to medium-height zinnias as hedges, planting them close together so their dense branches formed natural barriers. They also experimented with zinnias as specimen plants, placing just one in the middle of a lawn; but the plants are much more effective, of course, in colorful masses. Lilliput was sold by Peter Henderson & Company in 1910.

CUT AND COME AGAIN

Cut armfuls of these candy-colored zinnias, and the plants will rebloom all summer. The 2- to 3-inch blooms appear on vigorous plants in 60 to 70 days from sowing. Single, semidouble, and fully doubled forms are available, and the long, sturdy stems produce an abundance of bright yellow, pink, salmon, scarlet, orange, and cream flowers.

GREEN ENVY

Green as a Granny Smith apple, this variety grows 24 to 30 inches tall. For a quirky color scheme, limit this zinnia to a bed of green and white flowers. Other envy green plants include Bells of Ireland; Rudbeckia Green Wizard; Green Ice roses, which open white and mature to pale green; Marguerite, a chartreuse-

colored, ornamental sweet potato vine; green gladiolas; and Lime Green *Nicotiana alata*. Of all the zinnias, Green Envy is the most shade-tolerant.

PERSIAN CARPET—*Z. X HAAGEANA*

Seed sellers of the early 1900s listed these two-foot-tall plants as "Mexican hybrids." The semidouble flowers come in southwestern shades of gold, orange, yellow, chestnut, and deep red. They are also available in cream, chocolate brown, and bicolors. An All-American Selections winner from 1952, this variety produces long-lasting cut flowers. Be careful when handling the tiny seeds.

RED SPIDER—*Z. TENUIFLORA*

Botanists first described these odd flowers in 1801. Each bloom will remind you of a spider, with its "legs" of narrow, bright red petals and a dark central "body." Don't let the resemblance put you off. These compact plants are fun

Green Envy.
(Courtesy of Renee's Garden)

Persian Carpet.
(Courtesy of Renee's Garden)

to grow and bear prolifically from midsummer until frost. The 1-inch flowers appear in 9 to 12 weeks from sowing.

Growing Tips

Zinnias are heat-loving annuals whose seeds can be started indoors or planted directly in the garden. If you are planting indoors, sow the seeds 4 to 6 weeks before the last frost, and watch for them to germinate in 5 to 7 days.

Some growers warn that zinnias dislike transplanting, but others insist that the plants don't mind if you start them in individual pots or seed trays. But be sure to wait until the seedlings have their first true leaves before you harden them off and move them outside. Zinnias are sensitive to the cold and will not thrive until the temperature rises above 50°F.

Zinnias can be spaced from 4 to 24 inches apart in the garden and prefer full sun and fertile, well-drained soil. The variety dictates the spacing, and taller types, as you would guess, need more room. All zinnias will appreciate good air circulation, which helps prevent powdery mildew.

Pinch the tips of your zinnias when they reach 4 to 6 inches high to keep the plants bushy. You won't need to do this for short varieties.

Deadheading or cutting the flowers for bouquets will encourage reblooming from summer until frost. You can also sow more zinnia seeds every 2 to 4 weeks for a continuous supply of flowers.

Plant Zinnias and They Will Come

Zinnias rank among the three most popular flowers in American gardens, and it's not just people who love them. Butterflies can't resist them. Cut and Come Again zinnias have big blooms that make a fine landing pad for swallowtails, while other types lure Painted Ladies, Red Admirals, sulphurs, and hairstreaks. The kind of butterflies you'll lure depends on where you live, so try a mix of colors and flower forms to see what your native species prefer. Then stand back and watch as your nectar-loving visitors float over the garden.

Old 66

Most of our modern zinnia hybrids can be traced to an experimental zinnia bred by Burpee's. This parent plant came from the 66th row of a trial garden, hence the name.

Cut and Come Again, Granny's Bouquet, Green Envy, and Persian Carpet zinnia seeds. (Courtesy of Renee's Garden)

The Garden in Fall

If you are lucky enough to have a shed with a tin roof, like one gardener I know, you've got a built-in warning system for the turn of the weather. All she has to do is listen for the plunk of acorns to know that colder temperatures are on the way. While the squirrels mobilize to stash the nuts, the rest of us have our flowers and vegetables to gather.

It's time now to bring in any tomatoes that are still growing in the garden. If they are hit by a freeze, they will quickly turn to mush. You can even save your green tomatoes by wrapping them in newspapers and storing them at 60° to 65°F. They'll continue to ripen over the next few weeks. Carrots can stay in the ground if you live where the winters are warm. The rest of us will need to pull them up, but at least we'll have plenty of fresh salads and delicious side dishes until the mercury plummets. Eggplants and okra are usually in by now, but you'd better grab any peppers still hanging on your plants. Look around and you may also spot a few heads of cabbage that still need cutting, or some cream-colored turnip roots to dig.

In the flower bed, it's time to snip any blossoms you left to dry. Shake or shred them for the seeds, if you like, or bring the stems inside for everlasting arrangements. Cosmos and cornflowers preserve nicely in silica gel.

Ripened sunflower heads can be stored until you're ready to use them. If you are going to feed the birds this fall, don't bother to strip the heads for their seeds. The birds will do that for you. Just nail a couple of dried heads to a tree, or suspend them from some strong branches, and stand aside. Once the buffet's open, the diners will fly in.

If you sowed annual aster seeds in the spring or carried over any perennial types from last year, your beds and borders will soon be a sea of gold, bronze, pink, garnet, yellow, white, and amethyst. But don't feel bad if your spring seeds didn't do much. There is always next year.

Although autumn is traditionally our harvest season, it's not too late to sow a second crop of many cool-weather vegetables. Count backward from

"They began now to gather in the small harvest they had, and to fit up their houses and dwellings against winter, being all well recovered in health and strength and had all things in good plenty."
  William Bradford,
  History of Plymouth
  Plantation (ca. 1621)

....
....
....
....
....
....
....
....
....
....
....
....
....
....
....
....
....
....
....
....
....
....
....
....
....
....
....
....
....
....

the average date of your first frost, and you may be able to slip in more beets, cabbages, chards, mustards, rutabagas, spinach, and turnips. The nice thing about fall is that the ground is still relatively loose from the spring tilling, so you won't have to work it much.

Heirloom radish seeds can go in now, too. Plant quick-sprouting German Beer radishes by midfall, and you'll have a crop to enjoy into the New Year. Just give their rough skins a scrub under cold running water and serve them with coarse salt for dipping. They'll be good with an icy beer while you're watching the Superbowl—or maybe you'd prefer them with a salad while bird-watching.

For spring flowers, gardeners in zones 6 through 8 can start the seeds of cold-hardy annuals now; try Shirley poppies, violas, snapdragons, and larkspurs. Biennials can also be sown in autumn for blooms the following year.

By the time Halloween rolls around, your jack-o'-lanterns should be waiting on the porch to greet the trick-or-treaters. Pie pumpkins are on the kitchen sideboard, too, waiting for the family cook to bake flaky shells for Thanksgiving. In the somber landscape, they are food for the eyes as well as the table in autumnal shades of burnt orange, ghostly white, ocher, gold, and deep yellow. Leave a length of stem for a handle on the carving types, so you can slip a candle behind their toothy grins.

As you collect the last of the heirloom seeds, remember that biennials will not form seeds until their second year, so gardeners who live in cold climates will need to find new stock. Other plants with tough, bristly pods or tiny, hard-to-handle seeds might also be good candidates for buying or trading.

You have probably noticed that some of your flowers or vegetables grew unusually vigorously or prolifically throughout the season or held up nicely to bugs and disease. These specimens have traits you will want to preserve, natural adaptations to the climate and conditions in your particular garden, so look to them for your seeds.

Of course, hungry animals and birds are watching, too. Help our wild friends and leave some seeds for their use. As the natural food supply diminishes throughout the fall and winter, you may spot goldfinches plucking at your leftover coneflowers or a turtle munching on a shriveled muskmelon. You'll have the satisfaction of knowing you helped them survive, and the birds may even help redistribute some of your seeds. The turtle won't help much with seed dispersal, but that's okay. One small melon isn't a bad trade-off for the pleasure of watching him on a dreary autumn day. And after all, heirloom gardening is as much about giving as about it is about getting.

As you store your seeds, remember that some are exceptionally long-lived, while others, like onion seeds, soon lose their ability to germinate. Label each variety and include the date of collection, a use-by date, and details about the plant's color or height or spread.

When your seeds are tucked away, take some time to clean and repair your tools. Small clippers, trowels, and garden forks can be rinsed, dried, and plunged into a bucket of sand mixed with a little motor oil. The oil will give them a protective coating while the grit scrapes off traces of dirt or rust. Other garden gear might need maintenance, too. Maybe there's a hoe to sharpen or a leaky hose that wants a patch.

Back outside, spend a fair-weather day tilling up any vacant flower beds or garden areas—just make sure the ground is dry. If you can squeeze a handful of soil into a ball and the ball doesn't break when you drop it, wait. It's too wet to dig or till. But if the ground is dry, go ahead. If you wait until next spring to till, heavy rains may delay you. Turning the ground now also exposes many weed seeds to killing temperatures.

Finally, this is the best time to submit a soil sample to your county extension agent. Mention what you plan to grow, so he or she can recommend specific fertilizers and additives to adjust your pH level and improve your soil's texture.

If you have a large garden, you may want to sow a fall cover crop to help control erosion. Cover crops also add valuable nitrogen and organic materials to the soil when you plow them under in spring. Again, your county extension agent can suggest a crop that is suited to your needs and advise you on when and how to plant.

There is much to be thankful for as autumn ends and we shut our gardens down. A harvest of flowers and vegetables and heirloom seeds will keep our spirits green as the first dark days of winter approach.

notes

ASTER—*Aster*, also known as Michaelmas Daisy, Starwort, Frost Flower

Asters cross-pollinate freely, and identifying various species is tricky. Asa Gray, a nineteenth-century American botanist, once complained, "Never was there so rascally a genus; they reduce me to despair."

By fall, the colors of the garden are starting to fade. Drying cornstalks turn paper-bag brown and rustle in the cooling air. Melon vines turn pale and shrivel after their fruits are picked. In the flower bed, the sunflowers droop heavy heads toward the ground. Everything is winding down for the coming winter.

Everything, that is, except autumn-blooming asters. These hardy flowers take center stage in August, September, and October, blanketing the earth with rich golds, burgundies, pinks, lavenders, purples, and cream while many flowers decline.

Asters are old English garden favorites, dating back to at least 1596, when a blue flower known as *Aster amellus* was introduced to Britain. This was probably the blue Italian starwort. The poet Virgil once spotted it growing on the banks of Italy's Mella River and described the flowers around 29 B.C. in *The Georgics*:

> There's a meadow flower also, the Italian starwort,
> That farmers call *amellus*, easy for searchers to find:
> Since it lifts a large cluster of stems from a single root,
> Yellow-centered, but in the wealth of surrounding petals
> There's a purple gleam in the dark blue: often the gods' altars
> Have been decorated with it in woven garlands.

Asters, which look like some chrysanthemums, take their name from the Latin word for "star." The "wort" in their old English appellation, "starwort," originally meant "root," and probably refers to the medicinal uses of the plants. In the 1600s, herbalist John Parkinson recommended making a nasty-sounding poultice from asters. It was helpful, he assured his readers, for treating "the biting of a mad dogge, the greene herb being beaten with old hogs grease, and applyed."

By 1710, the violet-blue perennial aster, *A. novi-belgii*, was known in Britain. It is also called the New York aster or Michaelmas daisy, because it typically blooms around the feast of St. Michael.

The New England aster, *A. novae-angliae*, is our second most common perennial aster. A North American native, its seeds were sent home to Britain by colonial settlers. English gardeners welcomed these fall-blooming beauties into their gardens, admiring the rosy lilac or deep purple blossoms studded with yellow centers.

In the early 1900s, flower hobbyist Ernest Ballard began working to improve asters in his garden in Worcestershire, England. Some of his cultivars are still available, although they can be hard to find. Marie Ballard, which opens luminous, pale blue to lavender-blue double flowers, is especially attractive to bees and butterflies. Blue Climax, introduced around 1906, and Blue Gown, a pre-1945 variety, bear clusters of light blue blossoms with buttery centers and dark green leaves.

If you're a butterfly gardener, plant *A. novae-angliae* to give visiting Monarchs to a valuable source of late-season nectar. They will fuel up at the flowers before starting their yearly migration to Mexico. If you would rather cultivate a cutting garden, you'll appreciate the long stems on these flowers. Try underplanting them with a few shorter, bushy plants to disguise the stems when they start to look shaggy, or cut the stems back hard in late spring so they don't become lanky.

HARRINGTON'S PINK—*A. NOVAE-ANGLIAE*

New England heirloom asters are not easy to find, although Harrington's Pink, a variety that dates to the 1930s, is still offered commercially. Its daisy-like blooms range in color from salmon pink to clear pink and grow atop 48- to 60-inch plants. The flowers have a nice mounding habit, providing waves of color until frost. You can stake them or let them lean against other plants.

CHINESE ASTER—*CALLISTEPHUS CHINENSIS*

This one is not a true aster, but a lovely impostor. Discovered in the 1730s by a Jesuit missionary to Peking, Chinese or China asters were popular a century ago as long-lasting cut flowers. The original Chinese aster was a single blossom with purple petals arranged in rays around a yellow center. Modern

Harrington's Pink. (Courtesy of David Cavagnaro)

hybridizers have since developed fuller, frillier flowers in jewel-like tones including garnet red, amethyst, pale ruby, pink, blue, and white.

In 1865, nurseryman James Vick raved about many of the new varieties that had come onto the market: "They are now as double as the chrysanthemum or the dahlias, and almost as large and showy as the peony, and constitute the principal adornment of our gardens during the autumn months."

Unfortunately, a disease called yellow aster nearly wiped out *Callistephus chinensis*. Newer, disease-resistant types have been developed, but avoid problems by planting your asters in a different location each year.

Growing Tips

Asters are usually sold as rooted cuttings, and for good reason: they are difficult to grow from their slow-sprouting seeds, which can take from 21 to 45 days to germinate. At least one commercial seed seller cautions his customers not to expect more than a 40 percent success rate.

But if you're game for the challenge, you can plant your aster seeds directly into the garden after the last frost. Remember that these flowers attract bees, so choose a spot away from doors or decks or anyplace that the visiting insects might become a nuisance. Remember, too, that the flowers can grow quite tall, so try using them at the back of beds and borders.

If you prefer, the seeds can be started indoors 6 to 8 weeks before the last frost. Cover them with $\frac{1}{8}$ to $\frac{1}{4}$ inch of fine soil. When the seedlings emerge and produce two or three true leaves, thin them to 12 to 15 inches apart and harden them off before transplanting them. The seeds can also be sown directly in the garden after the last spring frost. Asters can tolerate full sun to light shade.

New York and New England asters are perennials. While they will grow in poor soil and dry conditions, you'll need to keep them well watered for the lushest, showiest blooms. Water the ground underneath them, rather than sprinkling the leaves from above, to help prevent powdery mildew.

Pinch back the flowering tips of your plants when they are 3 to 5 inches long, to encourage them to stay short and bushy. If necessary, stake the plants as soon as they begin to look leggy. Stop pinching by midsummer or you won't have many flowers.

Chinese asters can be grown from seed in the same way as other asters,

notes

although they are annuals rather than perennials. If you plan to cut the blossoms for bouquets, sow more seeds every 2 to 4 weeks.

Remember, to help control or eliminate disease in the garden, don't plant asters in the same spot two years in a row.

For the nicest arrangements, wait until your asters are completely open before you bring them inside. Unlike some flowers, these blossoms don't continue to open if you snip too soon.

Seed savers, take note: aster seeds are slender bits of fluff that soar on the wind to find new homes. Because they're fine and often light in color, they are among the most difficult flower seeds to handle. If you want to collect the seeds, let the blossoms dry and turn almost completely brown before cutting them from the plants. Then hold the blossoms over a sheet of white paper or a paper bag and shred them. The seeds are held together in a tight cluster, but they will separate easily. Don't worry about cleaning away the chaff. It's hard to remove all the tiny plant parts, and it won't hurt if you simply sow the seeds and chaff together the following year.

CHARD—*Beta vulgaris* var. *cicla*, also known as Swiss Chard

"The 'Five Color Silverbeet' was offered by Thompson and Morgan from 1970 to 1989, but we don't know much about its history beyond that. I cook it in quiches, and grow it for decoration, too."
John Coykendall, heirloom gardener

Chard, as some wit once remarked, is like a beet "without the beet." Although they are related to those vegetables, chards are grown only for their thick leaves and celery-like stems, not their inedible roots. If you've never tried chard, you may have heard that it has a pungent, slightly salty flavor. That's true, and some people don't like the raw foliage, which can taste bitter, like beet greens. But others enjoy tossing the nutritious leaves into salads for color and crunch, or sautéing, boiling, or steaming them to serve like cooked spinach.

Despite its common name, Swiss chard, this vegetable is believed to be a native of the Mediterranean area, and it has probably been cultivated for at least 2,000 years. Its only real link to Switzerland may come from the nineteenth-century Swiss botanist who named it in honor of his homeland.

Part of the difficulty in tracing the exact origin of chard comes from its various nicknames. It is thought that the word "chard" comes from the French

Neon-colored chard brightens the table. (Courtesy of David Cavagnaro)

carde, meaning "cardoon," a plant with edible leafstalks and roots, or the French and Latin words for "thistle," which once referred to plants with chard-like ribs. The leafy vegetables have also been known as white beet, perpetual spinach, Roman kale, sea kale beet, leaf beet, Chilean beet, and silverbeet.

In ancient Greece, chard was used for medicinal purposes. Juice from the plants is also an old-time folk remedy for congestion, while the leaves are said to help soothe an upset stomach.

ARGENTATA, also known as Bionda á Costa

Gourmet chefs like to use this Italian heirloom, which matures in 60 days from planting, as a substitute for spinach. The large, deep green leaves and silvery midribs have a sweet, mild taste. Try steaming them with a squeeze of fresh lemon. You may see this variety packaged commercially as Italian Silver Rib.

MAGENTA SUNSET

This modern chard is both tender-tasting and heat tolerant. The medium green leaves start out smooth and become more crumpled-looking as they age, while the stalks turn an attractive hot pink or purple-red. The plants mature 50 to 60 days from sowing, but you can begin harvesting the baby leaves after about 28 days.

RHUBARB

Crimson veins highlight the purplish-green leaves of this old favorite. The stalks are a dark ruby, and some gardeners swear the color becomes more intense after a light frost. Rhubarb is an 1857 introduction that is equally nice for kitchen gardens or ornamental beds. Try combining the crinkly leaves with a handful of wildflowers for a unique bouquet. The plants are resistant to summer heat and mature at 2 feet tall.

LUCULLUS

This vigorous variety can tolerate extremes of hot and cold weather and may overwinter in your garden if it is heavily mulched. The stalks, which resemble pale celery, and the juicy leaves are ready to pick about 52 days from sowing. Lucullus yields nicely into the fall but needs adequate water to discourage bolting. It is named for Lucius Lucullus, a Roman general who reputedly threw extravagant banquets for his friends.

RAINBOW

Victorian-era gardeners admired the pink, red, violet, orange, white, and gold colors of Rainbow chard in their ornamental beds and borders, but this New Zealand heirloom has a mild flavor that is also fine for table use. The multicolored stalks and green or bronze leaves grow to 2 feet tall and are ready in

55 days. Jazz up plain green salads with the leaves or the chopped ribs, which have a pleasant, crunchy texture. Unlike most chard leaves, which turn dull or gray when cooked, Rainbow often holds its electric colors even if it is briefly microwaved. Seed catalogs sometimes list this All-American Selections winner as Bright Lights or Five Color Silverbeet.

FORDHOOK GIANT

Introduced by Burpee's in 1934, this sturdy chard has thick, snowy white stalks with a delicate taste and crisp bite. The heavily crinkled leaves are blue-green to dark green and grow to 10 inches across. The plants mature around 2 feet high and stay productive even in the heat. Give it 60 days to maturity.

Bright Lights.
(Courtesy of Renee's Garden)

....
....
....
....
....
....
....
....
....
....
....
....
....
....
....
....
....
....
....
....
....
....
....
....
....
....
....

RUBY RED

This crimson beauty bears juicy, dark green leaves with ruby-colored veins and stalks. The plants grow 2 feet tall about 55 days after sowing. Ruby Red tends to bolt, but try it for its leaves, which are tender, juicy, and sweet. It can take hot weather and light shade.

Growing Tips

Chards like well-drained, rich soil and full sun. They will tolerate some shade in hot climates, although they may not grow as prolifically. Although chards, like beets, can withstand mild to moderate frosts, they are generally grown as annuals.

Most people don't start this fast-growing vegetable indoors, and it isn't necessary. Simply plant the seeds directly in the garden 2 to 3 weeks before the last spring frost. Gardeners in mild climates can plant outside in the fall for a winter or early spring crop. Northerners can sow from early spring into summer for a fall harvest.

Chard seeds come in clusters that produce more than one plant, so separate the seeds as much as possible. Then plant the seeds ½ inch deep and 1 inch apart, in rows spaced 18 inches apart. When the seedlings are up, thin them to every 10 or 12 inches, but don't worry if your spacing isn't exact. Chards can handle some crowding. Four to 6 rows will usually produce plenty for an average family.

Few pests or diseases are a serious problem for these plants. They are a great substitute for spinach because many chards resist bolting in hot weather and stay productive until late in the growing season.

You can pick chard leaves at any size, but most gardeners say that cold weather improves their crunchy texture and sweet flavor. When you harvest them, remove the outer leaves first (discard them if the bugs have riddled them with holes). Don't forget to cut the leafstalks, too, which can be prepared like asparagus or eaten along with the leaves. One note: Do not cook chard in aluminum pots. This vegetable contains oxalates, naturally occurring substances that can interact with the metal and discolor your pans.

If a hard freeze threatens, you can dig up your plants, leaving some soil around the roots, and store them for a short time in a cool, moist location while you continue to pick the leaves.

This rainbow chard, from old New Zealand stock, has a mild flavor. (Courtesy of Renee's Garden)

Chards are biennials, so if you want to save seeds, the plants will have to survive into their second year. If you live in a mild climate, you may be able to carry the plants over the winter by mulching around them. After they flower the following year, pick the brown seed pods and allow them to dry. Beets and chards will cross, however, so you will probably want to obtain fresh stock rather than trying to isolate your plants and save your own seeds. Chard seeds should remain viable for up to 3 years if stored properly.

Eat Your Chard

Chard is packed with vitamins A and C as well as calcium, magnesium, potassium, fiber, and iron. Best of all, it's economical to buy and often available year-round. If you are new to chards, try using them to flavor soups or chowders. The big leaves also make nice appetizers when wrapped around creamy cheeses and other fillings.

KALE AND COLLARDS—*Brassica oleracea* var. *acephala*

Looseleaf collards and kale, which are actually nonheading wild cabbages, have never been widely popular. That is not surprising, because their strong flavor takes some getting used to, and their leaves become tough if they are not harvested at the right time. On top of that, they're downright smelly while they are cooking.

In fact, early people might never have eaten these greens, except that they were among the few vegetables that grew in cold weather. It's too bad that more cooks don't serve them, because kale and collards contain calcium, potassium, and vitamins A and C, and they are delicious when prepared properly.

There is almost no difference, botanically speaking, between kale, collards, and cabbages, and some seed companies even list collards as a kind of kale. Both collards and kale probably descended from plants that grew in prehistoric Asia Minor.

The taste of heirloom collards improves with frost. (Courtesy of David Cavagnaro)

Collards, which have not changed much in the last 2,000 years, were introduced to the colonies by British settlers. African slaves who worked on southern plantations learned how to make a meal from the greens by seasoning them with whatever meat scraps were available. Today southerners still cook up a "mess of greens," simmering their collards with a ham hock or piece of salt pork.

Kale

BLACK TUSCAN KALE, also known as Dinosaur and Black Tuscan Palm Tree Kale

This Italian heirloom, listed by Seed Savers Exchange as Lacinato, dates to the eighteenth century. Its long, strappy leaves are dark blue or grayish-black, with primitive-looking "warts" that seem to resemble a dinosaur's hide. As the leaves grow, they curl over the plant's central stem like ostrich plumes. Expect this 3-foot-tall variety to mature in 50 days. It is very cold hardy.

"This kale illustrates the form of the most ancient of kales. I find it has a mild, peppery flavor that is very good with meat dishes."
Wesley Greene,
Garden Historian,
Colonial Williamsburg
Foundation

Black Tuscan kale. (Courtesy of David Cavagnaro)

RED RUSSIAN

Russian traders brought this rare kale to Canada in the late 1800s. Nineteenth-century gardening authority Fearing Burr referred to it as Buda Kale, while French botanist Vilmorin-Andrieux called it Ragged Jack. Its frilly young leaves are gray-green but turn reddish-purple as the weather gets colder. They are tender and mild enough to eat raw in salads; but they tend to wilt fast, so use or refrigerate the leaves soon after harvesting. The cold-hardy plants grow 2 to 3 feet tall in 50 to 55 days from sowing.

Collards

GEORGIA

Southern gardeners have favored this blue-green variety, named for the Peach State, since before 1880. The plants reach up to 3 feet tall, with tender, cabbagelike leaves that sweeten up after a light frost. Tolerant of heat or cold, this variety holds up well during droughts and performs in sandy or poor soils. The juicy leaves have a mild flavor and are ready for harvest 70 to 80 days after sowing.

GEORGIA SOUTHERN, also known as Creole or the True Collard

Atlantic Coast gardeners with sandy soil often choose this sweet, tender collard, which can thrive where other members of the cabbage family struggle. The 3-foot plants produce loose, open heads of bluish-green leaves 75 days after planting. This is a traditional southern favorite that reseeds well; try it for canning or freezing.

VATES

Mid-Atlantic and southern gardeners favor this nonheading type, which is slow to bolt. The big, blue-green leaves are frost resistant and have a mild cabbagelike flavor when boiled. Give this one 75 days to harvest.

WALKING STICK—*BRASSICA OLERACEA* VAR. *LONGATA*

English Channel Island gardeners have been cultivating this odd ornamental, which can grow to 8 or more feet, for more than 200 years. Sometimes listed as a cabbage, Walking Stick is actually a type of kale that forms leafy heads.

Vates collards. (Courtesy of David Cavagnaro)

It also appeared in late 1880s seed lists under such names as Tree Cabbage, Jersey Kale, and Chou Cavalier.

You can make your own walking canes by cutting the plant's long stems and allowing them to dry at the end of the growing season. One source pegs the record length for a stem at 18 feet—quite a walking stick!

Planting Flowering Kales and Cabbages

Savvy plant breeders have realized that some of us will never acquire a taste for kale or cabbage. Instead of trying to convince us to grow these vegetables for the table, they have turned their attention to developing beautiful ornamental types for our flower beds.

Flowering kales or cabbages, ornamental forms of *Brassica oleracea*, truly

··

··

··

··

··

··

··

··

··

··

··

··

··

··

··

··

··

··

··

··

··

··

··

··

··

are spectacular in the fall and winter. Over the course of a few chilly weeks, the plants lose the chlorophyll that makes them appear green and reveal hidden colors like pink, lavender, red, and purple.

For a showy autumn-through-spring display, plant flowering kales in drifts, or use them alongside cold-tolerant pansies, violas, and snapdragons. Their colors become richer as the temperature drops.

Growing Tips

Kale is usually grown as a fall crop. Most gardeners can start the seeds outdoors in early summer, in rich, well-drained soil and full sun. In the South, kale can take some shade during the hottest part of the summer. Gardeners who live where the winters are mild can plant kale in late summer for a winter harvest.

Sow your kale seeds directly in the garden, covering them ¼ to ½ inch deep in rows spaced 18 inches apart. Thin the seedlings to every 8 to 14 inches, and keep the plants watered during dry spells.

Cold temperatures sweeten the taste of kale, so wait until the first light frost to pick the outer leaves as needed. Although kale is a biennial, it may not survive the winter in areas where the temperature drops below about 20°F.

Collards can be grown as a spring or fall crop. They also like well-drained soil in full sun, but they may live longer in the South if given partial shade during the summer. For an early start, plant the seeds indoors 4 to 6 weeks before the last frost. Harden off the seedlings and transplant them into the garden, spacing them 8 inches apart, after the last heavy frost.

If you prefer, sow collards directly outdoors after the last heavy frost, covering them ¼ to ½ inch deep in rows spaced 30 inches apart. Thin the seedlings to every 8 inches.

For a fall harvest, plant collards in midsummer. The plants can survive until the temperature drops well below freezing, so some gardeners can grow these biennials year-round.

Collards need weekly watering. To harvest, cut the entire plant when it reaches 8 inches tall, or let it continue to grow and pick the leaves from the bottom as needed. Like kale, collards taste sweeter after they are exposed to frost.

Saving kale and collard seeds takes some effort, because these plants don't set seeds until their second year. They also cross-pollinate with one another and with cabbage, so you will need to isolate them to keep the seeds pure.

If you live where the plants would perish in the winter, dig them up before a killing freeze and store them in an area that stays between 32° and 45°F. The following spring, move the plants back outside after the last heavy frost, and watch for the seeds to develop. Avoid growing them in the same spot for 2 consecutive years, to help prevent disease. Kale and collard seeds can remain viable for up to 5 years.

PANSY—*Viola*, also known as Ladies' Delight, Three-Faces-under-a-Hood, Love-in-Idleness, Cuddle-Me, and Jack-Jump-Up-and-Kiss-Me

Of all the flowers, pansies seem especially old-fashioned. Maybe it's because they were commonly used in Victorian illustrations or gathered into tussie-mussies, small bouquets carried by ladies of that era. They are also at home in traditional settings, spilling out of cottage window boxes and lifting their cheerful faces around porch steps.

But pansies have not been around as long as you might think—at least not the huge, brightly colored blossoms sold at modern nurseries. Prior to the 1800s, gardeners were cultivating much smaller ancestors of modern-day pansies, including Johnny-Jump-Ups (*Viola tricolor*), yellow mountain violets (*V. lutea*), and horned violets (*V. cornuta*).

With the onset of the Victorian period, these modest flowers began to change. English gardeners learned to use steel, which had dropped in price as a building material, to construct private greenhouses and conservatories. Suddenly anyone could grow pansies, which required cool temperatures and semishaded conditions, and the demand for the little plants increased.

By 1835, breeders had created more than 400 different varieties of pansies. Still, the standards for the ideal pansy became quite strict, and the only exhibitors who took ribbons home were those who showed pansies with nice, round blooms.

Fancier pansies showed up after growers launched a search for a wider range of colors. Flower patterns began to change, too, so that what once looked

"The Pansy is the flower for all. Cheap, hardy, beautiful, bright, cheerful, etc."
Harriet Keeler,
Our Garden Flowers
(1910)

"These lowly plants are amongst the most floriferous, most showy, most pleasantly fragrant flowers in the outdoor garden."
William Cuthbertson,
Pansies, Violas and
Violets *(1910)*

simply like a blotch in the middle of each bloom evolved into bigger, facelike markings. Breeders continued to tinker with pansies until around 1870, when the charming plants were at last recognizable as the big, colorful pansies, *V.* x *wittrockiana*, that we grow today.

Pansies and violets come from the *Violaceae* family, and the resemblance is easy to see. In fact, the wild form, also known as Heartsease or *V. tricolor*, is often simply called a "pansy." The term comes from the French word *pensée*, meaning "thought" or "remembrance." In the Middle Ages, the blue, purple, and yellow or white faces of *Viola tricolor* were believed to represent the Christian trinity.

Viola *x* wittrockiana

VICTORIAN POSY

Today's pansies are shorter than these leggy posies, which reach 4 to 6 inches tall. Still, their delicately marked faces and fancy petals, which are as ruffled as the hem of a lady's ball gown, make them a pleasure to grow. Just use this variety a little further back in the border than usual, so it won't shade shorter plants. Look for velvety shades of dark gold, royal purple, and mahogany, as well as ivory and lavender.

BOWLES BLACK

This small, black beauty was introduced by the famous nineteenth-century gardener E. A. Bowles. Each satiny blossom has a sunny yellow eye and bears a slight fragrance. The plants, which grow 3 to 6 inches high, produce flowers for a long time and reseed nicely. Watch them closely when the temperature rises, and you may notice that the petals undergo a color change, taking on a purple hue.

CHALON

Gardeners did not have really big pansies until Chalon debuted in 1870. Smaller violas and Johnny-Jump-Ups soon took a backseat to these showy blooms with a wonderful fragrance. The flowers are available in canary yellow, bright blue and white, or violet-red with chocolate brown or black faces. The petals are so heavily ruffled as to look doubled, and some growers insist that the scallops get deeper and more prominent as the weather gets colder. A newer form, Chalon Improved, remains true to the frilly original but adds a thin, white band along the edge of some petals. Chalon Supreme is another entry in the series. Its deeply ruffled petals come in dark, rich colors.

Viola

BULLION

This golden yellow viola bears charming black "whiskers" on its face. Some early gardeners described the flowers as more lemon colored than gold and insisted they had a mild, sweet scent. Developed in 1867 by Englishman James Grieve, Bullion was once the oldest viola under cultivation, but it has become rare and very hard to find.

JACKANAPES

A flower named for a monkey? Jackanapes is believed to have been bred in the early 1900s by garden designer Gertrude Jekyll and named in honor of her pet monkey. Its markings look more like dashes or chocolate-colored cat's whiskers than the familiar face seen on modern pansies. The medium-sized flowers are two-toned, with upper petals ranging from crimson to maroon or brown and lower petals that are bright or deep yellow. The plants are vigorous and dependable. Britain's Royal Horticultural Society has honored it with an Award of Garden Merit. The society recommends starting it from cuttings rather than seeds, which do not grow true to type.

Growing Tips

If pansies and violas seem rather delicate—well, it's because they are, at least when summer rolls around. The plants are not hard to grow; in fact, they are generally carefree. They are, however, very sensitive to heat.

Because flowering often shuts down in midsummer, southern gardeners

Pansies in antique shades make romantic nosegays.
(Courtesy of Renee's Garden)

should start their pansy seeds outdoors in early fall. Put them in well-worked, well-raked soil in a sunny to partly shady location and cover them lightly. Water gently to settle the seeds, so they don't float away. After the seedlings emerge, in about 6 to 10 days, thin them to every 4 inches. Space large varieties 6 to 12 inches apart. Blooms appear in 12 to 14 weeks from sowing and continue throughout the winter and following spring.

Pansies planted in the fall develop better root systems and usually produce flowers that are twice as big as those set out in spring. But if you do wait until spring to sow, plant before the temperature reaches 70° to 75°F or your pansy seeds may not germinate.

In the North, pansy seeds can be started in a cool room of the house or directly outdoors. After the seedlings emerge, give them plenty of bright, cool light to make them strong and sturdy. Harden them off and transplant them into a sunny garden spot after they put out two or three true leaves. Pansies have fine, densely matted roots, so handle them carefully, gently separating the root balls.

Because they are heavy feeders, be prepared to fertilize your pansies regularly with a specialty pansy food. Water as needed, but don't let the plants stand in puddles, which can lead to rotting.

When the flowers fade, deadhead them to keep the show going. During the long, hot days of summer, pansies often become weak and floppy. Rejuvenate them by cutting them back, and you may be rewarded with a flush of more flowers. Eventually the heat will overtake them, though, so while pansies are cold-hardy biennials, it's best to treat them as annuals.

One of the nicest things about pansies is their ability to survive in cold weather. The plants may wilt and turn grayish-green, but they generally recover unless the temperature stays below 15°F. If the temperature remains low for some time, or if strong winds threaten to dehydrate their foliage, you will need to protect your pansies with a layer of insulating mulch.

Pansies and violas can cross-pollinate, so keep each variety isolated to ensure seed purity. You can either collect the seeds and store them for later use or allow them to ripen on the plants and drop to the ground for self-sowing. Even in good conditions, only about 60 percent of saved pansy seeds will germinate, so save some extra seeds in case you have to replant. Or just sow more heavily than you normally would on your first pass through the garden.

PUMPKIN—*Cucurbita*

If you think you can't grow pumpkins because you don't have enough room, you are probably right. Pumpkins, like watermelons, are exuberant creatures, and their sprawling vines can easily overtake a garden. They also need lots of water and fertilizer. But don't be put off by their demands. These thick-skinned beauties often hide a sweet, moist flesh that is delicious in breads, soups, and pies sprinkled with nutmeg and cinnamon.

Stout orange pumpkins have traditionally been used as decorations. We have been turning them into glowing jack-o'-lanterns since the early 1800s, when Irish immigrants accustomed to warding off evil spirits with candlelit turnips, gourds, rutabagas, beets, and potatoes discovered that New World pumpkins were easier to carve and more widely available.

Botanically speaking, pumpkins, gourds, and squash are all related, as they belong to the family of vining crops called *Cucurbitaceae*. Whether we call one plant a pumpkin and another a squash really depends more on custom than on scientific classification. For most of us, if it's round and orange, it's a pumpkin.

The monsters of the pumpkin patch fall into the *C. maxima* group. If you want to grow a giant, choose King Mammoth Gold, an old Kentucky favorite that bulks up to 50 pounds, or Big Max, an orange-skinned behemoth that earns ribbons at county fairs.

The name "pumpkin" comes from the Greek *pepon*, for large melon. Apparently French and English gardeners put their distinctive spins on the word until it evolved into *pumpion*, today's "pumpkin."

Pumpkins have a long history in the New World. Arriving colonists found Native Americans roasting them for food or drying strips of pumpkins to weave into mats. Historians believe that by the first Thanksgiving feast, in 1621, the settlers had learned to prepare tasty pies by filling hollowed pumpkins with honey, milk, and spices and baking them in hot ashes. And just in case you're wondering, botanists classify pumpkins as fruits, not vegetables.

C. pepo

CASPER

White as a ghost, these 10- to 20-pound pumpkins have a bluish cast, so they're great for spooky decorations. The sunset orange flesh is also good in pies and can be cooked and eaten like winter squash. Casper is ready in about 100 days from planting. If you're not handy with a knife, try painting a Halloween face on the light skin.

AMISH PIE

Hailing from a farm in the Maryland mountains, this variety is fine for processing, freezing, or making into pies. The moist flesh is unusually thick, reaching almost 5 inches deep. Make room in your pantry if you are processing these; each fruit can weigh 60 to 80 pounds.

CONNECTICUT FIELD, also known as Big Tom

Prior to the 1700s, New England settlers saw their Native American neighbors cultivating orange Big Toms in their cornfields. These can fatten up to 25 pounds apiece and grow as round as the harvest moon. There is some debate over the tastiness of these fruits. Some growers will only feed them to their livestock, while others insist they are fine for eating fresh or canning. Try some and decide for yourself.

SMALL SUGAR

From the 1800s, this is a smaller version of the Connecticut Field pumpkin, but it lacks the stringy fibers. The fruits grow to 5 to 8 pounds, with dark orange skins and meaty flesh. Burpee's, offering the Small Sugar in 1887, boasted that it was "a very prolific and handsome little pumpkin; usual size about 10 inches in diameter, skin is a deep orange-yellow. It is very fine-grained, sweet and sugary, and keeps well." Small Sugar matures in 80 to 110 days.

ROUGE VIF D'ETAMPES—*C. MAXIMA*

This is one of the so-called true or French pumpkins. Although it's rather flat in shape, it is a classic beauty with brilliant orange skin. Burpee's first offered this heirloom variety to American gardeners in 1883. Also known as Cinderella or Cinderella's Carriage, it reportedly inspired the artist who drew the fairy-tale coach. *Rouge vif* translates as "vivid red," although the color of the fruits can range from neon orange to burnt orange.

Some cooks have dubbed this variety the gourmet's pumpkin, citing its custardlike flesh and sweet, mild flavor. Gardening author Amy Goldman, who cultivates many wonderful heirloom squashes and pumpkins, disagrees, calling it "insipid and watery," not worthy of gracing a humble pie crust. One note for seed savers: this pumpkin does not produce many seeds, so plan accordingly.

Eat Your Pumpkin Seeds

Roasted pumpkin seeds make a great snack, and they're nutritious, too, packed with potassium and vitamin A. English botanist John Gerard, a barber-surgeon by profession, suggested eating them if you were "troubled with the stone of the kidnies."

Growing Tips

Pumpkin seeds will not germinate in cold soil, so wait until the ground is thoroughly warm before sowing. For a Halloween harvest in the North, plant

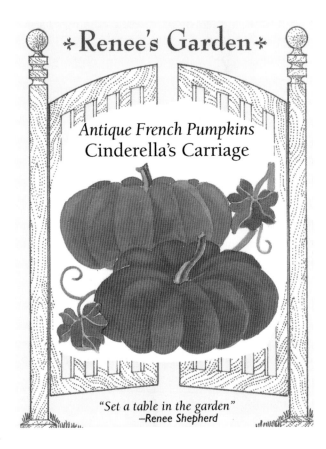

This old French variety is still a European favorite. (Courtesy of Renee's Garden)

Renee's Garden

Antique French Pumpkins
Cinderella's Carriage

"Set a table in the garden"
—Renee Shepherd

pumpkins in the late spring. If you live in the South, you can wait until mid- to late July to tuck your seeds into the earth. Timing is important, because you do not want the pumpkins to mature, and possibly soften and rot, before you can carve them for the holiday or process them for the kitchen.

Start your seeds indoors 3 to 4 weeks before the last frost, or sow them outdoors in hills, tucking 4 to 5 seeds per hill. Leave 5 to 10 feet in all directions, and thin to 3 seedlings per hill.

Miniature varieties give you a little break on the spacing. Sow 2 or 3 seeds every 2 feet in a row, and leave 6 to 8 feet between rows. Thin to the strongest plant every 2 feet.

Pumpkins are heavy feeders, so grow them in soil enriched with manure and compost. The plants can take short dry spells, but water them regularly if rainfall is sparse. Hoe lightly to prevent weeds; you don't want to injure the roots.

Casper and Cinderella's Carriage (courtesy of Renee's Garden) pumpkin seeds.

If bugs are a problem, wait until late afternoon or early evening to apply insecticides. The pumpkin's blossoms will close at the end of the day, so there is less chance then of killing any bees that do the important work of pollinating.

Most varieties will signal their readiness for harvest when they turn completely orange. You will also know they are ready to pick when the rinds become hard and the vines die back. That is usually in late September or early October for most of the country, or at least before the first heavy frost arrives. Leave a few inches of stem when you cut your pumpkins from the vines, so you'll have a handle for making jack-o'-lanterns.

Store the fruits in a dry location where the temperature is between 50° and 55°F. If the pumpkins are not completely mature or if they have been damaged, they will not keep, so check them often and handle them gently.

Varieties within the same botanical species can cross-pollinate, so if you are also growing plants like zucchinis and acorn squash, they can cross with your pumpkins. This means that if you are saving seeds for the coming year, you may get some odd results. It won't necessarily help to grow just one variety of pumpkin, either, unless you keep bees away from your plants and hand-pollinate. It can be fun to save seeds anyway and see what you get, or you can start with fresh seeds next year.

TURNIP—*Brassica rapa* var. *rapifera*

Maybe it was culinary payback. Native Americans had introduced the colonists to indigenous crops like beans, squash, and pumpkins, but it fell to the early settlers to introduce Native Americans to turnips.

These earthy, nutritious vegetables probably originated in Europe or western Asia some 4,000 years ago. Early Romans preferred their taste to carrots, and while it may be hard to swallow, legend says that a Roman general once turned down an offer from his enemies to trade his meal of roasted turnips for a bag of pure gold.

If that story is true, humble turnips, along with their close relatives, rutabagas, lost their high standing somewhere over the years. They are not very popular in the United States anymore except among southerners, who still enjoy an occasional side dish of cooked turnip greens. Gardeners have traditionally fed the plants to livestock, although people have regularly consumed them, too, especially during times of economic scarcity. That may be why some gardeners still call them "poor man's food."

Sorting out turnips from other members of the *Brassica* family can be tricky. Turnips often have green leaves and whitish roots with rosy shoulders (although there are golden and reddish varieties). Rutabagas, which arose during the Middle Ages as a cross between turnips and cabbages, generally have blue-green leaves and larger roots.

GOLDEN BALL, also known as Orange Jelly

American farmers tested the seeds of this variety in 1855, at the request of a London seed company. Of a total of 26 turnips grown in field trials, only Golden Ball performed so well that it is still widely offered. Its roots are more golden yellow than orange, ready for picking in 45 to 65 days. They are sweet, tender, and mild. While the roots cook nicely for mashing, they also store very well. Pull them when they are 3 to 4 inches in diameter.

SEVEN TOP, also known as Foliage Turnip and Southern Prize

Cut the leafy tops of this 1845 heirloom when they are young and supple, and they will regrow several times. But leave the small roots alone, as they are tough and woody at any size. Seven Top is grown strictly for its greens, but it's a favorite in the South, where the 16- to 22-inch leaves are delicious in winter or early spring. Give the plants 45 to 50 days to mature. Southern Exposure Seed Exchange recommends sowing this variety to attract harlequin bugs and then turning chickens loose in your garden to gobble up the destructive pests.

WALDOBORO GREENNECK

Are these plants really turnips? Some gardeners insist that the big roots, topped by bluish-gray leaves, are more akin to rutabagas. This 1780s variety takes its name from a town in Maine, although France may be its true homeland. Waldoboro seeds supposedly washed ashore from the nineteenth-century shipwreck of the *Cambridge*. The plants form fine-textured roots that are white with green shoulders. They are ready in about 50 days from sowing. If you're looking for seeds, fellow heirloom gardeners may be your best bet for this turnip, since it is rare and hard to find.

Golden Ball. (Courtesy of David Cavagnaro)

GILFEATHER

John Gilfeather, of Wardsboro, Vermont, is credited with developing this sweet turnip in the late 1800s. The egg-shaped roots are creamy white with a green blush and mature in 70 to 85 days from planting. Cook them before they become large and woody, and you'll find they have a sweet flavor. The spineless green tops are also tasty when harvested early.

PURPLE TOP WHITE GLOBE, also known as Veitch's Red Globe

Still the standard for the marketplace as well as the backyard, this turnip has been cultivated since at least 1880. The round, white roots are bicolored, with bright purple or purplish red tops and creamy white bottoms. For best

Purple Top White Globe. (Courtesy of Seed Savers Exchange)

results, use the roots when they're three to four inches in diameter, and the leaves when they're 14 to 22 inches long. Try the sweet roots fresh or mashed; they're ready for harvest in 45 to 65 days from sowing.

SNOWBALL

These round, white roots really do look a bit like snowballs when they mature 50 days after planting. Pull them when they are 3 to 4 inches across, while the flesh has a juicy, crisp bite. If the roots are left to grow much larger, they will become woody and pithy. Snowball is thought to have been introduced prior to 1865.

WHITE EGG

Gardeners have been sowing this early turnip, which matures in about 48 days, since the 1880s. The egg-shaped roots have a smooth, white skin and a tender, sweet flesh. You will see some green tinting on the roots as they develop partially aboveground. This is a bunching variety developed in the United States.

Rutabagas—Brassica napus *var.* napobrassica, also known as Swede or Swedish Turnips

MACOMBER, also known as Sweet German

Garden author Fearing Burr recommended this long-keeping rutabaga in 1863 for its fine flavor. There is hardly any neck on the round, white roots, which are topped with pinkish-red crowns. At maturity, the roots reach 5 to 6 inches in diameter and weigh up to 5 pounds. For a sweet side dish, peel them and roast them in a little olive oil. This variety needs 80 to 90 days from sowing.

LAURENTIAN, also known as Improved Purple Top

These 4- to 6-inch, globe-shaped roots become pale or creamy yellow below ground and dark purple above. Don't worry if they turn orange when cooked; they will still have a good flavor. From Canada, this variety predates 1920 and keeps very well. The roots are ready in 90 to 120 days and taste delicious when baked or fried.

AMERICAN PURPLE TOP

Developed from the Purple Top Yellow strain prior to 1920, this rutabaga is ready in 90 days. The round, yellow roots have short necks and purple shoulders and grow to 6 inches in diameter. When peeled, they reveal a fine-grained, light yellow flesh with a robust taste. This is the standard market rutabaga in the United States, good for table use or processing.

Growing Tips

Cool-season turnips are easy to grow. Although you can sow the seeds in spring, late summer, or fall, crops that are harvested in autumn usually taste better and keep longer.

Plant turnip seeds ½ inch deep in rows spaced 1 to 2 feet apart. Keep them well watered until the seedlings appear. Thin the seedlings to every 6 inches apart if you are growing the plants for their roots, or leave them closer together if you're only interested in the tops.

Allow your turnip leaves to become about 4 inches long before you pick them. The plants should grow another set, as long as you don't remove all of the leaves at once. For an extended harvest, plant additional seeds at 10-day intervals.

Rutabagas are also cool-weather crops, but they need more time to mature than turnips. Unless your winters are mild, you probably won't have time to sow them more than once. For best results, aim for a fall harvest. Otherwise, cultivate them as you would turnips.

Rutabagas and turnips should be pulled or cut when the roots reach the recommended size for the particular variety you choose to grow. Frost sweetens their flavor, turning their starch into sugar, but be sure to use or store them before a killing freeze.

If you are saving seeds, remember that turnips and rutabagas will cross-pollinate. Because the plants are also biennials and don't set seeds until their second season, obtaining fresh seeds every year is easier than trying to collect your own.

Golden Ball and White Egg turnip seeds.

The Garden in Winter

Change sweeps over the garden along with the wintery winds. There is very little to do outside once the ground is too wet or too frozen to work. Many of the seeds lying under a tangle of dead vegetation and fallen leaves have gone to sleep and are waiting for spring to rouse them from dormancy. They won't need our prompting to know when to burst their seed coats and push green shoots toward the sun. Nature has built in the only clock they need, and they will wake up and grow when they are ready.

Most gardeners will admit that they are not altogether sorry to see the end of the growing season. After tending and processing the summer's bounty—speckling the kitchen countertops with juice and seeds from sun-ripened tomatoes and snapping and stringing beans until our fingers are sore and there's no more room in the freezer—we are tired. We have stored the autumnal harvest, too, braided the tops of paper-shelled onions into thick, ropey strands and pickled the last peppers with vinegar and spices for tasty Christmas gifts. The seeds of many heirloom plants have dropped to the earth where they will rest for awhile, and we gardeners are ready for a rest of our own.

But if you're like me, your desire for gardening downtime ends about as soon as you flip to a new calendar and put away the New Year's party hats. It's dreary, lingering inside when you could be outdoors doing—something. Anything.

Even the mildest winter day can lure you back into the yard. Thick, woolly socks notwithstanding, you stuff your feet into a pair of old boots stashed by the back door. They are stiffened, caked with dried mud, and slightly shrunken from the mornings you wandered through the grass before the dew burned away or the late afternoons when a rain shower caught you far from the house, a bunch of pulled chickweed in each hand.

No matter. The boots will stretch back out. You shrug a jacket over your shoulders and button up—maybe it doesn't fit quite as well as it did a couple of months ago, when bending and stooping to pick the zucchinis kept

"I have great faith in a seed."
Henry David Thoreau

the old stomach muscles tight. A warm hat for your head, and you're ready to explore.

There's not much to see, at first glance. Then you plunder up and down the rows, kicking away the decaying mulch, nudging aside the remnants of pea plants and peppers. If you're lucky, and if you live where the weather stays warm enough, you might still have a bed of sky-blue-and-canary-colored pansies to visit in the faded landscape.

But there's no escaping it. You are not needed out here. Not right now, anyway. Come back in a few weeks or months, and things will be different.

So you mosey back inside, shuck off the cold weather clothing like an old husk, and drag a chair from the kitchen table. You'll have to be patient. Winter isn't the season for planting seeds.

But it is the season for seed catalogs.

It's hard to resist browsing through the offers for flowers and vegetables that pour in at this time of year. Seed sellers have long recognized our midwinter yearnings for color and flavor. Bernard McMahon, a Philadelphia nurseryman and gardening mentor to President Thomas Jefferson, must have known this when he published the first of the American seed catalogs. Jefferson himself confessed a lifelong urge to plan and plant. "No occupation is so delightful to me as the culture of the earth," he wrote, "and no culture comparable to that of the garden."

Savvy seed purveyors soon recognized Jefferson had plenty of kindred spirits and they have been enticing us ever since. We have welcomed their efforts, glad to open the squeaky mailbox door and find their promises stashed inside. In 1894, W. Atlee Burpee & Company proudly announced how busy it had become: no less than 110,000 customers at "select addresses" eagerly awaited its new list that year.

"Cash should always accompany the order," Burpee's gently reminded its customers. "Money can be sent safely either by post-office order, bank draft, express, or cash by registered letter." If you placed an order for more than one dollar—a whole dollar—Burpee's would reimburse you for the cost of your eight-cent stamp with free extra seeds.

One newspaper of the era, *The Philadelphia Inquirer*, gave Burpee's a nod of approval. "It is one of the most astonishing things about the firm of W. Atlee Burpee & Co. that it has built up in seeds one of the largest mail, express, and freight businesses of any kind in the United States. During the months of February, March, and April its mail is the heaviest of any firm in the country, and its order books show that it keeps in touch with more sections of this and other countries than any other firm known."

Burpee's also sent out an annual farm catalog. Anyone who purchased seeds from it, the company explained happily, would receive a free copy for the asking. But if you weren't a seed buyer but merely a "looker" desiring "a nice book," well, Burpee's earnestly hoped you would help cover the nearly fifteen-cent cost of producing their catalog. "You should enclose us ten cents," Burpee's reasoned amiably, "which is only part of the cost; put yourself in our place."

Burpee's has plenty of competition these days. Remarkably, most seed catalogs are still free or available for just a little of our hard-earned money. And the orders we mail during the winter for the plants we can't resist still choke the mailrooms of seed sellers across the country.

The majority of catalogs that turn up on our doorsteps are packed with modern hybrids, many of which are undeniably beautiful, prolific, and disease resistant. But the antique flowers and vegetables grown by our grandparents and their parents before them are equally rewarding to cultivate, rich with their own unique beauty and personalities.

Maybe instead of dreading the winter season that keeps us housebound, we can learn to think of it as nature's prelude to the next garden, a time to browse the seed catalogs and plan the heirloom treasures we will grow.

If there are old-fashioned flowers and vegetables you would like to try, but you have trouble finding them through commercial sources, don't despair. Advocacy groups like the American Horticultural Society may be able to help.

You can also look for seed swaps or exchanges sponsored by the horticultural or agricultural departments of your local colleges and universities. Heirloom gardeners may come from miles around to trade for an elusive butterbean that someone's granddaddy used to grow, or the seeds of a sunflower they've noticed in a forgotten field. Precious varieties are bartered for and counted out, seed by seed, into tiny bags or envelopes, while memories, stories, and gardening tips are shared.

If you can't find a seed swap in your area, consider starting one; humble beginnings are fine. When word gets around—and gardeners are always look-

....
....
....
....
....
....
....
....
....
....
....
....
....
....
....
....
....
....
....
....
....
....
....
....
....
....
....
....

ing for "new" plants they haven't tried before—your swap may grow as well as your heirloom plants.

Don't forget to check with your state agricultural department, too, about subscribing to any market bulletins it may publish for consumers and farmers. Historical gardens like those at Monticello or living history museums are also excellent resources for information about heirloom seeds.

When you finally come home with a handful of Moon and Stars watermelon seeds or a pocket of prickly nigella pods, remember what heirloom gardening is all about. Enjoy your heirlooms in the landscape garden and at the table, and then pass their seeds along. Share.

May you always grow a bountiful garden.

BIBLIOGRAPHY

Adams, Denise Wiles. *Restoring American Gardens: An Encyclopedia of Heirloom Ornamental Plants, 1640–1940*. Portland, Oreg.: Timber Press, 2004.

Armitage, Allan, Maureen Heffernan, Chela Kleiber, and Holly H. Shimizu. *Burpee Complete Gardener*. New York: Macmillan, 1995.

Bender, Steve, and Felder Rushing. *Passalong Plants*. Chapel Hill: University of North Carolina Press, 1993.

Buff, Shelia. *The Great Tomato Book*. Short Hills, N.J.: Burford Books, 1999.

Bush-Brown, Louise, and James Bush-Brown. *America's Garden Book*. New York: Macmillan, 1996.

Colborn, Nigel, and Jacqui Hurst. *The Old-Fashioned Gardener: Lessons from the Past for the Gardener of Today*. New York: Lorenz Books, 1995.

Creasy, Rosalind. *The Edible Heirloom Garden*. Boston: Periplus Editions, 1999.

Fairbairn, Neil. *A Brief History of Gardening*. Emmaus, Pa.: Rodale, 2001.

Gardner, Jo Ann. *The Heirloom Garden: Selecting and Growing over 300 Old-Fashioned Ornamentals*. Pownal, Vt.: Storey Communications, 1992.

Goldman, Amy. *The Compleat Squash: A Passionate Grower's Guide to Pumpkins, Squash, and Gourds*. New York: Artisan, 2004.

———. *Melons for the Passionate Grower*. New York: Artisan, 2002.

Grimshaw, Dr. John, and consultant Dr. Bobby Ward. *The Gardener's Atlas: The Origins, Discovery and Cultivation of the World's Most Popular Garden Plants*. Buffalo, N.Y.: Firefly Books, 2002.

Henderson, Peter. *Henderson's Handbook of Plants*. New York: Peter Henderson & Co., 1881.

Jabs, Carolyn. *The Heirloom Gardener*. San Francisco: Sierra Club Books, 1984.

Leighton, Ann. *Early American Gardens "For Meate or Medicine."* Boston: Houghton Mifflin, 1970.

Luebbermann, Mimi, and Faith Echtermeyer. *Heirloom Gardens: Simple Secrets for Old-Fashioned Flowers and Vegetables*. San Francisco: Chronicle Books, 1997.

Martin, Laura C. *Grandma's Garden: A Celebration of Old-Fashioned Gardening*. Atlanta: Longstreet Press, 1990.

———. *Wildflower Folklore*. Charlotte, N.C.: East Woods Press, 1984.

Martin, Tovah. *Heirloom Flowers: Vintage Flowers for Modern Gardens*. New York: Gaia Books, 1999.

———. *Once upon a Windowsill: A History of Indoor Plants*. Portland, Oreg.: Timber Press, 1988.

Nazarea, Virginia D. *Heirloom Seeds and Their Keepers: Marginality and Memory in the Conservation of Biological Diversity*. Tucson: University of Arizona Press, 2005.

Neal, Bill. *Gardener's Latin*. Chapel Hill, N.C.: Algonquin Books, 1992.

Skinner, Charles M. *Myths and Legends of Flowers, Trees, Fruits, and Plants in All Ages and All Climes*. Philadelphia: Lippincott, 1939.

Stewart, Martha. *Gardening 101: Learn How to Plan, Plant, and Maintain a Garden*. New York: Clarkson Potter, 2000.

Strickland, Sue, Kent Whealy, and David Cavagnaro. *Heirloom Vegetables: A Home Gardener's Guide to Finding and Growing Vegetables from the Past*. New York: Simon and Schuster, 1998.

Stuart, David, and James Sutherland. *Plants from the Past*. New York: Viking, 1987.

Sumner, Judith. *American Household Botany: A History of Useful Plants, 1620–1900*. Portland, Oreg.: Timber Press, 2004.

Swain, Roger B. *The Practical Gardener: Mastering the Elements of Good Growing*. New York: Galahad Books, 1998.

Thoreau, Henry David, Bradley P. Dean, Abigail Rorer, and Robert D. Richardson Jr. *Faith in a Seed: The Dispersion of Seeds and Other Late Natural History Writings*. Washington, D.C.: Island Press, 1996.

Viola, Herman J., and Carolyn Margolis, eds. *Seeds of Change: A Quincentennial Commemoration*. Washington, D.C.: Smithsonian Institution Press, 1991.

Watson, Benjamin. *Taylor's Guide to Heirloom Vegetables*. Boston: Houghton Mifflin, 1996.

Weaver, William Woys. *100 Vegetables and Where They Came From*. Chapel Hill, N.C.: Algonquin Books, 2000.

———. *Heirloom Vegetable Gardening: A Master Gardener's Guide to Planting, Seed Saving, and Cultural History*. New York: Henry Holt, 1997.

Welch, William, and Greg Grant. *The Southern Heirloom Garden*. Dallas: Taylor Publishing, 1995.

Wells, Diana. *100 Flowers and How They Got Their Names*. Chapel Hill, N.C.: Algonquin Books, 1997.

Whealy, Kent, and Arllys Ademann, eds. *Seed Savers Exchange: The First Ten Years*. Decorah, Iowa: Seed Saver Publications, 1986.

Whiteside, Katherine. *Antique Flowers: A Guide to Using Old-Fashioned Species in Contemporary Gardens*. New York: Villard Books, 1989.

Wilder, Louise Beebe. *The Fragrant Path*. New York: Dover Publications, 1932.

———. *My Garden*. New York: Doubleday, Page, 1920.

Yepsen, Roger. *A Celebration of Heirloom Vegetables: Growing and Cooking Old-Time Varieties*. New York: Artisan, 1998.

WHERE TO FIND HEIRLOOM SEEDS OR VISIT HEIRLOOM GARDENS

Canada

Agrestal Organic Heritage Seed Co.
<www.agrestalseeds.com>
Box 646
Gormley, ON LoH 1Go
Phone (905) 888-1881

Circle Dance Seeds
<www.cdseeds.ca>
RR 3, 84354 McNabb Line
Brussels, ON NoC 1Ho
email circledanceseeds@
scsinternet.com

The Cottage Gardener Heirloom Seed
& Plant Nursery
<www.cottagegardener.com>
4199 Gilmore Road, RR1
Newtonville, ON LoA 1Jo
Phone (905) 786-2388

Ecogenesis
<www.ecogenesis.ca>
1267-2384 Yonge St.
Toronto, ON M4P 3E5
Phone 416-485-8333

Eternal Seed
657 Pritchard Road
Farrellton, QC JoX 1To
819-827-8881
email edecas@travel-net.com

Florabunda Seeds
<www.florabundaseeds.com>
Box 3,
Indian River, ON KoL 2Bo
Phone (705) 295-6440
Fax (705) 295-4035

Full Circle Seeds
<www.fullcircleseeds.com>
P.O. Box 807
Sooke, BC VoS 1No
Phone (250) 642-3671

Gardenimport, Inc.
(sellers of Sutton's Seeds)
<www.gardenimport.com>
Box 760, 135 West Beaver Creek Road
Richmond Hill, Ontario L4B 1C6
Canada
Phone 905.731.1950 and
800.339.8314
Fax 905.881.3499

Lindenberg Seeds
<www.lindenbergseeds.ca>
803 Princess Avenue
Brandon, MB R7A oP5
Phone (204) 727-0575
Fax (204) 727-2832

Ontario Seed Company
<www.oscseeds.com>
Box 7, 330 Phillip Street
Waterloo, ON N2J 3Z6
Phone (519) 886-0557

Prairie Garden Seeds
<www.prseeds.ca>
Box 118
Cochin, SK, SoM oLo
Phone (306) 386-2737
or (306) 682-1475 (Humboldt)

Richter's Herbs
<www.richters.com>
357 Highway 47, Goodwood
ON LoC 1Ao
Phone 905 640-6677
Fax 905 640-6641

Sage Garden Herbs
<www.herbs.mb.ca>
3410 St Mary's Road
Winnipeg, MB R2N 4E2
Phone (204) 257-2715

Salt Spring Seeds
<www.saltspringseeds.com>
Box 444, Ganges P.O.
Salt Spring Island, BC V8K 2W1
Phone (250) 537-5269

Seeds of Diversity Canada —
Canada's Heritage Seed Program
<www.seeds.ca>
P.O. Box 36, Stn Q
Toronto ON M4T 2L7
Phone 1-866-509-SEED

Seeds of Victoria
<www.earthfuture.com/gardenpath/
Seeds_Catalogue.htm>
395 Conway Road
Victoria, BC V9E 2B9
Phone (250) 881-1555

Terra Edibles
<www.terraedibles.ca>
535 Ashley Street
Foxboro, ON KoK 2Bo
Phone (613) 961-0654

Two Wings Farm
<www.twowingsfarm.com>
4768 William Head Rd.
Victoria, BC V9C 3Y7
Phone (250) 478-3794

Upper Canada Seeds
8 Royal Doulton Drive
Toronto, ON M3A 1N4
Phone (416) 447-5321

Veseys Seeds
<www.veseys.com>
PO Box 9000
Charlottetown, PEI C1A 8K6
Phone 1-800-363-7333
Fax 1-800-686-0329

West Coast Seeds
<www.westcoastseeds.com>
3925 64th Street RR 1
Delta, BC V4K 3N2
Phone (604) 952-8828

Yuko Horiuchi
<www.yuko.ca>
202 Arklan Road
Carleton Place, ON K7C 3R9
Phone (613) 253-0787

In the United States

Abundant Life Seeds
<www.abundantlifeseeds.com>
P.O. Box 157
Saginaw, OR 97472
Phone 541.767.9606
Fax 866.514.7333

Artistic Gardens & Le Jardin
du Gourmet
<www.artisticgardens.com>
P.O. Box 75
St. Johnsbury Center, VT 05863-0075
Phone/fax 802.748.1446

Aunt Martha's Garden
<www.auntmarthasgarden.com>
731 E. Valley Road
Willits, CA 95490

Baker Creek Heirloom Seeds
<www.rareseeds.com>
2278 Baker Creek Road
Mansfield, MO 65704
Phone 417.924.8917
Fax 417.924.8887

Bountiful Gardens
<www.bountifulgardens.org>
18001 Shafer Ranch Road
Willits, CA 95490-9626
Phone 707.459.6410
Fax 707.459.1925

W. Atlee Burpee & Company
<www.burpee.com>
300 Park Avenue
Warminster, PA 18974
Phone 800.888.1447
Fax 800.487.5530

Canyon Creek Nursery
<www.canyoncreeknursery.com>
3527 Dry Creek Road
Oroville, CA 95965
Phone 530.533.2166

Colonial Williamsburg Foundation
<www.colonialwilliamsburg.org>
P.O. Box 1776
Williamsburg, VA 23187-1776
Phone 757.229.1000

Comstock, Ferre & Company
<www.comstockferre.com>
263 Main Street
Wethersfield, CT 06109
Phone 800.733.3773 or 860.571.6590
Fax 860.571.6595

The Cook's Garden
<www.cooksgarden.com>
P.O. Box C5030
Warminster, PA 18974
Phone 800.457.9703
Fax 800.457.9705

Eastern Native Seed Conservancy
<www.enscseeds.org>
P.O. Box 451
Great Barrington, MA 01230
Phone 413.229.8316

Garden State Heirloom Seed Society
<www.historyyoucaneat.org/>
P.O. Box 15
Delaware, NJ 07833

Good Seed Company
<www.goodseedco.net/>
195 Bolster Road
Oroville, WA 98844

The Gourmet Gardener
<www.gourmetgardener.com>
12287 117th Drive
Live Oak, FL 32060
Fax 407.650.2691

Heirloom Seeds
<www.heirloomseeds.com>
P.O. Box 245
West Elizabeth, PA 15088-0245
Phone 412.384.0852

High Mowing Seeds
<www.highmowingseeds.com>
813 Brook Road
Wolcott, VT 05680
Phone 802.888.1800
Fax 802.888.8446

J. L. Hudson, Seedsman
<www.JLHudsonseeds.net>
Star Route 2, Box 337
La Honda, CA 94020-9733

Ed Hume Seeds
<www.humeseeds.com/>
P.O. Box 73160
Puyallup, WA 98373
Phone 253.435.4414
Fax 253.435.5144

Thomas Jefferson Center for
Historic Plants
<www.monticello.org>
Monticello
P.O. Box 316
Charlottesville, VA 22902
General information: 434.984.9800
Catalog phone orders: 800.243.1743

Johnny's Selected Seeds
<www.johnnyseeds.com>
955 Benton Avenue
Winslow, ME 04901
Phone 800.879.2258
Fax 800.437.4290

Landis Valley Heirloom Seed Project
<www.landisvalleymuseum.org>
Landis Valley Museum
2451 Kissel Hill Road
Lancaster, PA 17601
Phone 717.569.0401
Fax 717.560.2147

D. Landreth Seed Company
<www.landrethseeds.com>
P.O. Box 16380
Baltimore, MD 21210-2229
Phone 800.654.2407

Mount Vernon House and Gardens
<www.mountvernon.org>
3200 Mount Vernon Memorial
Highway
Mount Vernon, VA 22121
mailing address:
Mount Vernon Ladies' Association
P.O. Box 110
Mount Vernon, VA 22121
Phone 703.780.2000

Native Seeds/SEARCH
<www.nativeseeds.org>
526 N. 4th Avenue
Tucson, AZ 85705-8450
Phone 520.622.5561
Fax 520.622.5591

The Natural Gardening Company
<www.naturalgardening.com>
P.O. Box 750776
Petaluma, CA 94975-0776
Phone 707.766.9303
Fax 707.766.9747

Nichols Garden Nursery
<www.nicholsgardennursery.com>
1190 Old Salem Road NE
Albany, OR 97321-4580
Phone 800.422.3985
Fax 800.231.5306

Old Salem Gardens
<http://www.oldsalem.org/>
P.O. Box F, Salem Station
Winston-Salem, NC 27108-0346
Located southwest of the intersection
of business 40 and U.S. highway 52.
Phone 888.653.7253
Fax 336.721.7335

Old Sturbridge Village
<www.osv.org>
1 Old Sturbridge Village Road
Sturbridge, MA 01566
Phone 508.347.3362

Park Seed Company
<www.parkseed.com>
1 Parkton Avenue
Greenwood, SC 29647
Phone 800.213.0076
Fax 800.275.9941

The Pepper Gal
<www.peppergal.com>
P.O. Box 23006
Fort Lauderdale, FL 33307-3006
Phone 954.537.5540
Fax 954.566.2208

Pinetree Garden Seeds
<www.superseeds.com/home.htm>
P.O. Box 300
New Gloucester, ME 04260
Phone 207.926.3400
Fax 888.527.3337

Plants of the Southwest
<www.plantsofthesouthwest.com>
3095 Agua Fria Road
Santa Fe, NM 87507
Phone 800.788.7333
Fax 505.438.8800

Reimer Seeds
<www.reimerseeds.com>
P.O. Box 236
Mount Holly, NC 28120-0236
Fax 704.644.3762

Renee's Garden
<www.reneesgarden.com>
7389 W. Zayante Road
Felton, CA 95018
Phone 888.880.7228
Fax 831.335.7227

Revolution Seeds
<www.walkinginplace.org/seeds>
204 North Waverly Street
Homer, IL 61849
Phone 217.896.3267

P. L. Rohrer & Bro., Inc.
<www.rohrerseeds.com>
2472 Old Philadelphia Pike
P.O. Box 250
Smoketown, PA 17576
Phone 717.299.2571
Fax 800.468.4944

Sand Hill Preservation Center
<www.sandhillpreservation.com>
1878 230th Street
Calamus, IA 52729-9659
Phone 563.246.2299

John Scheepers Kitchen
Garden Seeds
<www.kitchengardenseeds.com>
23 Tulip Drive
P.O. Box 638
Bantam, CT 06750
Phone 860.567.6086
Fax 860.567.5323

Seed Savers Exchange
<www.seedsavers.org>
3094 North Winn Road
Decorah, IA 52101
Phone 563.382.5990
Fax 563.382.5872

Seeds of Change
<www.seedsofchange.com>
1 Sunset Way
Henderson, NV 89014
Phone 888.762.7333

Seeds Trust
<www.seedstrust.com>
P.O. Box 596
Cornville, AZ 86325
Phone 928.649.3315
Fax 928.649.8181

Seeds West Garden Seeds
<www.seedswestgardenseeds.com>
317 14th Street NW
Albuquerque, NM 87104
Phone 505.843.9713

Select Seeds Antique Flowers
<www.selectseeds.com>
180 Stickney Hill Road
Union, CT 06076
Phone 800.684.0395
Fax 800.653.3304

Skyfire Garden Seeds
<www.grapevine.net/~mctaylor/>
1313 23rd Road
Kanopolis, KS 67454-9225

South Carolina Foundation
Seed Association
<http://virtual.clemson.edu/groups/
seed/index.htm>
1162 Cherry Road, Box 349952
Clemson, SC 29634
Phone 864.656.2520

Southern Exposure Seed Exchange
<www.southernexposure.com>
P.O. Box 460
Mineral, VA 23117
Phone 540.894.9480
Fax 540.894.9481

Southern Seed Legacy Project
<http://www.uga.edu/~ebl/
southernheirloom/>
10 Legacy Road
Crawford, GA 30630

Harriett Beecher Stowe Center
<http://www.
harrietbeecherstowecenter.org/>
77 Forest Street
Hartford, CT 06105
Phone 860-522-9258
Fax 860-522-9259

INDEX